Privacy and Data Protection Law in the Philippines

Privacy and Data Protection Law in the Philippines

Leandro Angelo Y. Aguirre
Celine Melanie A. Dee

This book was originally published as a monograph in the International Encyclopaedia of Laws/Privacy and Technology Law.

Founding Editor: Roger Blanpain
General Editor: Frank Hendrickx
Volume Editors: Jos Dumortier, Pieter Gryffroy, Ruben Roex & Yung Shin Van Der Sype

Wolters Kluwer

Published by:
Kluwer Law International B.V.
PO Box 316
2400 AH Alphen aan den Rijn
The Netherlands
E-mail: lrs-sales@wolterskluwer.com
Website: www.wolterskluwer.com/en/solutions/kluwerlawinternational

Sold and distributed by:
Wolters Kluwer Legal & Regulatory U.S.
7201 McKinney Circle
Frederick, MD 21704
United States of America
E-mail: customer.service@wolterskluwer.com

ISBN 978-94-035-0726-2

e-Book: ISBN 978-94-035-0876-4
web-PDF: ISBN 978-94-035-0886-3

The Authors

Leandro Angelo Y. Aguirre is the Deputy Commissioner of the Philippine National Privacy Commission and has served in that role since February 2018.

He received his Juris Doctor degree from the University of the Philippines College of Law and his Master of Laws from Harvard Law School, Boston. He is a member of both the Philippine Bar and the New York State Bar.

He is also a member of the academe having taught various subjects at the University of the Philippines College of Law since 2013. He served as an advisor on the bill that eventually became the Data Privacy Act of 2012.

Celine Melanie A. Dee, Chief of Staff to Deputy Commissioner Leandro Angelo Y. Aguirre, is a licensed lawyer in the Philippines with several locally and internationally published works in technology and intellectual property laws.

Her work and research centres on innovation policy and development. Her insights from private practice and involvement in the academe provide her with a grounded approach to the legal controversies of emerging technologies.

She received her Juris Doctor degree from the Ateneo de Manila University School of Law, Philippines. She holds an LL.M (Distinction) in Technology and Intellectual Property Law from the University of Hong Kong. In 2012, she clerked for Roberto A. Abad (Ret.), Justice of the Philippine Supreme Court.

The Authors

Table of Contents

List of Abbreviations

Constitution	1987 Constitution of the Republic of the Philippines
ASD	Administrative Services Division
APEC-CPEA	APEC Cross-Border Privacy Enforcement Arrangement
CBPR System	APEC Cross-Border Privacy Rules System
DMF	ASEAN Data Management Framework
MCCs	ASEAN Model Contract Clauses
APEC	Asia-Pacific Economic Cooperation
CDO	Cease and Desist Order
CCTV	Closed-Circuit Television
CID	Complaints and Investigation Division
CMD	Compliance and Monitoring Division
COP	Compliance Officer for Privacy
DPA	Data Privacy Act of 2012
DPA	Data Protection Officer
DPO ACE	Data Protection Officer Accountability, Compliance, and Ethics
DSTSD	Data Security and Technology Standards Division
DSA	Data Sharing Agreement
DICT	Department of Information and Communications Technology
DOJ	Department of Justice
DPA and other privacy regulations	DPA, its IRR, and other issuances of the Commission
EnD	Enforcement Division
1995 EU Privacy Directive	European Union Data Privacy Directive of 1995
FFR	Fact-Finding Report
FAO	Finance and Administrative Office

List of Abbreviations

FPMD	Financial, Planning, and Management Division
FOI	Freedom of Information
GPA	Global Privacy Assembly
HRDD	Human Resources Development Division
IRR	Implementing Rules and Regulations of the Data Privacy Act of 2012
ICT	Information and Communications Technology
IT-BPO	Information Technology – Business Process Outsourcing
ICCPR	International Covenant on Civil and Political Rights
LEO	Legal and Enforcement Office
LD	Legal Division
National ID System	National Computerized Identification Reference System
the Commission	National Privacy Commission
Civil Code	New Civil Code of the Philippines
PDS	Personal Data Sheet
PIC	Personal Information Controller
PIP	Personal Information Processor
PhilSys	Philippine Identification System
PSA	Philippine Statistics Authority
PSN	PhilSys Number
PDD	Policy Development Division
PRD	Policy Review Division
PEA	Privacy Enforcement Authority
PIA	Privacy Impact Assessment
PPO	Privacy Policy Office
PIAD	Public Information and Assistance Division
T3P	Training the Trainers Program

Acknowledgements

The authors wish to express their sincere gratitude to Dianne Lane B. Lopez, Ma. Angela G. Butalid, Elaine I. Pineda, Jelica D.R. Perez, Ariel Rocelle B. Dayu, Jocelyn H. Baylon, Christian D. Sorongon, Joshu E. Villanueva, and Pio Mari G. Aguilar for their valuable contribution to this monograph.

Acknowledgements

General Introduction

1. The Republic of the Philippines is an archipelagic country in Southeast Asia with more than seven thousand islands.[1] It is a democratic and republican state, where sovereignty resides in the people.[2]

2. The prevailing Constitution is the 1987 Philippine Constitution, which provides three separate and equal branches of government – the Executive, the Legislative, and the Judiciary.[3]

3. The head of the Executive Department is the President, who is elected by a majority vote of the Filipino people.[4] Executive power consists of the execution of laws, which is exercised by the President through government agencies.[5] The Legislative Department is characterized by bicameralism where legislative power or the power to make statutory laws is vested in the Senate and House of Representatives.[6] The Judicial Department, where judicial power is vested, is composed of the Supreme Court and other lower courts established by law.[7]

4. The Philippine Legal System is a mixture of civil and common legal systems. As such, judicial decisions that apply or interpret statutory laws or the Constitution are recognized as part of the Philippine Legal System.[8] Judicial decisions are 'evidence of what the laws mean'[9] and 'assume the same authority' as statutory laws themselves.[10]

5. This monograph examines the right to privacy in general, as discussed in the 1987 Philippine Constitution and cases decided by the Supreme Court before the passage of the Data Privacy Act of 2012. It also analyses the right to data privacy,

1. *See* PHIL. CONST. art. I, §1.
2. *Ibid.*, art. II, §1.
3. *See ibid.*, arts VI, VII, & VIII.
4. *Ibid.*, art. VII, §1.
5. *See ibid.*, art. VII, §1.
6. *Ibid.*, art. VI, §1.
7. *Ibid.*, art. VIII, §1.
8. An Act to Ordain and Institute the Civil Code of the Philippines [CIVIL Code], Republic Act No. 386, art. 8 (1949).
9. *Columbia Pictures, Inc. v. Court of Appeals*, G.R. No. 110318 (1996).
10. *Caltex (Philippines), Inc. v. Palomar*, G.R. No. L-19650 (1966).

particularly the right to informational privacy, grounded on the Data Privacy Act of 2012, its Implementing Rules and Regulations, and other issuances of the National Privacy Commission.

Part I. Privacy Protection in the Philippines

Chapter 1. Privacy Protection in the Constitution

§1. The Right to Privacy of Communication

6. The right to privacy in the 1987 Constitution of the Republic of the Philippines (Constitution) focuses on the privacy of communication and correspondence and freedom from government interference in one's communication.[11] As stated in Article III of the Bill of Rights of the Constitution:

> Section 3. (1) The privacy of communication and correspondence shall be inviolable except upon lawful order of the court, or when public safety or order requires otherwise, as prescribed by law.
> (2) Any evidence obtained in violation of this or the preceding section shall be inadmissiblc for any purposc in any procccding.[12]

7. The right to privacy of communication and correspondence was introduced in Philippine law as early as the 1935 Constitution.[13] The right is intended to protect forms of communication in order to prevent arbitrary violations of privacy.[14]

8. The Constitutional right to privacy is qualified with 'of communication and correspondence', which stems from the notion that 'intrusion of communication and correspondence is [a] kind of search'.[15]

9. The term 'communication and correspondence' is understood in its general sense,[16] which means it includes all forms of communication such as letters, messages, wiretaps, and electronic eavesdropping.[17]

---

11. Phil. Const. Art. III, §3(1); *See Kilusang Mayo Uno v. Director-General*, G.R. Nos. 167798 & 167930 (2006).
12. Phil. Const. Art. III, §3(1).
13. 1935 Phil. Const. Art. III, §1(5) (superseded in 1973).
14. Joaquin G. Bernas, S.J., The 1987 Constitution of the Republic of the Philippines: A Commentary 218 (2009).
15. *Ibid.*, 217.
16. *Ibid.*, 218.
17. *Ibid.*,.

10. The guarantee of the privacy of communication and correspondence is not absolute and may be lawfully infringed by the State in certain cases. The State may infringe on the privacy of communication upon lawful order of the court, or when required by public safety and order.[18] The Constitutional provision is further qualified by the phrase 'as prescribed by law', which means that a lawful infringement requires a supporting law that permits the infringement.[19]

11. The Supreme Court recognized that 'the privacy right is but an aspect of the right to be secure in one's person'.[20] The right to privacy in the Constitution, however, does not specifically refer only to the right to informational privacy or data privacy.

12. As succinctly explained by Chief Justice Reynato S. Puno in his speech, 'The Common Right to Privacy', there are three aspects of the right to privacy, namely: (1) locational or situational privacy, (2) decisional privacy, and (3) informational privacy.[21] Locational or situational privacy pertains to 'privacy felt in a physical space', which covers violations by trespass or through an unlawful search and seizure.[22] Decisional privacy refers to the 'right of individuals to make certain kinds of fundamental choices with respect to their personal and reproductive autonomy'.[23] Informational privacy, which is the 'right of individuals to control information about themselves',[24] is the strand of privacy protected by the Data Privacy Act of 2012 (DPA).

§2. Recognition of the Constitutional Right to Privacy in Jurisprudence

13. Philippine law recognizes Supreme Court decisions that apply or interpret the laws as part of its legal system:[25]

> [T]he decisions of this Court form part of the [Philippines'] legal system. While these decisions are not laws pursuant to the doctrine of separation of powers, they evidence the laws' meaning, breadth, and scope and, therefore, have the same binding force as the laws themselves.[26]

---

18. *Ibid.*, 220; Public order and safety are defined as 'the security of human lives, liberty and property against the activities of invaders, insurrectionists and rebels'. *Ibid.*, 220 (citing 1971 Constitutional Convention, Session of Nov. 25, 1972).
19. *Ibid.*, 221.
20. *Ibid.*, 219 (citing *Material Distributors, Inc. v. Natividad* (1949)).
21. *Vivares v. St. Theresa's College*, G.R. No. 202666 (2014).
22. *See ibid.*, (citing Reynato S. Puno, Chief Justice, Supreme Court, The Common Right to Privacy (12 Mar. 2008)).
23. *See ibid.*,.
24. *Ibid.*
25. An Act to Ordain and Institute the Civil Code of the Philippines [Civil Code], Republic Act No. 386, art. 8 (1949).
26. *Philippine Long Distance Telephone Company v. Alvarez*, G.R. No.179408 (2014).

14. The Supreme Court has penned several cases on the right to informational or data privacy. These cases, however, were all decided before the Philippine Congress passed the DPA, which is the current law on data privacy.

15. As early as 1968, the Supreme Court recognized that the right to privacy 'fully deserv[es]' constitutional protection.[27] In *Morfe v. Mutuc*, the Supreme Court highlighted that the protection of the dignity and integrity of the individual is paramount considering the technological developments in modern society.[28]

16. In this case, the Supreme Court ruled on the constitutionality of the compulsory revelation of a public official's sworn statement of his or her assets, liabilities, and net worth.[29] It held that such a requirement is not a violation of the public official's individual right to privacy since it is a valid exercise of police power to 'promote morality in public service' and prevent unscrupulous corrupt practices of public officials.[30]

17. In reaching this determination, the Supreme Court delved into a discussion on the individual's right to privacy.[31] The court recognized the right to privacy as laid down in *Griswold v. Connecticut*:

> In that respect the question is one of first impression, no previous decision having been rendered by this Court. It is not so in the United States where, in the leading case of *Griswold v. Connecticut*, Justice Douglas, speaking for five members of the Court, stated: 'Various guarantees create zones of privacy. The right of association contained in the penumbra of the First Amendment is one, as we have seen. The Third Amendment in its prohibition against the quartering of soldiers 'in any house' in time of peace without the consent of the owner is another facet of that privacy. The Fourth Amendment explicitly affirms the 'right of the people to be secure in their persons, houses, papers, and effects, against unreasonable searches and seizures.' The Fifth Amendment in its Self-Incrimination Clause enables the citizen to create a zone of privacy which government may not force him to surrender to his detriment. The Ninth Amendment provides: 'The enumeration in the Constitution, of certain rights, shall not be construed to deny or disparage others retained by the people.' After referring to various American Supreme Court decisions, Justice Douglas continued: 'These cases bear witness that the right of privacy which presses for recognition is a legitimate one.'[32]

18. The court recognized that the right to privacy is underpinned by the right to liberty and due process, right against unreasonable searches and seizures, right to

---

27. *Morfe v. Mutuc*, G.R. No. 20387 (1968).
28. *Ibid.*
29. *Ibid.*
30. *Ibid.*
31. *Ibid.*
32. *Ibid.* (citing *Griswold v. Connecticut*, 381 U.S. 479 (1965)).

liberty of abode, and right against self-incrimination.[33] In fact, in Chief Justice Puno's speech, he explained that: '*Morfe* recognized the constitutional right to privacy as laid down in *Griswold v. Connecticut*.'[34] Referring to *Griswold*, he said: 'The Court then held that the right to privacy was a fundamental right under the Constitution and it came from penumbras of the Bill of Rights through the First, Third, Fourth, Fifth and Ninth Amendments.'[35] The right to privacy, as such, is accorded recognition independently of its identification with liberty; in itself, it is fully deserving of constitutional protection.[36]

19. Later, in *Ople v. Torres*, the Supreme Court expounded on the constitutional right to privacy it recognized in *Morfe v. Mutuc*.[37] Here, the Supreme Court struck down a proposed administrative order on the National Computerized Identification Reference System (National ID System) as unconstitutional.[38]

20. The Supreme Court determined that the proposed administrative order violated the fundamental right to privacy.[39] It held that the proposed National ID System lacked sufficient parameters that safeguard the right to privacy.[40] The Supreme Court observed that the proposed administrative order failed to concisely enumerate the (1) necessary information sought to be collected; (2) purpose they are to be collected for; (3) means of collecting such information; and (4) means for the individual to verify the collected information about him or her.[41] It also failed to inform individuals of the authorities who shall have control and access over the collected information, and to install adequate security features to guard against unauthorized disclosure of information.[42] In recognizing the right to privacy, the Supreme Court decided that the absence of these safeguards may very well result in the abuse and misuse of information since the individual lacks sufficient control over the pieces of information collected from him or her.[43] It also emphasized that the right to privacy is not limitless and it is 'not intended to stifle scientific and technological advancements that enhance public service and the common good. It merely requires that the law be narrowly focused and a compelling interest justify such intrusions'.[44] The court further stressed that intrusions into the right must be subject to adequate safeguards and sufficient standards.[45]

---

33. *Ibid.*
34. *See Vivares v. St. Theresa's College*, G.R. No. 202666 (2014) (citing Reynato S. Puno, Chief Justice, Supreme Court, The Common Right to Privacy (12 Mar. 2008)).
35. *See ibid.,.*
36. *Ople v. Torres*, G.R. No. 127685 (1998).
37. *Ibid.*
38. *Ibid.*
39. *Ibid.*
40. *Ibid.*
41. *Ibid.*
42. *Ibid.*
43. *Ibid.*
44. *Ibid.*
45. *Ibid.*

§3. Reasonable Expectation of Privacy Test

Application of the Reasonable Expectation of Privacy Test Before the DPA

21. Prior to the enactment of the DPA, the Supreme Court applied the 'reasonable expectation of privacy test' expounded by the United States Supreme Court in *Katz v. US*[46] to determine whether to uphold an individual's right to privacy in relation to a particular situation.[47]

22. The reasonable expectation of privacy test requires a positive determination of the following: first, whether by his conduct, the individual has exhibited an expectation of privacy, and second, whether this expectation is one that society recognizes as reasonable.[48]

23. The Supreme Court first applied this test in deciding the unconstitutionality of the proposed administrative order on the National ID System in *Ople v. Torres*. The Supreme Court resolved that a minimum standard for a reasonable expectation of privacy is not evident in the proposed administrative order because it failed to specify the means of technology that will be used in the National ID System.[49] The lack of sufficient safeguards, such as the failure to specify the technological means to be used in collecting information, renders the proposed administrative order as too broad.[50]

24. In *Hing v. Choachuy*, the Supreme Court had an opportunity to discuss the reasonable expectation of privacy test first mentioned in *Ople v. Torres*. It emphasized that reasonableness is determined based on the factual circumstances of a case.[51] In this case, the Supreme Court pronounced that the installation of video surveillance cameras directly facing another's property, without securing the consent of the owner of the property, is a violation of that person's right to privacy.[52] The Supreme Court reasoned that the property owners had a reasonable expectation of privacy in their property.[53]

25. In *Pollo v. Constantino*, the Supreme Court applied the reasonable expectation of privacy test in relation to a search conducted on the personal files of a government employee's government-issued computer.[54] Applying the test, the Supreme Court found that there was no violation of the right to privacy.[55] It held that there

46. *Katz v. United States*, 389 U.S. 347 (1967).
47. *Ople v. Torres*, G.R. No. 127685 (1998).
48. *Ibid.*
49. *Ibid.*
50. *Ople v. Torres*, G.R. No. 127685 (1998).
51. *Spouses Hing v. Choachuy*, G.R. No. 179736 (2013).
52. *Ibid.*
53. *Ibid.*
54. *Pollo v. Constantino*, G.R. No. 181881 (2011).
55. *Ibid.*

was no reasonable expectation of privacy since the actions of the government employee did not show an expectation of privacy and that society does not recognize his expectation as reasonable.[56] The court determined that the government employee could not have reasonably expected privacy in his government-issued computer since not only did he fail to allege that he limited access to his government-issued computer and his work area but he also welcomed visitors to his office and permitted their use of his government-issued computer.[57] A policy regulating the use and monitoring of the government-issued computer was similarly in place.[58] Considering the foregoing, the court reasoned that the government employee had no reasonable expectation of privacy because his acts surrounding the use of the government-issued computer failed to demonstrate the same.[59] The files, albeit personal, were stored in the government-issued computer, which the government could rightfully regulate and monitor.[60]

26. In *Vivares v. St. Theresa's College*, the Supreme Court explained that there was no expectation of privacy over photographs of oneself posted on online social network sites if the user's privacy settings did not limit the possibility that such photographs would be disclosed.[61] It explained that there was no expectation of privacy over the photographs posted on Facebook since the default privacy settings were set to public.[62] Petitioners also failed to present evidence that the privacy settings were changed to limit access to the photographs.[63] It determined that it was the user's friends who showed the photographs to the respondent, which makes the latter a mere recipient.[64] There was also no showing that respondents committed unlawful acts to gain access to the photographs, and that they disclosed or broadcasted the photographs other than appending the photographs to its submissions before the court.[65] Taking the foregoing and the social nature of Facebook into consideration, the Supreme Court determined that the right to informational privacy over the photographs was not violated.[66]

27. To reiterate, the Supreme Court decided the cases using the reasonable expectation of privacy test before the effectivity of the DPA.

56. *Ibid.*
57. *Ibid.*
58. *Ibid.*
59. *Ibid.*
60. *Ibid.*
61. *Vivares v. St. Theresa's College*, G.R. 202666 (2014).
62. *Ibid.*
63. *Ibid.*
64. *Ibid.*
65. *Ibid.*
66. *Ibid.*

Application of the Reasonable Expectation of Privacy Test with the Passage of the DPA

28. The DPA protects the right to informational privacy. With the passage and implementation of the DPA, any reference to the reasonable expectation of privacy test within the context of informational privacy points to the rights and obligations provided in the DPA:

> Considering that *Ople* itself recognized the idea of statutory zones of privacy, it follows that with respect to the zone of privacy specifically covered and protected by the Data Privacy Act, the strand of privacy known as informational privacy, the determination of the metes and bounds of the right to privacy should necessarily be grounded in the Act itself.[67]

29. The first test of 'whether by his conduct, the individual has exhibited an expectation of privacy' is understood in relation to the DPA.[68] The DPA already provides for an individual's expectations of his right to privacy and the permissible means by which his personal information may be processed.[69] An individual no longer needs to demonstrate any expectations of privacy before his or her rights and the obligations of personal information controllers (PICs) or personal information processors (PIPs),[70] under the law, are recognized.[71] The second test of 'whether this expectation is one that society recognizes as reasonable' is appreciated by the very existence of the DPA as a law.[72] The codification of the DPA is a manifestation of the data subjects' expectations regarding their privacy:[73]

> Given the specific standards the Data Privacy Act provides with regard to the obligations it imposes on those who process personal data and the rights it gives to data subjects, it follows that reference should first be made to these clear and objective standards before going into an abstract and general examination that is the 'reasonable expectation of privacy' test in *Katz* – a test that was traditionally applied for locational or situational privacy cases to determine when a search can be considered as an intrusion into the right to privacy of individuals.

---

67. *JV v. JR*, CID 17-047, 13 Aug. 2019, at 9, *available at* https://www.privacy.gov.ph/wp-content/uploads/2020/10/CID-17-047-JV-v.-JR-Decision-PSD-10Aug2020.pdf (last accessed 28 Apr. 2022).
68. *Ibid.*, at 10.
69. *Ibid.*, at 9.
70. '*Personal information processor* refers to any natural or juridical person qualified to act as such under this Act to whom a personal information controller may outsource the processing of personal data pertaining to a data subject.' An Act Protecting Individual Personal Information in Information and Communications Systems in the Government and the Private Sector, Creating for this purpose a National Privacy Commission, and For Other Purposes [Data Privacy Act of 2012], Republic Act No. 10173 §3(i) (2012).
71. *JV v. JR*, CID 17-047, 13 Aug. 2019, at 10, *available at* https://www.privacy.gov.ph/wp-content/uploads/2020/10/CID-17-047-JV-v.-JR-Decision-PSD-10Aug2020.pdf (last accessed 28 Apr. 2022).
72. *Ibid.*, at 11.
73. *Ibid.*,.

. . .

In fact, even applying the reasonable expectation of privacy test within the context of informational privacy, the result still points to the Data Privacy Act.

The first part asks 'whether by his conduct, the individual has exhibited an expectation of privacy.' This expectation of privacy has to be examined taking into consideration what the Act itself provides. An individual's expectation of privacy does not depend on a particular action on their part before they are granted the rights provided under the law; these rights are not waived, and the obligations of controllers and processors cannot be ignored simply because there is no overt exhibition of this expectation of privacy. As to the second part, which asks 'whether this expectation is one that society recognizes as reasonable,' this determination should be considered as having been made when Congress and the President, as representatives of the people, codified what data subjects should expect with regard to their privacy.[74]

---

74. *Ibid.*, at 10–11.

Chapter 2. National Application of Regional and International Conventions

30. In 2017, the National Privacy Commission (the Commission) joined the APEC Cross-Border Privacy Enforcement Arrangement (APEC-CPEA) to solidify its status as the Privacy Enforcement Authority (PEA) of the Philippines.[75] Its membership in the APEC-CPEA allows it to facilitate information-sharing among privacy enforcement authorities of the different APEC economies.[76]

31. The Commission signified its intent to join the APEC Cross-Border Privacy Rules System (CBPR System) in September 2019.[77] The CBPR System is a 'regional, multilateral cross-border data transfer mechanism and enforceable privacy code of conduct developed for businesses by the APEC economies'.[78] Through the Commission's membership, it seeks to achieve cross-border privacy cooperation with other APEC economies by adopting common standards to eliminate data flow barriers and promote the free transfer of data across the participating countries.[79]

32. On 28 June 2021, the Commission issued an Advisory on the use of the ASEAN Model Contract Clauses (MCCs) and ASEAN Data Management Framework (DMF) as part of the ASEAN Framework on Digital Data Governance.[80]

33. The Commission is also accredited by the Global Privacy Assembly (GPA).[81] As a member of the GPA, the Commission refers to the Resolutions adopted by the assembly to guide its actions on emerging issues on data privacy.[82]

34. The Commission's international commitments are further discussed in Part VII.

---

75. National Privacy Commission, *PH Strengthens Extraterritorial Reach through the APEC Cross Border Privacy Enforcement Arrangement,* National Privacy Commission Website (5 Dec. 2017), https://www.privacy.gov.ph/2017/12/ph-strengthens-extraterritorial-reach-apec-cross-border-privacy-enforcement arrangement/.
76. *Ibid.*
77. National Privacy Commission, *PH Joins APEC Privacy System,* National Privacy Commission Website (20 Sep. 2019), https://www.privacy.gov.ph/2019/09/ph-joins-apec-privacy-system/.
78. National Privacy Commission, *PH Strengthens Extraterritorial Reach through the APEC Cross Border Privacy Enforcement Arrangement,* National Privacy Commission Website (5 Dec. 2017), https://www.privacy.gov.ph/2017/12/ph-strengthens-extraterritorial-reach-apec-cross-border-privacy-enforcement-arrangement/.
79. National Privacy Commission, *PH Joins APEC Privacy System,* National Privacy Commission Website (20 Sep. 2019), https://www.privacy.gov.ph/2019/09/ph-joins-apec-privacy-system/.
80. National Privacy Commission, Guidance for the Use of the ASEAN Model Contract Clauses and ASEAN Data Management Framework, Advisory No. 02, Series of 2021 (28 Jun. 2021).
81. Global Privacy Assembly, *List of Accredited Members*, Global Privacy Assembly Website, https://globalprivacyassembly.org/participation-in-the-assembly/list-of-accredited-members/.
82. Global Privacy Assembly, *Adopted Resolutions,* Global Privacy Assembly Website, https://globalprivacyassembly.org/document-archive/adopted-resolutions/.

Chapter 3. Privacy in Electronic Communications

35. Specific Philippine statutory laws relating to privacy in electronic communications are Republic Act No. 4200 or the Anti-Wiretapping Law and Republic Act No. 10175 or the Cybercrime Prevention Act of 2012.

36. The Anti-Wiretapping Law penalizes the 'tap[ping] of any wire or cable, or use of any other device or arrangement, to secretly overhear, intercept, or record such communication or spoken word by using a device commonly known as a dictaphone or dictagraph . . . or walkie-talkie or tape recorder, or however otherwise described'.[83] It also prohibits the possession of:

> [A]ny tape record, wire record, disc record, or any other such record, or copies thereof, of any communication or spoken word secured ... or to replay the same for any other person or persons; or to communicate the contents thereof, either verbally or in writing, or to furnish transcriptions thereof, whether complete or partial, to any other person.[84]

37. The Cybercrime Prevention Act of 2012 was enacted 'to regulate access to and use of the cyberspace'.[85] The law penalizes offences against the confidentiality, integrity, and availability of computer data and systems, computer-related systems, and content-related offences.[86] Section 4 of the Cybercrime Prevention Act states:

> Section 4. *Cybercrime Offenses.* The following acts constitute the offense of cybercrime punishable under this Act:
>
> (a) Offenses against the confidentiality, integrity and availability of computer data and systems:
>   (1) Illegal Access. – The access to the whole or any part of a computer system without right.
>   (2) Illegal Interception. – The interception made by technical means without right of any non-public transmission of computer data to, from, or within a computer system including electromagnetic emissions from a computer system carrying such computer data.
>   (3) Data Interference. – The intentional or reckless alteration, damaging, deletion or deterioration of computer data, electronic document, or electronic data message, without right, including the introduction or transmission of viruses.
>   (4) System Interference. – The intentional alteration or reckless hindering or interference with the functioning of a computer or computer network by inputting, transmitting, damaging, deleting, deteriorating,

83. An Act to Prohibit and Penalize Wire Tapping and Other Related Violations of the Privacy of Communication, and for other Purposes [Anti-Wiretapping Law], Republic Act No. 4200, Sec. 1 (1965).
84. *Ibid.*, Sec. 2.
85. *Disini v. Secretary of Justice*, G.R. No. 203335 (2014).
86. *Ibid.*

altering or suppressing computer data or program, electronic document, or electronic data message, without right or authority, including the introduction or transmission of viruses.

(5) Misuse of Devices.

(i) The use, production, sale, procurement, importation, distribution, or otherwise making available, without right, of:

(aa) A device, including a computer program, designed or adapted primarily for the purpose of committing any of the offenses under this Act; or

(bb) A computer password, access code, or similar data by which the whole or any part of a computer system is capable of being accessed with intent that it be used for the purpose of committing any of the offenses under this Act.

(ii) The possession of an item referred to in paragraphs 5(i)(aa) or (bb) above with intent to use said devices for the purpose of committing any of the offenses under this section.

(6) Cyber-squatting. – The acquisition of a domain name over the internet in bad faith to profit, mislead, destroy reputation, and deprive others from registering the same, if such a domain name is:

(i) Similar, identical, or confusingly similar to an existing trademark registered with the appropriate government agency at the time of the domain name registration:

(ii) Identical or in any way similar with the name of a person other than the registrant, in case of a personal name; and

(iii) Acquired without right or with intellectual property interests in it.

(b) Computer-related Offenses:

(1) Computer-related Forgery. –

(i) The input, alteration, or deletion of any computer data without right resulting in inauthentic data with the intent that it be considered or acted upon for legal purposes as if it were authentic, regardless whether or not the data is directly readable and intelligible; or

(ii) The act of knowingly using computer data which is the product of computer-related forgery as defined herein, for the purpose of perpetuating a fraudulent or dishonest design.

(2) Computer-related Fraud. – The unauthorized input, alteration, or deletion of computer data or program or interference in the functioning of a computer system, causing damage thereby with fraudulent intent: *Provided*, That if no damage has yet been caused, the penalty imposable shall be one (1) degree lower.

(3) Computer-related Identity Theft. – The intentional acquisition, use, misuse, transfer, possession, alteration or deletion of identifying information belonging to another, whether natural or juridical, without right: *Provided*, That if no damage has yet been caused, the penalty imposable shall be one (1) degree lower.

(c) Content-related Offenses:

(1) Cybersex. – The willful engagement, maintenance, control, or operation, directly or indirectly, of any lascivious exhibition of sexual organs or sexual activity, with the aid of a computer system, for favor or consideration.

(2) Child Pornography. – The unlawful or prohibited acts defined and punishable by Republic Act No. 9775 or the Anti-Child Pornography Act of 2009, committed through a computer system: *Provided*, That the penalty to be imposed shall be (1) one degree higher than that provided for in Republic Act No. 9775.[87]

38. The Supreme Court, however, declared certain provisions of the Cybercrime Prevention Act void and unconstitutional.[88] In *Disini v. Secretary of Justice, et al.*, the Supreme Court held that the offence penalizing the transmission of unsolicited commercial communications is unconstitutional.[89] Section 4(c)(3) states:

> Section 4. *Cybercrime Offenses*. The following acts constitute the offense of cybercrime punishable under this Act:
>
> . . .
>
> (c) Content-related Offenses:
>
> . . .
>
> (3) *Unsolicited Commercial Communications. – The transmission of commercial electronic communication with the use of computer system which seek to advertise, sell, or offer for sale products and services are prohibited unless:*
>
> (i) *There is prior affirmative consent from the recipient; or*
>
> (ii) *The primary intent of the communication is for service and/or administrative announcements from the sender to its existing users, subscribers or customers; or*
>
> (iii) *The following conditions are present:*
>
> (aa) *The commercial electronic communication contains a simple, valid, and reliable way for the recipient to reject. receipt of further commercial electronic messages (opt-out) from the same source;*
>
> (bb) *The commercial electronic communication does not purposely disguise the source of the electronic message; and*

87. An Act Defining Cybercrime, Providing for the Prevention, Investigation, Suppression and the Imposition of Penalties therefor and for other Purposes [Cybercrime Prevention Act of 2012], Republic Act No. 10175, Sec. 4 (2012).
88. *Disini v. Secretary of Justice*, G.R. No. 203335 (2014).
89. *Ibid.*

> (cc) *The commercial electronic communication does not purposely include misleading information in any part of the message in order to induce the recipients to read the message.*[90]

39. The court explained that prohibiting unsolicited commercial communications or spam results is a violation of the constitutionally guaranteed right to freedom of expression because a person would be denied his right to read email addressed to him or her, including unsolicited advertisements, which are legitimate forms of expression.[91]

40. The Supreme Court also distinguished between the original author of a post and the recipients of the post on the constitutionality of section 4(c)(4) on libel committed through a computer system.[92] Section 4(c)(4) provides:

> Section 4. *Cybercrime Offenses.* – The following acts constitute the offense of cybercrime punishable under this Act:
>
> . . .
>
> (c) Content-related Offenses:
>
> . . .
>
> (4) Libel. – The unlawful or prohibited acts of libel as defined in Article 355 of the Revised Penal Code, as amended, committed through a computer system or any other similar means which may be devised in the future.[93]

41. The Supreme Court declared that section 4(c)(4) on libel remains constitutional only 'with respect to the original author of the post'.[94] It, however, declared the provision unconstitutional 'with respect to others who simply receive the post and react to it'.[95] It is explained as follows:

> The Court agrees with the Solicitor General that libel is not a constitutionally protected speech and that the government has an obligation to protect private individuals from defamation. Indeed, cyber libel is actually not a new crime since Article 353, in relation to Article 355 of the penal code, already punishes it. In effect, Section 4(c)(4) above merely affirms that online defamation constitutes 'similar means' for committing libel.

90. An Act Defining Cybercrime, Providing for the Prevention, Investigation, Suppression and the Imposition of Penalties therefor and for other Purposes [Cybercrime Prevention Act of 2012], Republic Act No. 10175, Sec. 4(c)(3). Emphasis supplied.
91. *Disini v. Secretary of Justice*, G.R. No. 203335 (2014).
92. *Ibid.*
93. An Act Defining Cybercrime, Providing for the Prevention, Investigation, Suppression and the Imposition of Penalties therefor and for other Purposes [Cybercrime Prevention Act of 2012], Republic Act No. 10175, Sec. 4(c)(4).
94. *Disini v. Secretary of Justice*, G.R. No. 203335 (2014).
95. *Ibid.*

> *But the Court's acquiescence goes only insofar as the cybercrime law penalizes the author of the libel[l]ous statement or article.* Cyber libel brings with it certain intricacies, unheard of when the penal code provisions on libel were enacted. The culture associated with internet media is distinct from that of print.
>
> The internet is characterized as encouraging a freewheeling, anything-goes writing style. In a sense, they are a world apart in terms of quickness of the reader's reaction to defamatory statements posted in cyberspace, facilitated by one-click reply options offered by the networking site as well as by the speed with which such reactions are disseminated down the line to other internet users.[96]

42. In effect, the original authors of libellous posts may still be held liable under section 4(c)(4) of the Cybercrime Prevention Act. Penalizing recipients who react to the libellous post or those who aid or abet in the commission of cyber libel and other offenses affecting the freedom of expression 'creates a chilling effect on the constitutionally-protected freedom of expression':[97]

> The old parameters for enforcing the traditional form of libel would be a square peg in a round hole when applied to cyberspace libel. Unless the legislature crafts a cyber libel law that takes into account its unique circumstances and culture, such law will tend to create a chilling effect on the millions that use this new medium of communication in violation of their constitutionally-guaranteed right to freedom of expression.[98]

---

96. *Ibid.* Emphasis supplied.
97. *Ibid.*
98. *Ibid.*

Chapter 4. Other Relevant National Legal Provisions Regarding the Protection of Privacy

43. Statutory legislation relevant to the right to privacy includes laws of general application as well as sector-based legislation.

44. The New Civil Code of the Philippines (Civil Code) recognizes an individual's right to privacy against prying into the privacy of another person's resident or meddling with or disturbing the private life or family relations of another.[99] It provides civil remedies in the form of damages, prevention, and other relief against abuses committed against an individual.[100]

45. The Revised Penal Code penalizes crimes of security that infringe upon another person's privacy. These crimes include trespass to one's dwelling,[101] the discovery of secrets through the seizure of correspondence,[102] and revealing secrets with abuse of office.[103]

46. The Rules of Court disqualifies testimonial evidence on matters learned in confidence from the privileged communication between husband and wife, attorney and client, physician and patient, priest and penitent, and public officer subject to certain conditions.[104]

47. The Writ of Habeas Data provides a remedy to any person against the violation or threat to his or her right to privacy in life, liberty, or security.[105] The violation or threat arises from an unlawful act or omission of a public official or of a private individual or entity engaged in the collection and storage of data on the person, family, home, and correspondence of the aggrieved party.[106]

48. Other laws of general application include laws against wiretapping,[107] and voyeurism,[108] and laws on confidentiality of health information.[109]

---

99. An Act to Ordain and Institute the Civil Code of the Philippines [Civil Code], Republic Act No. 386, art. 26 (1949).
100. *Ibid.*,.
101. An Act Revising the Penal Code and Other Penal Laws [Rev. Penal Code], Act No. 3815, art. 280–281 (1930).
102. *Ibid*, art. 292 (1930).
103. *Ibid.*
104. 2019 Amendments to the 1989 Revised Rules on Evidence, rule 130, §24.
105. The Rule on the Writ of Habeas Data, A. M. No. 08-1-16-SC, §1 (22 Jan. 2008).
106. *Ibid.*
107. An Act to Prohibit and Penalize Wire Tapping and Other Related Violations of the Privacy of Communication, and for other Purposes [Anti-Wiretapping Law], Republic Act No. 4200 (1965).
108. An Act Defining and Penalizing the Crime of Photo and Video Voyeurism, Prescribing Penalties Therefor, and for Other Purposes [Anti-Photo and Video Voyeurism Act of 2009], Republic Act No. 9995 (2009).
109. An Act Strengthening the Philippine Comprehensive Policy on Human Immunodeficiency Virus (HIV) and Acquired Immune Deficiency Syndrome (AIDS) Prevention, Treatment, Care, and Support, and, Reconstituting the Philippine National Aids Council (PNAC), Repealing for the Purpose

49. Sector-based legislation includes laws on secrecy of bank deposits[110] and foreign currency deposits,[111] and laws protecting women and children against violence, abuse, and discrimination,[112] among others.

Republic Act No. 8504, otherwise known as The 'Philippine Aids Prevention and Control Act of 1998', and Appropriating Funds Therefor [Philippine HIV and AIDS Policy Act], Republic Act No. 11166 (2018).

110. An Act Prohibiting Disclosure of or Inquiry into Deposits with any Banking Institution and Providing Penalty Therefor, Republic Act No. 1405 (1955).

111. An Act Instituting a Foreign Currency Deposit System in the Philippines, and for other Purposes [Foreign Currency Deposit Act of the Philippines], Republic Act No. 6426 (1974).

112. An Act Establishing a Comprehensive Juvenile Justice and Welfare System, Creating the Juvenile Justice and Welfare Council Under the Department of Justice, Appropriating Funds Therefor and For Other Purposes [Juvenile Justice and Welfare Act of 2006], Republic Act No. 9344 (2006); An Act Providing for Stronger Deterrence and Special Protection Against Child Abuse, Exploitation and Discrimination, and For Other Purposes [Special Protection of Children Against Child Abuse, Exploitation and Discrimination Act], Republic Act No. 7610 (1992); An Act Defining Violence Against Women and Their Children, Providing for Protective Measures for Victims, Prescribing Penalties Therefore, and For Other Purposes [Anti-violence Against Women and their Children Act of 2004], Republic Act No. 9262 (2004).

Part II. National Data Protection Law

Chapter 1. Background

§1. General Overview

50. The prevailing law on the right to privacy of personal data or informational privacy is Republic Act No. 10173, otherwise known as the DPA.[113]

51. The Philippine Legislature passed the DPA into law with the intent of establishing a legal regulatory framework on personal data protection that promotes a balance between ensuring fair practices and the free flow of data.[114] It aims to protect the integrity of data by providing safeguards and limiting the unchecked collection of data that leads to a person's identification.[115] It also intends to advance the Philippine economy, particularly in the Information Technology – Business Process Outsourcing (IT-BPO) industry and other Information and Communications Technology (ICT-) driven sectors, by improving the country's information security systems and processes and establishing privacy controls.[116]

52. The DPA finds footing in Senate Bill No. 2965 and House Bill No. 4115.[117] The Philippine Legislature consolidated the Senate version and the House version of the Bills to develop the current law on data privacy protection.[118] In the process of developing the different legislative bills, the Legislature extensively looked at

113. An Act Protecting Individual Personal Information in Information and Communications Systems in the Government and the Private Sector, Creating for this purpose a National Privacy Commission, and For Other Purposes [Data Privacy Act of 2012], Republic Act No. 10173 (2012).
114. An Act Protecting Individual Personal Data in Information and Communications Systems in the Government and the Private Sector, Creating for this Purpose a National Data Privacy Commission, and For Other Purposes, Committee on Information and Communication Technology, H. Comm. Rep., at 26, 15th Cong., 1st Reg. Sess. (2010).
115. S. Journal No. 50, at 958-959, 15th Cong., 2d Reg. Sess. (8 Feb. 2012).
116. S. Journal No. 22, at 360, 15th Cong., 2d Reg. Sess. (21 Sep. 2011).
117. An Act to Establish Fair Practices in the Processing of Information Relating or Personal to Individuals Creating for the Purpose a Personal Data protection Commission, and For Other Purposes, Committee on Government Reorganization and Information and Communications Technology, H. Comm. Rep No. 554, 15th Cong., 1st Reg. Sess. (2011).
118. An Act to Establish Fair Practices in the Processing of Information Relating or Personal to Individuals Creating for the Purpose a Personal Data protection Commission, and For Other Purposes, Committee on Government Reorganization and Information and Communications Technology, H. Comm. Rep No. 554, 15th Cong., 1st Reg. Sess. (2011).

international standards on data privacy and protection.[119] It particularly highlighted the Asia-Pacific Economic Cooperation (APEC) Privacy Framework and the European Union Data Privacy Directive of 1995 (1995 EU Privacy Directive).[120]

53. The DPA upholds the State's policy to protect the fundamental human right to privacy of communication to ensure the free flow of information for innovation and growth.[121] The law is likewise aligned and requires continued compliance with international standards for data protection.[122] It also aims to ensure the security and protection of personal data in information and communication systems in the government and private sectors.[123]

54. The law was promulgated on 15 August 2012 and took effect fifteen days after its publication.[124]

55. The DPA created the Commission as the central administrative agency to administer and implement its provisions.[125] The Commission is mandated by law to enforce the legal regulatory framework on personal data protection in the Philippines and interpret the provisions of the DPA and other data privacy laws.[126]

56. Although the DPA was passed in 2012, the Commission was only constituted in March 2016 when the first set of Commissioners were appointed by then President Benigno C. Aquino III.[127]

57. In 2016, in accordance with its rule-making power as an administrative agency and the express mandate under the DPA, the Commission enacted the Implementing Rules and Regulations of the Data Privacy Act of 2012 (IRR).[128]

---

119. S. Journal No. 55, at 1066, 15th Cong., 2d Reg. Sess. (7 Mar. 2012).
120. *Ibid.*
121. An Act Protecting Individual Personal Information in Information and Communications Systems in the Government and the Private Sector, Creating for this purpose a National Privacy Commission, and For Other Purposes [Data Privacy Act of 2012], Republic Act No. 10173 §2 (2012).
122. S. Journal No. 22, at 360, 15th Cong., 2d Reg. Sess. (21 Sep. 2011); An Act Protecting Individual Personal Information in Information and Communications Systems in the Government and the Private Sector, Creating for this purpose a National Privacy Commission, and For Other Purposes [Data Privacy Act of 2012], Republic Act No. 10173 §7 (2012).
123. An Act Protecting Individual Personal Information in Information and Communications Systems in the Government and the Private Sector, Creating for this purpose a National Privacy Commission, and For Other Purposes [Data Privacy Act of 2012], Republic Act No. 10173 §2 (2012).
124. *Ibid.*, §45.
125. *Ibid.*, §7 (2012).
126. *Ibid.*, §7(l) (2012).
127. *DOST Exec Named First Commissioner of National Privacy Commission*, Newsbytes.PH, 07 Mar. 2016, *available at* https://newsbytes.ph/2016/03/07/dost-exec-named-first-commissioner-of-national-privacy-commission-2/ (last accessed 28 Apr. 2022).
128. National Privacy Commission, Rules and Regulations Implementing the Data Privacy Act of 2012, Republic Act No. 10173 (2016).

58. An IRR is an administrative regulation enacted by an administrative agency to implement and interpret the law which it is entrusted to enforce.[129] An administrative agency, such as the Commission, is enjoined with the power to formulate rules and regulations to implement the law.[130] The rule-making power may fill details of the law or ascertain facts necessary to bring the law into actual operation.[131]

59. The purpose of the IRR is to supplement and further enforce the DPA and adopt generally accepted international principles and standards for personal data protection.[132] The IRR promulgated by the Commission has the force and effect of law and enjoys the presumption of constitutionality and legality until and unless it is set aside with finality by a competent court.[133]

60. The IRR took effect on 9 September 2016.[134]

§2. Privacy Regulatory Framework

61. The data privacy regulatory framework in the Philippines encompasses the DPA, its IRR, the Circulars and Advisories issued by the Commission, and the decisions and resolutions of the Commission interpreting and applying all of these (DPA and other privacy regulations). Aside from these, there are also other pieces of statutory legislation outside the DPA that regulate data protection and confidentiality of personal information.

62. The Commission issues Circulars to fill in the details or supplement the provisions of the DPA or provide means for carrying out the law.[135] It issues Advisories to provide guidance on interpreting the law in relation to specific matters affecting data privacy.[136] The Commission also issues Advisory Opinions pursuant to its Advisory function.[137]

63. Since 2016, the Commission has issued Circulars that interpret the DPA on matters relating to data privacy and data protection. The Circulars supplement the

129. *Abakada Guro Party List v. Purisima*, G.R. No. 166715 (2008).
130. *Ibid.*
131. *Ibid.*
132. National Privacy Commission, Rules and Regulations Implementing the Data Privacy Act of 2012, Republic Act No. 10173, §2 (2016).
133. *Abakada Guro Party List v. Purisima*, G.R. No. 166715 (2008).
134. National Privacy Commission, Rules and Regulations Implementing the Data Privacy Act of 2012, Republic Act No. 10173, §72 (2016); The IRR was promulgated 24 Aug. 2016. National Privacy Commission, Rules and Regulations Implementing the Data Privacy Act of 2012, Republic Act No. 10173 (2016).
135. Instituting the 'Administrative Code of 1987' [Admin. Code], Executive Order No. 292 bk. IV, ch. 11, §50(1) (1987).
136. National Privacy Commission, Rules and Regulations Implementing the Data Privacy Act of 2012, Republic Act No. 10173, §9(b) (2016).
137. *Ibid.*, §9(b)(1).

provisions of the DPA and its IRR in order to strengthen the protection of personal data.[138] The Commission has published Circulars on Security of Personal Data in Government Agencies,[139] Data Sharing Agreements,[140] Personal Data Breach Management,[141] Registration of Data Processing Systems and Notifications Regarding Automated-Decisions-Making,[142] Compliance Checks,[143] and Processing of Personal Data for Loan-Related Transactions.[144]

64. It also published a set of procedural rules that govern proceedings before the Commission, such as the Rules of Procedure,[145] Rules on Mediation,[146] and Rules on the Issuance of Cease and Desist Orders.[147]

65. The Commission also issues Advisories that provide guidance on the processing of personal data in relation to particular matters or situations.[148] These Advisories aim to clarify the application of the DPA and its IRR in certain circumstances and guide the public in its understanding of the privacy regulatory framework. To date, the Commission has issued Advisories that discuss Designation of Data Protection Officers,[149] Access to Personal Data Sheets of Government Personnel,[150] Guidelines on Privacy Impact Assessments,[151] Guidelines and

---

138. *Ibid.*, §9(c)(3).
139. National Privacy Commission, Security of Personal Data in Government Agencies, Circular No. 01, Series of 2016 [NPC Circ. No. 16-01] (10 Oct. 2016).
140. National Privacy Commission, Data Sharing Agreements Involving Government Agencies, Circular No. 02, Series of 2016 [NPC Circ. No. 16-02] (10 Oct. 2016); National Privacy Commission, Data Sharing Agreements, Circular No. 03, Series of 2020 [NPC Circ. No. 20-03] (23 Dec. 2020).
141. National Privacy Commission, Personal Data Breach Management, Circular No. 03, Series of 2016 [NPC Circ. No. 16-03] (15 Dec. 2016).
142. National Privacy Commission, Registration of Data Processing and Notifications regarding Automated Decision-Making, Circular No. 01, Series of 2017 [NPC Circ. No. 17-01] (31 Jul. 2017).
143. National Privacy Commission, Guidelines on Compliance Checks, Circular No. 02, Series of 2018 [NPC Circ. No. 18-02] (20 Sep. 2018).
144. National Privacy Commission, Guidelines on the Processing of Personal Data for Loan-Related Transactions, Circular No. 01, Series of 2020 [NPC Circ. No. 20-01] (14 Sep. 2020). The Circular is in the process of being amended.
145. National Privacy Commission, 2021 Rules of Procedure of the National Privacy Commission, Circular No. 01, Series of 2021 [NPC Circ. No. 21-01] (28 Jan. 2021).
146. *See ibid.*
147. National Privacy Commission, Rules on the Issuance of Cease and Desist Orders, Circular No. 02, Series of 2020 [NPC Circ. No. 20-02] (6 Oct. 2020).
148. *See* National Privacy Commission, Guidelines on the Processing of Personal Data for Election Campaign or Partisan Political Activity, Advisory No. 03, Series of 2021 [NPC Advisory No. 21-03] (5 Nov. 2021); National Privacy Commission, Guidelines for Workplaces and Establishments Processing Personal Data for COVID-19 Response, Advisory No. 03, Series of 2020 [NPC Advisory No. 20-03] (23 Oct. 2020).
149. National Privacy Commission, Designation of Data Protection Officers, Advisory No. 01, Series of 2017 [NPC Advisory No. 17-01] (14 Mar. 2017).
150. National Privacy Commission, Access to Personal Data Sheets of Government Personnel, Advisory No. 02, Series of 2017 [NPC Advisory No. 17-02] (3 Apr. 2017).
151. National Privacy Commission, Guidelines on Privacy Impact Assessments, Advisory No. 03, Series of 2017 [NPC Advisory No. 17-03] (31 Jul. 2017).

Templates[152] on Security Incident and Personal Data Breach Reportorial Requirements,[153] Data Subject Rights,[154] Guidance for the Use of the ASEAN Model Contract Clauses and ASEAN Data Management Framework,[155] and on the Use of Closed-Circuit Television (CCTV) Systems.[156]

66. The Commission likewise issues Advisory Opinions on a wide variety of topics with the aim of assisting entities or persons in the government or private sector on matters relating to informational privacy.[157] The purpose of an Advisory Opinion is to guide the requesting party and the general public.[158] In an Advisory Opinion, the Commission makes a determination on a data privacy issue based on the facts and circumstances provided by the requesting party.[159] The Commission applies the DPA and other privacy regulations on the matter, and other relevant laws in making its determination.[160]

67. An entity or person may request for an Advisory Opinion on the following subjects: (1) interpretation of the DPA and other privacy regulations; (2) compliance requirements under the DPA and related issuances; (3) enforcement of the DPA and the IRR; and (4) other related matters on personal data privacy, security, and protection.[161]

Section 5. Subject of an advisory opinion.

a. The following may be the subject of an advisory opinion:
    1. Interpretation of the provisions of the DPA, its Implementing Rules and Regulations (IRR) and NPC Issuances;
    2. Compliance requirements under the DPA and related issuances;
    3. Enforcement of data privacy laws and regulations; and
    4. Other related matters on personal data privacy, security, and protection.
b. A request for advisory opinion shall not be accommodated if:
    1. The request is on an issue which has been finally decided by the courts or is pending in a case in litigation;

152. National Privacy Commission, Updated Templates on Security Incident and Personal Data Breach Reportorial Requirements, Advisory No. 02, Series of 2018 [NPC Advisory No. 18-02] (26 Jun. 2018).
153. *See also* National Privacy Commission, Personal Data Breach Management, Circular No. 03, Series of 2016 [NPC Circ. No. 16-03] (15 Dec. 2016).
154. National Privacy Commission, Data Subject Rights, Advisory No. 01, Series of 2021 [NPC Advisory No. 21-01] (29 Jan. 2021).
155. National Privacy Commission, Guidance for the Use of the ASEAN Model Contract Clauses and ASEAN Data Management Framework, Advisory No. 02, Series of 2021 [NPC Advisory No. 21-02] (28 Jan. 2021).
156. National Privacy Commission, Guidelines on the Use of Closed-Circuit Television (CCTV) Systems, Advisory No. 04, Series of 2020 [NPC Advisory No. 20-04] (16 Nov. 2020).
157. National Privacy Commission, Rules of Procedure on Requests for Advisory Opinions, Circular No. 01, Series of 2018 [NPC Circ. No. 18-01], §1 (10 Sep. 2018).
158. *Ibid.*
159. *Ibid.*
160. *Ibid.*
161. *Ibid.*, §5(a).

2. The request is related to any matter before the NPC, or is subject of an ongoing investigation or compliance check;
3. The request has previously been the subject of an advisory opinion;
4. The request posits questions, issues or concerns that are too general in scope, overly abstract, anticipatory and speculative;
5. The request requires a review and interpretation of contracts or an opinion on the validity of contracts; or
6. It involves a request for review of a privacy notice, privacy manual, consent form, organization terms and conditions, or other privacy policies.[162]

68. An Advisory Opinion is neither intended to be used for adjudicating issues between conflicting parties nor imposing sanctions or awarding damages.[163] While of educational value, an Advisory Opinion is not considered in the nature of a standing rule that binds the Commission when it evaluates other cases.[164]

162. *Ibid.*, §5(b).
163. *Ibid.*, §2.
164. *Ibid.*

Chapter 2. Scope of the National Law

69. The DPA and other privacy regulations apply to the processing of all types of personal information by any natural or juridical persons[165] in the government or private sector.[166] Its scope encompasses acts of processing personal information performed in and outside the Philippines.[167] It applies to an entity who processes the personal information of any Philippine citizen or resident.[168] The DPA and other privacy regulations continue to apply even if personal information is publicly available or accessible.[169]

70. A natural or juridical person processing personal information is covered by the national law if such entity is found or established in the Philippines.[170] The application of the DPA and other privacy regulations, however, is not limited to entities that are registered or incorporated under Philippine law.[171]

71. It also includes entities with links to the Philippines, such as when: (1) a contract is entered in the Philippines; (2) a juridical entity that is not registered under Philippine law but exercises central management and control[172] in the country; (3)

---

165. An Act Protecting Individual Personal Information in Information and Communications Systems in the Government and the Private Sector, Creating for this purpose a National Privacy Commission, and For Other Purposes [Data Privacy Act of 2012], Republic Act No. 10173 §4 (2012).
166. National Privacy Commission, Rules and Regulations Implementing the Data Privacy Act of 2012, Republic Act No. 10173, §4 (2016).
167. An Act Protecting Individual Personal Information in Information and Communications Systems in the Government and the Private Sector, Creating for this purpose a National Privacy Commission, and For Other Purposes [Data Privacy Act of 2012], Republic Act No. 10173 §6 (2012); National Privacy Commission, Rules and Regulations Implementing the Data Privacy Act of 2012, Republic Act No. 10173, §4 (2016).
168. An Act Protecting Individual Personal Information in Information and Communications Systems in the Government and the Private Sector, Creating for this purpose a National Privacy Commission, and For Other Purposes [Data Privacy Act of 2012], Republic Act No. 10173 §6(a) (2012); National Privacy Commission, Rules and Regulations Implementing the Data Privacy Act of 2012, Republic Act No. 10173, §4(b) (2016).
169. National Privacy Commission, Re: Request for Official List of Legitimate Taxi Operators, Advisory Opinion No. 008, Series of 2021, at 4 (15 Mar. 2021).
170. An Act Protecting Individual Personal Information in Information and Communications Systems in the Government and the Private Sector, Creating for this purpose a National Privacy Commission, and For Other Purposes [Data Privacy Act of 2012], Republic Act No. 10173 §4 (2012).
171. National Privacy Commission, Rules and Regulations Implementing the Data Privacy Act of 2012, Republic Act No. 10173, §4(a) (2016).
172. 'Mere legal title is insufficient to meet the 60 percent Filipino-owned 'capital' required in the Constitution. Full beneficial ownership of 60 percent of the outstanding capital stock, coupled with 60 percent of the voting rights, is required. The legal and beneficial ownership of 60 percent of the outstanding capital stock must rest in the hands of Filipino nationals in accordance with the constitutional mandate. Otherwise, the corporation is 'considered as non-Philippine national[s].' ... The legal and beneficial ownership of 60 percent of the outstanding capital stock must rest in the hands of Filipinos in accordance with the constitutional mandate. Full beneficial ownership of 60 percent of the outstanding capital stock, coupled with 60 percent of the voting rights, is constitutionally required for the State's grant of authority to operate a public utility'. *Gamboa v. Teves*, G.R. No. 176579 (2011).

an entity that has established a branch, agency, office, or subsidiary in the Philippines and the parent or affiliate of the Philippine entity has access to personal information; (4) the entity carries out business in the Philippines; (5) an entity collects or holds personal information in the Philippines; and (6) an entity uses equipment located in the Philippines.[173] In such cases, the nationality or resident of the data subjects is immaterial.[174]

72. The DPA and other privacy regulations do not apply to: (1) personal information that relates to positions or functions of public officials or employees;[175] (2) information relating to any discretionary financial benefit granted by the government to an individual;[176] and (3) information necessary to carry out functions of public authority and to comply with the law, including the central monetary board, law enforcement and regulatory agencies,[177] and registered banks and other financial institutions.[178] For government agencies, personal information is outside the scope of the DPA if it is necessary to carry out the function of the public authority and the processing of such personal information is for the performance of a constitutional or statutory mandate.[179]

173. An Act Protecting Individual Personal Information in Information and Communications Systems in the Government and the Private Sector, Creating for this purpose a National Privacy Commission, and For Other Purposes [Data Privacy Act of 2012], Republic Act No. 10173 §6(b) (2012); National Privacy Commission, Rules and Regulations Implementing the Data Privacy Act of 2012, Republic Act No. 10173, §4(d) (2016).
174. National Privacy Commission, Re: Scope and Coverage of the Data Privacy Act, Advisory Opinion No. 22, Series of 2018, at 2 (30 Apr. 2018).
175. An Act Protecting Individual Personal Information in Information and Communications Systems in the Government and the Private Sector, Creating for this purpose a National Privacy Commission, and For Other Purposes [Data Privacy Act of 2012], Republic Act No. 10173 §4(a) (2012); National Privacy Commission, Rules and Regulations Implementing the Data Privacy Act of 2012, Republic Act No. 10173, §5(a) (1) (2016).
176. An Act Protecting Individual Personal Information in Information and Communications Systems in the Government and the Private Sector, Creating for this purpose a National Privacy Commission, and For Other Purposes [Data Privacy Act of 2012], Republic Act No. 10173 §4(c) (2012); National Privacy Commission, Rules and Regulations Implementing the Data Privacy Act of 2012, Republic Act No. 10173, §5(a)(3) (2016).
177. An Act Protecting Individual Personal Information in Information and Communications Systems in the Government and the Private Sector, Creating for this purpose a National Privacy Commission, and For Other Purposes [Data Privacy Act of 2012], Republic Act No. 10173 §4(e) (2012); National Privacy Commission, Rules and Regulations Implementing the Data Privacy Act of 2012, Republic Act No. 10173, §5(d) (2016).
178. An Act Protecting Individual Personal Information in Information and Communications Systems in the Government and the Private Sector, Creating for this purpose a National Privacy Commission, and For Other Purposes [Data Privacy Act of 2012], Republic Act No. 10173 §4(f) (2012); National Privacy Commission, Rules and Regulations Implementing the Data Privacy Act of 2012, Republic Act No. 10173, §5(e) (2016).
179. National Privacy Commission, Re: Authentication of a Marriage Contract for Purpose of Investigation, Advisory Opinion No. 79, Series of 2018, at 2 (23 Oct. 2018).

73. The DPA and other privacy regulations likewise do not apply to personal information processed for journalistic, artistic, or literary purposes to uphold freedom of speech, expression, or the press,[180] and personal information processed for research purposes intended for a public benefit.[181]

74. These exceptions to the law, however, are not absolute. The Commission has consistently interpreted that these exceptions apply only to the type of information processed and not to the entity processing the same.[182] This means that personal information covered by the exception may be processed without meeting any of the criteria for lawful processing of personal information and sensitive personal information provided under section 12 or section 13 of the DPA, respectively.[183]

75. The DPA and other privacy regulations also do not apply to personal information processed in the Philippines that have been originally collected from residents of foreign jurisdictions and in line with the respective foreign laws.[184] Under this exception, entities can continue processing in the Philippines the personal information collected in foreign jurisdictions without needing to comply with sections 12 and 13 of the DPA on the lawful criteria to process personal information. It remains incumbent upon the party seeking an exemption to prove (1) the law of the foreign jurisdiction applicable to the collection of personal information, and (2) that such law was complied with in the case of the personal information it is processing in the Philippines.[185]

76. The processing of personal information shall only be to the minimum extent necessary to achieve the specific purpose, function, or activity. The minimum extent necessary is determined on a case-by-case basis in relation to the general privacy principles of transparency, legitimate purpose, and proportionality.[186]

---

180. An Act Protecting Individual Personal Information in Information and Communications Systems in the Government and the Private Sector, Creating for this purpose a National Privacy Commission, and For Other Purposes [Data Privacy Act of 2012], Republic Act No. 10173 §4(d) (2012); National Privacy Commission, Rules and Regulations Implementing the Data Privacy Act of 2012, Republic Act No. 10173, §5(b) (2016).
181. National Privacy Commission, Rules and Regulations Implementing the Data Privacy Act of 2012, Republic Act No. 10173, §5(c) (2016).
182. National Privacy Commission, Re: Submission of Credit Information by Cooperatives to the Credit Information Corporation (CIC), Advisory Opinion No. 48, Series of 2017, at 3 (29 Aug. 2017).
183. National Privacy Commission, Re: Proposed Bangko Sentral ng Pilipinas and Department of Interior and Local Government Joint Memorandum Circular in the Issuance of Business License/ Permit for Pawnshops and Money Service Businesses, Advisory Opinion No. 14, Series of 2019, at 3 (5 Mar. 2019); National Privacy Commission, Re: Disclosure of Personal Information to the Bangko Sentral ng Pilipinas, Advisory Opinion No. 60, Series of 2018, at 2 (30 Aug. 2018).
184. An Act Protecting Individual Personal Information in Information and Communications Systems in the Government and the Private Sector, Creating for this purpose a National Privacy Commission, and For Other Purposes [Data Privacy Act of 2012], Republic Act No. 10173 §4(g) (2012); National Privacy Commission, Rules and Regulations Implementing the Data Privacy Act of 2012, Republic Act No. 10173, §5(f) (2016).
185. National Privacy Commission, Rules and Regulations Implementing the Data Privacy Act of 2012, Republic Act No. 10173, §5(f) (2016).
186. *Ibid.*

77. The exception from the DPA[187] only applies to lawful criteria. Notwithstanding the exception, the person or entity processing the personal information is still required to comply with the other provisions of the DPA and other privacy regulations, such as the other obligations of a PIC, particularly the need to implement reasonable and appropriate physical, organizational, and technical security measures, uphold the rights of data subjects, and adhere to the data privacy principles of transparency, legitimate purpose, and proportionality.[188]

78. Anonymized data is excluded from the scope of the DPA.[189] This is understood in relation to the concept of personal information. Personal information is defined as:

> Section. 3. *Definition of Terms.* Whenever used in this Act, the following terms shall have the respective meanings hereafter set forth:
>
> . . .
>
> (g) Personal information refers to any information whether recorded in a material form or not, *from which the identity of an individual is apparent or can be reasonably and directly ascertained by the entity holding the information, or when put together with other information would directly and certainly identify an individual.*[190]

79. A piece of information is deemed personal information if it can identify an individual. If information is truly anonymized, it can no longer lead to the identification of a data subject.[191] This, then, takes it out of the context of personal information and outside the scope of the DPA.[192] For personal information to be considered truly anonymized, anonymization must be irreversible that it is impossible or extremely impractical to identify the data subject.[193]

---

187. *See* An Act Protecting Individual Personal Information in Information and Communications Systems in the Government and the Private Sector, Creating for this purpose a National Privacy Commission, and For Other Purposes [Data Privacy Act of 2012], Republic Act No. 10173 §4 (2012).
188. National Privacy Commission, Re: Disclosure of Personal Information of Tenants by a Condominium Corporation to the Bureau of Internal Revenue, Advisory Opinion No. 28, Series of 2021, at 2 (16 Jul. 2021).
189. National Privacy Commission, Re: Storage and Sharing of Electronic Medical Records (EMR), Advisory Opinion No. 32, Series of 2019, at 4 (12 Sep. 2019); National Privacy Commission, Re: Phone Usage Data Records, Advisory Opinion No. 69, Series of 2018, at 1 (2 Oct. 2018).
190. An Act Protecting Individual Personal Information in Information and Communications Systems in the Government and the Private Sector, Creating for this purpose a National Privacy Commission, and For Other Purposes [Data Privacy Act of 2012], Republic Act No. 10173 §3(g) (2012). Emphasis supplied.
191. National Privacy Commission, Re: Anonymized Data for Marketing Analytics, Advisory Opinion No. 27, Series of 2017, at 2 (23 Jun. 2017).
192. *Ibid.*
193. National Privacy Commission, Re: Processing of Anonymized Personal Data by Electronic Medical Records Provider, Advisory Opinion No. 68, Series of 2018, at 2 (20 Nov. 2018).

80. Any form of pseudonymization, such as the replacement of an attribute of personal information in a record,[194] however, is not sufficient since the personal information remains to be personal data.[195] Pseudonymization only replaces some and not all categories of personal information and the remaining personal information may still be used to identify the data subject.[196] Since pseudonymization is reversible, as opposed to anonymization, the nature of the personal information remains unchanged and the DPA and other privacy regulations will continue to apply.

---

194. National Privacy Commission, Re: Compliance of Resident Physicians to the Requirement of Professional Societies for Diplomate Board Exam and Accreditation, Advisory Opinion No. 16, Series of 2018, at 2 (12 Apr. 2018).
195. National Privacy Commission, Re: Pseudonymization of Personal and Sensitive Personal Information, Advisory Opinion No. 29, Series of 2018, at 2 (0 Jun. 2018).
196. National Privacy Commission, Re: Compliance of Resident Physicians to the Requirement of Professional Societies for Diplomate Board Exam and Accreditation, Advisory Opinion No. 16, Series of 2018, at 2 (12 Apr. 2018).

Chapter 3. Concepts and Definitions

81. The DPA and its IRR discuss key concepts that are relevant to the administration and enforcement of the privacy regulatory framework of the Philippines.

82. Personal data encompasses all types of personal information.[197] This includes personal information, sensitive personal information, and privileged communication.[198]

83. Personal information is defined as any information from which the identity of an individual or a data subject is apparent or can be reasonably and directly ascertained by the entity holding the information.[199] Information is also considered personal information if such, when put together with other information, would directly and certainly identify an individual or a data subject.[200] Personal information need not be recorded in a material form.[201] Section 3 of the DPA states:

> Section. 3. *Definition of Terms.* Whenever used in this Act, the following terms shall have the respective meanings hereafter set forth:
>
> . . .
>
> (g) Personal information refers to any information whether recorded in a material form or not, *from which the identity of an individual is apparent or can be reasonably and directly ascertained by the entity holding the information, or when put together with other information would directly and certainly identify an individual.*[202]

84. Some examples of personal information include name,[203] a photograph of an identifiable individual,[204] employment details,[205] bank account number and bank

197. An Act Protecting Individual Personal Information in Information and Communications Systems in the Government and the Private Sector, Creating for this purpose a National Privacy Commission, and For Other Purposes [Data Privacy Act of 2012], Republic Act No. 10173 §3(g) (2012).
198. National Privacy Commission, Re: Rules Governing Certain Information Relating to Corporations, Advisory Opinion No. 10, Series of 2017, at 1 (16 Jan. 2017).
199. An Act Protecting Individual Personal Information in Information and Communications Systems in the Government and the Private Sector, Creating for this purpose a National Privacy Commission, and For Other Purposes [Data Privacy Act of 2012], Republic Act No. 10173 §3(g) (2012).
200. *Ibid.*
201. *Ibid.*
202. *Ibid.* Emphasis supplied.
203. National Privacy Commission, Re: Common Practices of Schools in Processing Personal Data of Students, Advisory Opinion No. 46, Series of 2020, at 3 (9 Nov. 2020).
204. National Privacy Commission, Re: Photographs and CCTV Footages in Hospitals, Advisory Opinion No. 53, Series of 2018, at 1 (26 Nov. 2018).
205. National Privacy Commission, Re: Collection Agency Communicating with Human Resource Department, Advisory Opinion No. 06, Series of 2020, at 2 (7 Feb. 2020).

account transaction history of a potential borrower,[206] names of members of a homeowners' association and their respective membership standing,[207] names of tenants and their respective unit numbers,[208] the last known address of a former employee,[209] college department,[210] and signature.[211]

85. In CID BN 18-072, the Commission held that an e-mail address is also considered as personal information, especially if it contains the name of the data subject or any other information from which the identity of the data subject may be apparent or reasonably and directly ascertained.[212]

86. Information is also considered personal information when such information, when put together with other information, would directly and certainly identify an individual.[213] To determine whether such information would result in the identification of an individual depends on whether the PIC or PIP used reasonable time, effort, and resources to directly and certainly identify an individual. Reasonableness is determined based on the circumstances of a particular case. If the use of unlimited time, effort, and resources is permitted, then all information will fall under the definition of personal information under the DPA. This, however, is not what the law contemplates.

87. Sensitive personal information consists of personal information which when processed, results in a higher degree of potential risk to the data subject and the enhanced protection necessary to avert such risk.[214] Section 3 of the DPA enumerates the following as sensitive personal information:

> Section 3. *Definition of Terms.* Whenever used in this Act, the following terms shall have the respective meanings hereafter set forth:
>
> . . .
>
> (l) *Sensitive personal information* refers to personal information:

---

206. National Privacy Commission, Re: Automated Retrieval of Bank Transaction History, Advisory Opinion No. 21, Series of 2020, at 2 (29 May 2020).
207. National Privacy Commission, Re: Disclosure of the Names of the Unit Owners/Members of a Condominium Association, Advisory Opinion No. 25, Series of 2019, at 1 (7 May 2019).
208. National Privacy Commission, Re: Disclosure of the Names of the Unit Owners/Members of a Homeowners' Association, Advisory Opinion No. 27, Series of 2019, at 1 (0 Jun. 2019).
209. National Privacy Commission, Re: Request for the Last Known Address of a Former Employee, Advisory Opinion No. 50, Series of 2019, at 2 (12 Dec. 2019).
210. *KRL v. University*, AA, MC, NCB, RG GV, GCT, RR, MR, PB, CID 17-K-003, 19 Nov. 2019, at 9, *available at* https://www.privacy.gov.ph/wp-content/uploads/2022/04/CID-17-K-003-KRL-v.-University-Decision-2019.11.19-.pdf (last accessed 28 Apr. 2022).
211. *Ibid.*
212. CID BN 18-072, 23 Jul. 2020, at 3 (NPC 2020) (unreported).
213. An Act Protecting Individual Personal Information in Information and Communications Systems in the Government and the Private Sector, Creating for this purpose a National Privacy Commission, and For Other Purposes [Data Privacy Act of 2012], Republic Act No. 10173 §3(g) (2012).
214. *EA and TA v. EJ*, NPC Case No. 17-018, 15 Jul. 2019, at 7, *available at* https://www.privacy.gov.ph/wp-content/uploads/2022/04/NPC-17-018-EA-and-TA-v-EJ-Decision-2019.07.15-.pdf (last accessed 28 Apr. 2022).

(1) About an individual's race, ethnic origin, marital status, age, color, and religious, philosophical or political affiliations;
(2) About an individual's health, education, genetic or sexual life of a person, or to any proceeding for any offense committed or alleged to have been committed by such person, the disposal of such proceedings, or the sentence of any court in such proceedings;
(3) Issued by government agencies peculiar to an individual which includes, but not limited to, social security numbers, previous or current health records, licenses or its denials, suspension or revocation, and tax returns; and
(4) Specifically established by an executive order or an act of Congress to be kept classified.[215]

88. Some specific examples of sensitive personal information are: educational records,[216] health and medical records, including out-patient records, autopsy records,[217] clinical photographs,[218] hospital billings, itemized hospital charges, other medical-related expenses,[219] government-issued identification numbers as well as their respective dates of issuance,[220] civil status,[221] and nationality[222].

89. Sensitive personal information that is specifically established by the Executive or Legislative departments to be kept classified refers to classified information or information that requires protection in the interest of national security.[223] These include the following information:

4. Definition. – Information and material (matter) the unauthorized disclosure of which would cause exceptionally grave damage to the nation, politically,

215. An Act Protecting Individual Personal Information in Information and Communications Systems in the Government and the Private Sector, Creating for this purpose a National Privacy Commission, and For Other Purposes [Data Privacy Act of 2012], Republic Act No. 10173 §3(l) (2012). Emphasis supplied.
216. NPC Case No. 18-141, 9 Jun. 2020, at 7 (NPC 2020) (unreported).
217. National Privacy Commission, Re: Access to and Processing of Medical Records for Cancer Registries, Advisory Opinion No. 31, Series of 2019, at 2 (5 Sep. 2019).
218. National Privacy Commission, Re: Photographs and CCTV Footages in Hospitals, Advisory Opinion No. 53, Series of 2018, at 2 (26 Nov. 2018).
219. National Privacy Commission, Re: Access to Employee 201 Files and Medical Records, Advisory Opinion No. 10, Series of 2019, at 3 (14 Jan. 2019).
220. NPC BN 20-149, 20 Aug. 2020, at 4 (NPC 2020) (unreported).
221. An Act Protecting Individual Personal Information in Information and Communications Systems in the Government and the Private Sector, Creating for this purpose a National Privacy Commission, and For Other Purposes [Data Privacy Act of 2012], Republic Act No. 10173 §3(l)(1) (2012).
222. *Ibid.*, Republic Act No. 10173 §3(l).
223. Office of the President, Amending Memorandum Circular 78 dated 14 Aug. 1964, Entitled 'Promulgating Rules Governing Security of Classified Matter in Government Offices.', Memorandum Circular No. 196 (19 Jul. 1968); Office of the President, Establishing a National Security Clearance System for Government Personnel with Access to Classified Matters and for Other Purposes, Executive Order No. 608 (30 Mar. 2007).

economically, or from a securing aspect. This category is reserved for the nation's closest secrets and is to be used with great reserve.[224]
11. Definition. – Information and material (matter) the unauthorized disclosure of which would endanger national security, cause serious injury to the interest or prestige of the nation or of any governmental activity or would be of great advantage to a foreign nation. [225]
17. Definition. – Information and material (matter) the unauthorized disclosure of which, while not endangering the national security, would be prejudicial to the interest or prestige of the nation or any government activity, or would cause administrative embarrassment or unwarranted injury to an individual or would be of advantage to a foreign nation.[226]

90. Sensitive personal information does not necessarily cover information characterized as 'confidential' by law. In such cases, confidential information is still identified as personal or sensitive personal information according to the definitions under the DPA.

91. Privileged information are data that arise from privileged communications under the Rules of Court and other relevant laws.[227] The Rules of Court is a set of laws on 'the protection and enforcement of constitutional rights, pleading, practice, and procedure in all courts'.[228] It also regulates the admission to the practice of law, the Integrated Bar, and the provision of legal assistance to the underprivileged.[229] The Rules of Court apply to all courts[230] and governs procedure in civil and criminal actions and special proceedings.[231]

92. Privileged information is discussed in section 24 of Rule 130 of the 2019 Amendments to the Revised Rules on Evidence:

> Section 24. *Disqualification by reason of privileged communication[s].* The following persons cannot testify as to matters learned in confidence in the following cases:
>
> (a) The husband or the wife, during or after the marriage, cannot be examined without the consent of the other as to any communication received in confidence by one from the other during the marriage except in a civil case by one against the other, or in a criminal case for a crime committed by one against the other or the latter's direct descendants or ascendants.

224. Office of the President, Promulgating Rules Governing Security of Classified Matter in Government Offices, Memorandum Circular No. 78, §II (4) (14 Aug. 1964).
225. *Ibid.*, §III (11).
226. *Ibid.*, §IV (17).
227. An Act Protecting Individual Personal Information in Information and Communications Systems in the Government and the Private Sector, Creating for this purpose a National Privacy Commission, and For Other Purposes [Data Privacy Act of 2012], Republic Act No. 10173 §3(k) (2012).
228. Phil. Const. art. VIII, §5(5).
229. *Ibid.*
230. 2019 Amendments to the 1997 Rules of Civil Procedure, rule 1, §2.
231. *Ibid.*, §3.

(b) An attorney or person reasonably believed by the client to be licensed to engage in the practice of law cannot, without the consent of the client, be examined as to any communication made by the client to him or her, or his or her advice given thereon in the course of, or with a view to, professional employment, nor can an attorney's secretary, stenographer, or clerk, or other persons assisting the attorney be examined, without the consent of the client and his or her employer, concerning any fact the knowledge of which has been acquired in such capacity, except in the following cases:
   (i) *Furtherance of crime or fraud.* If the services or advice of the lawyer were sought or obtained to enable or aid anyone to commit or plan to commit what the client knew or reasonably should have known to be a crime or fraud;
   (ii) *Claimants through same deceased client.* As to a communication relevant to an issue between parties who claim through the same deceased client, regardless of whether the claims are by testate or intestate or by *inter vivos* transaction;
   (iii) *Breach of duty by lawyer or client.* As to a communication relevant to an issue of breach of duty by the lawyer to his or her client, or by the client to his or her lawyer;
   (iv) *Document attested by the lawyer.* As to a communication relevant to an issue concerning an attested document to which the lawyer is an attesting witness; or
   (v) *Joint clients.* As to a communication relevant to a matter of common interest between two [(2)] or more clients if the communication was made by any of them to a lawyer retained or consulted in common, when offered in an action between any of the clients, unless they have expressly agreed otherwise.

(c) A physician, psychotherapist or person reasonably believed by the patient to be authorized to practice medicine or psychotherapy cannot in a civil case, without the consent of the patient, be examined as to any confidential communication made for the purpose of diagnosis or treatment of the patient's physical, mental or emotional condition, including alcohol or drug addiction, between the patient and his or her physician or psychotherapist. This privilege also applies to persons, including members of the patient's family, who have participated in the diagnosis or treatment of the patient under the direction of the physician or psychotherapist.

93. A 'psychotherapist' is:

(a) A person licensed to practice medicine engaged in the diagnosis or treatment of a mental or emotional condition, or
(b) A person licensed as a psychologist by the government while similarly engaged.
(c) A minister, priest or person reasonably believed to be so cannot, without the consent of the affected person, be examined as to any communication

or confession made to or any advice given by him or her, in his or her professional character, in the course of discipline enjoined by the church to which the minister or priest belongs.

(d) A public officer cannot be examined during or after his or her tenure as to communications made to him or her in official confidence, when the court finds that the public interest would suffer by the disclosure.

The communication shall remain privileged, even in the hands of a third person who may have obtained the information, provided that the original parties to the communication took reasonable precaution to protect its confidentiality.[232]

94. Communication is deemed privileged and thus, inadmissible as testimony, if it concerns matters learned in confidence by reason of relationship.[233]

95. Processing encompasses a wide set of operations that a PIC or a PIP performs on the personal data of a data subject.[234] As previously stated, it involves the collection, recording, organization, storage, updating or modification, retrieval, consultation, use, consolidation, blocking, until the erasure or destruction of data.[235] It may be performed through automated means or manual processing if the personal data are contained or intended to be contained in a filing system.[236] The DPA does not distinguish between the processing of personal data through digital means or in paper form.[237]

96. A data subject is an individual or a natural person whose personal data is processed.[238] The data subject is entitled to rights under the DPA. These are the right to be informed, the right to access, the right to object, the right to erasure and blocking, the right to rectify, the right to file a complaint, the right to damages, and the right to data portability.[239] The term 'data subject' excludes corporations or other juridical entities.[240]

---

232. 2019 Amendments to the 1989 Revised Rules on Evidence, rule 130, §24.
233. *Ibid.*
234. National Privacy Commission, Re: Processing of Anonymized Personal Data by Electronic Medical Records Provider, Advisory Opinion No. 68, Series of 2018, at 1 (20 Nov. 2018).
235. An Act Protecting Individual Personal Information in Information and Communications Systems in the Government and the Private Sector, Creating for this purpose a National Privacy Commission, and For Other Purposes [Data Privacy Act of 2012], Republic Act No. 10173 §3(j) (2012).
236. National Privacy Commission, Rules and Regulations Implementing the Data Privacy Act of 2012, Republic Act No. 10173, §3(o) (2016).
237. *EA and TA v. EJ*, NPC Case No. 17-018, 15 Jul. 2019, at 6, available at https://www.privacy.gov.ph/wp-content/uploads/2022/04/NPC-17-018-EA-and-TA-v-EJ-Decision-2019.07.15-.pdf (last accessed 28 Apr. 2022).
238. An Act Protecting Individual Personal Information in Information and Communications Systems in the Government and the Private Sector, Creating for this purpose a National Privacy Commission, and For Other Purposes [Data Privacy Act of 2012], Republic Act No. 10173 §3(c) (2012).
239. *Ibid.*, chapter IV (2012).
240. National Privacy Commission, Re: Publication of List of Cases Filed Against Employers for Non-Payment of Social Security Contributions, Advisory Opinion No. 28, Series of 2019, at 2 (1 Aug. 2019).

97. A PIC is a natural or juridical person or entity who controls the processing of personal data or instructs another (a PIP) to process the personal data on its behalf.[241] The decisive element is the existence and level of control over the processing of personal information.[242] Control over personal data exists if such person or entity decides on the type of information collected, its purpose, or the extent of processing such information.[243] A person or entity is not considered a PIC if (1) the processing has been instructed by another person or organization, in which case such person or entity is deemed a PIP, or (2) the processing is performed in connection with his or her personal, family, or household affairs.[244]

98. A PIP is a natural or juridical person or entity to whom a PIC outsources or instructs the processing of personal data.[245]

99. The definitions of a PIC and a PIP, however, are not mutually exclusive. An entity can be identified as both a PIC and a PIP depending on the specific processing undertaken by such entity. This is determined based on the information available on a case-by-case basis.

100. In certain cases, an entity acting under the instructions of another may still be considered as a PIC. If such entity exhibits control over the processing of the personal information and still determines what information is collected from the data subject and determines the processing and extent of the use of such information, then it is still acting as a PIC.[246]

---

241. An Act Protecting Individual Personal Information in Information and Communications Systems in the Government and the Private Sector, Creating for this purpose a National Privacy Commission, and For Other Purposes [Data Privacy Act of 2012], Republic Act No. 10173 §3(h) (2012).
242. National Privacy Commission, Re: Treatment of Insurance Agents under the DPA, Advisory Opinion No. 73, Series of 2018, at 2 (22 Nov. 2018).
243. National Privacy Commission, Rules and Regulations Implementing the Data Privacy Act of 2012, Republic Act No. 10173, §3(m) (2016).
244. An Act Protecting Individual Personal Information in Information and Communications Systems in the Government and the Private Sector, Creating for this purpose a National Privacy Commission, and For Other Purposes [Data Privacy Act of 2012], Republic Act No. 10173 §3(h) (2012).
245. *Ibid.*, Republic Act No. 10173 §3(i).
246. National Privacy Commission, Re: Deletion of Electronic Medical Records, Advisory Opinion No. 009, Series of 2020, at 2 (4 Feb. 2020); *RLA v. PLDT Enterprise*, NPC BN 18-010, 10 Dec. 2021, at 11, *available at* https://www.privacy.gov.ph/wp-content/uploads/2022/03/02-NPC_18_010_RLA_v_PLDT_Enterprise_Resolution_w_Dissenting_Opinion.pdf (last accessed 28 Apr. 2022).

Part III. General Privacy Principles

Chapter 1. Data Quality Principles

101. The processing of personal data has to conform with the general privacy principles of transparency, legitimate purpose, and proportionality:

> Section 11. *General Data Privacy Principles.* The processing of personal information shall be allowed, subject to compliance with the requirements of this Act and other laws allowing disclosure of information to the public and *adherence to the principles of transparency, legitimate purpose and proportionality.*[247]

102. The privacy principles serve as the cornerstone of the DPA and other privacy regulations. Section 18 of the IRR elaborates on these privacy principles:

> Section 18. *Principles of Transparency, Legitimate Purpose and Proportionality.* The processing of personal data shall be allowed subject to adherence to the principles of transparency, legitimate purpose, and proportionality.
>
> (a) Transparency. The data subject must be aware of the nature, purpose, and extent of the processing of his or her personal data, including the risks and safeguards involved, the identity of personal information controller, his or her rights as a data subject, and how these can be exercised. Any information and communication relating to the processing of personal data should be easy to access and understand, using clear and plain language.
> (b) Legitimate purpose. The processing of information shall be compatible with a declared and specified purpose which must not be contrary to law, morals, or public policy.
> (c) Proportionality. The processing of information shall be adequate, relevant, suitable, necessary, and not excessive in relation to a declared and specified purpose. Personal data shall be processed only if the purpose of the processing could not reasonably be fulfilled by other means.[248]

247. An Act Protecting Individual Personal Information in Information and Communications Systems in the Government and the Private Sector, Creating for this purpose a National Privacy Commission, and For Other Purposes [Data Privacy Act of 2012], Republic Act No. 10173 §11 (2012). Emphasis supplied.
248. National Privacy Commission, Rules and Regulations Implementing the Data Privacy Act of 2012, Republic Act No. 10173, §18 (2016).

103. Section 19 of the IRR also provides for general principles in the collection, processing, and retention of personal data.[249] In doing so, the IRR did not provide for additional general privacy principles but simply elaborated on the general privacy principles of transparency, legitimate purpose, and proportionality. Thus, processing should be understood in relation to the general privacy principles.

§1. Transparency

104. The principle of transparency requires the PIC to ensure that the data subject is aware of the nature, purpose, and extent of the processing of his or her personal data.[250]

105. Section 11 of the DPA illustrates the requirements for the collection of personal data, which are rooted in the principle of transparency:

> Section 11. *General Data Privacy Principles.*
>
> . . .
>
> Personal information must be:
>
> (a) *Collected for specified and legitimate purposes determined and declared before, or as soon as reasonably practicable after collection*, and later processed in a way compatible with such declared, specified and legitimate purposes only[.][251]

106. Section 19 of the IRR further elaborates on the general principles of collection, processing, and retention of personal data:

> Section 19. *General principles in collection, processing and retention.*
>
> The processing of personal data shall adhere to the following general principles in the collection, processing, and retention of personal data:
>
> a. Collection must be for a declared, specified, and legitimate purpose.
>   1. Consent is required prior to the collection and processing of personal data, subject to exemptions provided by the Act and other applicable laws and regulations. When consent is required, it must be time-bound in relation to the declared, specified and legitimate purpose. Consent given may be withdrawn.
>   2. *The data subject must be provided specific information regarding the purpose and extent of processing*, including, where applicable, the

249. *Ibid.*, §19.
250. *Ibid.*, §18.
251. An Act Protecting Individual Personal Information in Information and Communications Systems in the Government and the Private Sector, Creating for this purpose a National Privacy Commission, and For Other Purposes [Data Privacy Act of 2012], Republic Act No. 10173 §11 (2012). Emphasis supplied.

automated processing of his or her personal data for profiling, or processing for direct marketing, and data sharing.

. . .

b. Personal data shall be processed fairly and lawfully.
   1. Processing shall uphold the rights of the data subject, including the right to refuse, withdraw consent, or object. *It shall likewise be transparent, and allow the data subject sufficient information to know the nature and extent of processing.*
   2. *Information provided to a data subject must always be in clear and plain language to ensure that they are easy to understand and access.*[252]

107. The nature, purpose, and extent of the processing of personal data are usually conveyed by PICs to the data subjects through privacy policies, notices, or terms and conditions.[253] The principle of transparency requires that these materials should be easily accessible and understandable by the data subjects and should be in clear and plain language.[254]

108. The requirement to use clear and plain language means that information should be provided in as simple a manner as possible.[255] Complex sentence or language structures should be avoided and the information should be concrete and definitive.[256] The test to determine if the PIC has complied with the general privacy principle of transparency is to examine whether an average member of the target audience could have understood the information provided to them.[257] This, however, does not mean using layman's terms to substitute technical words at the risk of not capturing the complex concepts they represent.[258] The Commission also discourages the use of abstract or ambivalent terms or those that leave room for different interpretations[259] or vague and overbroad language such as 'including but not limited to'.[260] In NPC 19-450, the Commission emphasized the 'clear and plain language' requirement:

> While the Commission finds that the allegations of Complainant are not sufficiently substantiated to warrant a recommendation for prosecution, it finds it

252. National Privacy Commission, Rules and Regulations Implementing the Data Privacy Act of 2012, Republic Act No. 10173, §19 (2016). Emphasis supplied.
253. NPC Case No. 17-018, 05 Nov. 2020, at 4 (NPC 2020) (unreported).
254. National Privacy Commission, Rules and Regulations Implementing the Data Privacy Act of 2012, Republic Act No. 10173, §18 (2016).
255. *See* The Working Party on the Protection of Individuals with regard to the Processing of Personal Data, *Article 29 Working Party Guidelines on transparency under Regulation 2016/679,* at 8–11, WP260 rev.01 (11 Apr. 2018).
256. NPC Case No. 19-531, 21 May 2020, at 4 (NPC 2020) (unreported).
257. NPC Case No 19-498, 9 Jun. 2020, at 7 (NPC 2020) (unreported).
258. *Ibid.*
259. *Ibid.*
260. *JRG v. CXXX Lending Corporation*, NPC Case No. 19-450, 9 Jun. 2020, at 6, *available at* https://www.privacy.gov.ph/wp-content/uploads/2022/01/Decision_NPC-19-450-JRG-v.-CXXX.pdf (last accessed 22 Apr. 2022).

> necessary to emphasize the need for personal information controllers, such as Respondent, to inform their data subjects of the purpose of the processing of their personal information in 'clear and plain language.' The requirement to use clear and plain language does not mean using layman's terms to substitute technical words at the risk of not capturing the complex concepts they represent. Rather, this requirement means that information should be provided in as simple a manner as possible, avoiding sentence or language structures that are complex. The information provided should be concrete and definitive; it should not be phrased in abstract or ambivalent terms or leave room for different interpretations such as in the above-cited provision which uses the word 'any' several times, as well as wordings like 'including but not limited to'.[261]

109. In NPC Case No. 19-498, the Commission held that 'vague, overbroad, and confusing language cannot be said to comply with the requirements of the transparency principle'.[262] In this case, the PIC, an online lending company, presented a loan agreement to its data subjects with the following statement:

> Any information and data received from the Borrower by the Lender may be used and utilized by the Lender, either directly or indirectly in the performance of the terms under this Agreement.[263]

110. The PIC also requested its data subjects' 'permission to access and use the contacts of borrowers' by sending through its agents the following statement:

> Hello! [PIC] needs to safely process your data so that you are qualified for [sic] loan... [PIC] should be authorized for contact person and text message. We will process information for [sic] build your network with your financial record. Without your permission, we won't reach any of your contact.[264]

111. These statements fail to satisfy the transparency principle since the data subjects were not informed of the nature, purpose, and extent of the processing that the PIC is permitted to undertake, including what it can disclose.[265] The Commission explained as follows:

> This vague, overbroad, and confusing language cannot be said to comply with the requirements of the transparency principle and its objective of providing meaningful information to data subjects to enable them to understand the purpose, scope, nature, and extent of processing of their personal information. Taken plainly, what Respondent obtained was blanket consent to process the information they acquired from Complainant and not informed consent to process specific information for a specified and limited purpose.[266]

---

261. *Ibid.*
262. NPC Case No 19-498, 9 Jun. 2020, at 8 (NPC 2020) (unreported).
263. *Ibid.*, at 4. Emphasis omitted.
264. *Ibid.*, at 8.
265. *Ibid.*
266. *Ibid.*

112. The PIC should have informed the data subject that it will process specific personal data for a specific and limited purpose.[267]

113. The principle of transparency requires that the obligations enumerated in section 11(a) of the DPA and section 19(a) of the IRR should be provided to data subjects in a manner that enables them to understand the purpose, scope, nature, and extent of processing of their personal data.[268]

§2. LEGITIMATE PURPOSE

114. The legitimate purpose principle requires (1) the purpose of the processing must be specified and declared to the data subject; and (2) the purpose must not be contrary to law, morals, or public policy.[269]

115. The first requisite is understood in relation to the principle of transparency – the data subject must be informed of the legitimate purpose behind the processing of his or her personal data. Section 11 of the DPA provides that:

> Section 11. *General Data Privacy Principles.*
>
> . . .
>
> Personal information must be:
>
> (a) Collected for specified and legitimate purposes determined and declared before, or as soon as reasonably practicable after collection, and later processed in a way compatible with such declared, specified and legitimate purposes only;
> (b) Processed fairly and lawfully[.][270]

116. Section 19 of the IRR, which discusses the general principles in collection, processing, and retention of personal data, is also based on the principle of legitimate purpose:

> Section 19. *General principles in collection, processing and retention.*
>
> The processing of personal data shall adhere to the following general principles in the collection, processing, and retention of personal data:
>
> a. Collection must be for a declared, specified, and legitimate purpose.
>   1. Consent is required prior to the collection and processing of personal data, subject to exemptions provided by the Act and other applicable

267. *Ibid.*
268. *Ibid.*
269. National Privacy Commission, Rules and Regulations Implementing the Data Privacy Act of 2012, Republic Act No. 10173, §18 (2016).
270. An Act Protecting Individual Personal Information in Information and Communications Systems in the Government and the Private Sector, Creating for this purpose a National Privacy Commission, and For Other Purposes [Data Privacy Act of 2012], Republic Act No. 10173 §11 (2012).

laws and regulations. *When consent is required, it must be time-bound in relation to the declared, specified and legitimate purpose.* Consent given may be withdrawn.

2. The data subject must be *provided specific information regarding the purpose and extent of processing*, including, where applicable, the automated processing of his or her personal data for profiling, or processing for direct marketing, and data sharing.
3. Purpose should be determined and declared before, or as soon as reasonably practicable, after collection.
4. Only personal data that is necessary and compatible with declared, specified, and legitimate purpose shall be collected.

b. Personal data shall be processed fairly and lawfully.

. . .

3. *Processing must be in a manner compatible with declared, specified, and legitimate purpose.*

. . .

d. Personal Data shall not be retained longer than necessary.

1. Retention of personal data shall only for as long as necessary:
   (a) *for the fulfillment of the declared, specified, and legitimate purpose, or when the processing relevant to the purpose has been terminated*;
   (b) for the establishment, exercise or defense of legal claims; or
   (c) for legitimate business purposes, which must be consistent with standards followed by the applicable industry or approved by appropriate government agency.
2. Retention of personal data shall be allowed in cases provided by law.
3. Personal data shall be disposed or discarded in a secure manner that would prevent further processing, unauthorized access, or disclosure to any other party or the public, or prejudice the interests of the data subjects.

e. Any authorized further processing shall have adequate safeguards.

1. Personal data originally collected for a declared, specified, or legitimate purpose may be processed further for historical, statistical, or scientific purposes, and, in cases laid down in law, may be stored for longer periods, subject to implementation of the appropriate organizational, physical, and technical security measures required by the Act in order to safeguard the rights and freedoms of the data subject.
2. Personal data which is aggregated or kept in a form which does not permit identification of data subjects may be kept longer than necessary for the declared, specified, and legitimate purpose.
3. Personal data shall not be retained in perpetuity in contemplation of a possible future use yet to be determined.[271]

---

271. National Privacy Commission, Rules and Regulations Implementing the Data Privacy Act of 2012, Republic Act No. 10173, §19 (2016). Emphasis supplied.

117. The second requisite requires the purpose to be within the limitations of the law. Law is not limited to the DPA and other related privacy regulations; rather, it should be understood to include the entire body of laws, rules, and regulations. Aside from this, the purpose of the processing should also be fair and just that it does not go against prevailing morals or run counter to public policy.

118. The Commission succinctly discusses the principle of legitimate purpose in NPC Case No. 17-047:

> [A]ny person or entity that processes information should collect information only for legitimate purposes that have been made known to the data subject. They should only collect as much information as is needed to achieve business interests or to comply with the law.[272]

119. Once the declared, specified, and legitimate purpose of the processing has been fulfilled and no other criteria for lawful processing applies, then the PIC shall no longer retain the personal data.[273] The law, however, has provided for exceptions subject to adequate safeguards. Section 19 of the IRR provides:

> Section 19. *General principles in collection, processing and retention.*
>
> . . .
>
> e. Any authorized further processing shall have adequate safeguards.
> 1. Personal data originally collected for a declared, specified, or legitimate purpose may be processed further for historical, statistical, or scientific purposes, and, in cases laid down in law, may be stored for longer periods, subject to implementation of the appropriate organizational, physical, and technical security measures required by the Act in order to safeguard the rights and freedoms of the data subject.
> 2. Personal data which is aggregated or kept in a form which does not permit identification of data subjects may be kept longer than necessary for the declared, specified, and legitimate purpose.
> 3. Personal data shall not be retained in perpetuity in contemplation of a possible future use yet to be determined.[274]

§3. Proportionality

120. The principle of proportionality requires adequate, relevant, suitable, and necessary processing that is not excessive in relation to the declared and specified purpose.[275] The principle of proportionality also provides that '[p]ersonal data shall

---

272. NPC Case No. 17-047, 13 Aug. 2019, at 10 (NPC 2019) (unreported).
273. National Privacy Commission, Rules and Regulations Implementing the Data Privacy Act of 2012, Republic Act No. 10173, §19(d) (2016).
274. *Ibid.*, §19(e).
275. *Ibid.*, §18.

be processed only if the purpose of the processing could not reasonably be fulfilled by other means'.[276] Thus, the processing is deemed proportional if (1) processing is adequate, relevant, and necessary to the declared and specified purpose; and (2) the means by which processing is performed is the least intrusive means available.

121. The following General Data Privacy Principles enumerated in Section 11 of the DPA rest on the principle of proportionality:

> Section 11. *General Data Privacy Principles.*
>
> . . .
>
> Personal information must be:
>
> . . .
>
> (c) Accurate, *relevant* and, where necessary for purposes for which it is to be used the processing of personal information, kept up to date; inaccurate or incomplete data must be rectified, supplemented, destroyed or their further processing restricted;
>
> (d) *Adequate and not excessive in relation to the purposes for which they are collected and processed[.]*[277]

122. Section 19 of the IRR elaborates on the general principles in the collection, processing, and retention that hinge on the principle of proportionality:

> Section 19. *General principles in collection, processing and retention.*
> The processing of personal data shall adhere to the following general principles in the collection, processing, and retention of personal data:
>
> . . .
>
> b. Personal data shall be processed fairly and lawfully.
>
> . . .
>
> 4. Processed personal data should be *adequate, relevant, and limited to what is necessary in relation to the purposes for which they are processed.*
> 5. Processing shall be undertaken in a manner that ensures appropriate privacy and security safeguards.
>
> c. Processing should ensure data quality.
> 1. Personal data should be *accurate and where necessary for declared, specified and legitimate purpose, kept up to date.*
> 2. Inaccurate or incomplete data must be rectified, supplemented, destroyed or their further processing restricted.[278]

---

276. *Ibid.*, §18(c).

277. An Act Protecting Individual Personal Information in Information and Communications Systems in the Government and the Private Sector, Creating for this purpose a National Privacy Commission, and For Other Purposes [Data Privacy Act of 2012], Republic Act No. 10173, §11 (2012). Emphasis supplied.

278. National Privacy Commission, Rules and Regulations Implementing the Data Privacy Act of 2012, Republic Act No. 10173, §19 (2016). Emphasis supplied.

123. In NPC Case No. 19-528, the Commission ruled that the proportionality principle was violated since the collection and processing of personal information went beyond what was necessary to achieve the declared and specified purpose.[279] In this case, Respondent corporation owns the building where Complainant church is located.[280] In Respondent corporation's efforts to implement security measures in its premises, it required the collection and processing of government-issued identification cards containing sensitive personal information of Complainant church's members:[281]

> Respondents insisted that the collection and processing of Complainant's church members personal data from passports and government-issued IDs is proportional to their legitimate interest to ensure safety and order within the premises of the building. However, *the principle of proportionality requires that the processing of personal information must be relevant to, and must not exceed, the declared purpose. Personal data shall be processed only if the purpose of the processing could not reasonably be fulfilled by other means. Hence, proportionality is met when the processing is the least intrusive measure to achieve its purported aims.*
>
> . . .
>
> In this case, *the requirement of submission of passports, government-issued IDs, and colored ID pictures is not the least intrusive means to achieve the desired purpose.* The IDs issued by Complainant to its church members should suffice as an exhibit of the authorization as required under the building rules.[282]

124. The Commission held that Respondent corporation violated the proportionality principle since it could have achieved the declared and specified purpose through less intrusive means:

> The availability of a far less intrusive measure demonstrates that the measures employed by Respondents are disproportionate to the aim they seek to achieve.
>
> . . .
>
> By no stretch of reasoning can the involvement of the [Bureau of Immigration] be considered as necessary to fulfill the declared purpose of security measures in the building. The request for the [Bureau of Immigration]'s intervention in investigating the validity of the Korean nationals' visas only

279. NPC Case No. 19-528, 29 Oct. 2020, at 21 (NPC 2020) (unreported).
280. *Ibid.*, at 1.
281. *Ibid.*, at 13–14.
282. *Ibid.*, at 21–22. Emphasis supplied.

> strengthens the conclusion that the application of strict security measures were specifically targeted to the Complainants' members and hence excessive to the declared purpose of building security measures.[283]

The Court of Appeals upheld the Decision of the Commission on this case.[284]

283. *Ibid.*, at 23–24.
284. *PXXX v. MNLC, Inc.*, CA-G.R. SP No. 168952, 14 Dec. 2021, *available at* https://services.ca.judiciary.gov.ph/csisver3-war/faces/pages/ResultInformation.xhtml (last accessed 28 Apr. 2022).

Chapter 2. Legal Grounds for Processing Personal Information

125. The DPA characterizes personal information as (1) personal information and (2) sensitive personal information. The grounds for lawful processing of personal information and sensitive personal information are espoused in sections 12 and 13 of the DPA, respectively. The lawful criteria for processing sensitive personal information will be discussed in Chapter 3.

126. The processing of personal information is permitted if any of the criteria enumerated in section 12 is present:

> Section 12. *Criteria for Lawful Processing of Personal Information.* The processing of personal information shall be permitted only if not otherwise prohibited by law, and when at least one of the following conditions exists:
>
> (a) The data subject has given his or her consent;
> (b) The processing of personal information is necessary and is related to the fulfillment of a contract with the data subject or in order to take steps at the request of the data subject prior to entering into a contract;
> (c) The processing is necessary for compliance with a legal obligation to which the personal information controller is subject;
> (d) The processing is necessary to protect vitally important interests of the data subject, including life and health;
> (e) The processing is necessary in order to respond to national emergency, to comply with the requirements of public order and safety, or to fulfill functions of public authority which necessarily includes the processing of personal data for the fulfillment of its mandate; or
> (f) The processing is necessary for the purposes of the legitimate interests pursued by the personal information controller or by a third party or parties to whom the data is disclosed, except where such interests are overridden by fundamental rights and freedoms of the data subject which require protection under the Philippine Constitution.[285]

At the core of these criteria for lawful processing are the privacy principles of transparency, legitimate purpose, and proportionality. The Commission draws heavily on the concepts of privacy principles when deciding cases involving the grounds of lawful processing of personal information.

§1. Consent

127. Consent is a criteria for the lawful processing of personal information as provided in section 12 of the DPA:

---

285. An Act Protecting Individual Personal Information in Information and Communications Systems in the Government and the Private Sector, Creating for this purpose a National Privacy Commission, and For Other Purposes [Data Privacy Act of 2012], Republic Act No. 10173 §12 (2012).

> Section 12. *Criteria for Lawful Processing of Personal Information.* The processing of personal information shall be permitted only if not otherwise prohibited by law, and when at least one of the following conditions exists:
>
> (a) The data subject has given his or her consent[.][286]

128. Section 21 on Criteria for Lawful Processing of Personal Information further explains consent:

> Section 21. *Criteria for Lawful Processing of Personal Information.* Processing of personal information is allowed, unless prohibited by law. For processing to be lawful, any of the following conditions must be complied with:
>
> (b) The data subject must have given his or her consent *prior to the collection, or as soon as practicable and reasonable*[.][287]

129. The DPA defines consent as follows:

> Section 3. *Definition of Terms.* – Whenever used in this Act, the following terms shall have the respective meanings hereafter set forth:
>
> . . .
>
> (a) *Consent of the data subject* refers to *any freely given, specific, informed indication of will, whereby the data subject agrees to the collection and processing of personal information about and/or relating to him or her.* Consent shall be evidenced by written, electronic or recorded means. It may also be given on behalf of the data subject by an agent specifically authorized by the data subject to do so.[288]

130. The consent secured from the data subject must be: (1) freely given by the data subject; (2) specific; (3) informed; (4) indication of will; and (5) evidenced by written, electronic or recorded means.

131. Consent is freely given when it is without coercion or undue pressure.[289] In NPC 19-528, the Commission explained that:

> In determining whether consent was freely given, the data subject must be given a real choice where there is no risk of deception, intimidation, coercion

---

286. *Ibid.*
287. National Privacy Commission, Rules and Regulations Implementing the Data Privacy Act of 2012, Republic Act No. 10173, §21 (2016). Emphasis supplied.
288. An Act Protecting Individual Personal Information in Information and Communications Systems in the Government and the Private Sector, Creating for this purpose a National Privacy Commission, and For Other Purposes [Data Privacy Act of 2012], Republic Act No. 10173 §3(b). Emphasis supplied.
289. NPC Case No. 19-528, 29 Oct. 2020, at 16 (NPC 2020) (unreported).

> or significant negative consequences if he or she does not consent. If the consequences of giving consent undermine the individual's freedom of choice, consent would not be free.
>
> . . .
>
> Given all the pressure exerted on them, including being forced to choose between giving up their privacy or the exercise of their religion, it cannot be said that the church members were empowered to make a true and free choice. Clearly, this kind of consent is invalid.[290]

132. Consent is specific when the data subject is informed of the purpose of the processing, taking into consideration the principles of legitimate purpose and proportionality.[291] The consent given extends to processing for purposes that are related or necessary to the initial purpose of processing to which the data subject consented.[292] If there is a separate purpose distinct from and not directly related to the specific processing activity, then separate consent is necessary.[293]

133. This, however, does not mean that the PIC should provide the data subject with an exhaustive enumeration of each and every purpose. It would be sufficient for a PIC to inform the data subject of the context and purpose of the processing and the rights available to the data subject.[294] While a specific case has yet to be resolved in this area, it appears that the PIC may provide the data subject with the essential information concerning the specific processing activity and provide additional information through external links, when necessary.

134. Even if the PIC provides an enumeration of each and every purpose of the processing, it does not automatically meet the standard of specific consent:

> In its waiver provision, Respondent combines various purposes for disclosure and various parties to be given access of Complainant's information. This does not meet the requirement for consent to be specific. Having an enumeration of each and every purpose of the processing in a single paragraph still fails to provide the data subject with a genuine choice as he or she will be bound to sign off on the entire provision in toto.[295]

---

290. *Ibid.*, at 16, 18.
291. *Ibid.*, at 8.
292. *See* In re: FLI Operating ABC Online Lending Application, NPC Case No. 19-910, 17 Dec. 2020, at 22, *available at* https://www.privacy.gov.ph/wp-content/uploads/2021/02/NPC-19-910-In-re-FLI-Decision-LYA-Final-pseudonymized-17Dec2020-.pdf (last accessed 24 Apr. 2022).
293. *See ibid.*, at 21–26.
294. *JRG v. CXXX Lending Corporation*, NPC Case No. 19-450, 9 Jun. 2020, at 6, available at https://www.privacy.gov.ph/wp-content/uploads/2022/01/Decision_NPC-19-450-JRG-v.-CXXX.pdf (last accessed 22 Apr. 2022).
295. *Ibid.*, at 5.

135. Thus, a 'bundled' consent is not valid consent since it does not empower the data subject 'to make a true choice'.[296] A 'bundled' consent essentially requires the data subject to agree to the processing of his or her personal information for a wide range of purposes, including those not related or necessary to the service, sought to be availed.[297] Requiring the data subject to agree to these various unrelated or unnecessary purposes for processing does not meet the standard of specific consent. As discussed by the Commission in NPC 19-910:

> In this case, Respondent FLI requires the borrowers to click 'Agree' to the Privacy Policy, aside from the Credit Agreement, and subsequently relies on this as basis for the supposed consent obtained from the borrowers.
>
> . . .
>
> [T]he burden cannot be placed on the borrowers to have known what the ABC application was capable of, based on the information provided to them. The borrowers could have only expected that their entire contact lists will be utilized for collection purposes if they had known the scope, manner, and extent of Respondent FLI's processing of their information in the first place. This is all the more true considering the broad language used in the declared purposes of the Credit Agreement, i.e. 'in order to achieve the purposes of this agreement.' The declared purpose of 'collection purposes' in the Privacy Policy likewise does not contemplate the indiscriminate messaging of family, friends, and acquaintances, considering the Policy referred to personal information 'provided' by the borrowers. In the case of the ABC application, this pertains only to the reference contacts supplied upon the loan application.[298]

136. There is informed consent when the data subject is made aware of the content, manner, and purpose of the processing prior to the collection of his or her personal information or as soon as practicable and reasonable.[299] The data subject must be informed of all the personal information intended to be collected by the PIC.[300] In NPC 19-621, the Commission held that blanket consent is not informed consent.[301] A broad statement of purpose for processing does not meet the standard of informed consent since it is not compliant with the general privacy principle of transparency:

> The data subject must be informed of all the personal information intended to be collected. In this case, the Commission notes that the Privacy Policy and Authorization Letter of Information did not adequately inform the customer

---

296. In re: FLI Operating ABC Online Lending Application, NPC Case No. 19-910, 17 Dec. 2020, at 22, *available at* https://www.privacy.gov.ph/wp-content/uploads/2021/02/NPC-19-910-In-re-FLI-Decision-LYA-Final-pseudonymized-17Dec2020-.pdf (last accessed 24 Apr. 2022).

297. *See ibid.*

298. *Ibid.*, at 22, 29.

299. *See* National Privacy Commission, Rules and Regulations Implementing the Data Privacy Act of 2012, Republic Act No. 10173, §19(a)(3) (2016).

300. *AMP v. HXXX Lending Inc.*, NPC Case No. 19-621, 19 Nov. 2020, at 6, *available at* https://www.privacy.gov.ph/wp-content/uploads/2022/01/Decision_NPC-19-621-AMP-v.-HXXX-Lending.pdf (last accessed 25 Apr. 2022).

301. *Ibid.*

borrowers of the full extent of the intended processing. It only stated that it will process the customer-borrower's emergency contacts, which the Complainant may easily accept as an industry practice. This notice to the customer-borrower, however, is inconsistent with the allegations in the Complaint that all of Complainant's co-workers and family members received messages of his unsettled loan.

Uninformed consent cannot be considered as valid consent.

The Commission likewise notes that the Authorization Letter of Information contains ambiguous statements such as how '[PIC] can use the other contact ways and address provided for collection when the applicant is overdue for repayment.' The broad statement of purpose for processing cannot be considered as compliant with the general privacy principle of transparency.[302]

137. Consent also requires an indication of the will of the data subject.[303] The data subject must agree to the processing of his or her personal information for a specific and declared purpose.[304] The consent given must not go beyond the specific and declared purpose of the processing as communicated to the data subject. The PIC must ensure that there is no overcollection of data, even if consent was given by the data subject. Following the general privacy principle of proportionality, consent does not justify the overcollection and overprocessing of personal data. The general privacy principles, by their very nature, are considered part of each of the different lawful criteria to process. Compliance with these principles is therefore essential to any claim of lawful processing of personal information.

138. Consent of the data subject must be evidenced by written, electronic, or recorded means.[305] This may be in the form of a positive act such as a signature, an opt-in tick box, a confirmation email, or oral confirmation.[306]

139. The data subject must manifest his or her consent through a positive act; otherwise, his or her consent may not be considered meaningful consent as required by the DPA.[307]

140. The Commission has consistently held that 'the mere posting of a PIC's privacy policy or notice and requiring the consumers to agree thereon via the online

302. *Ibid.*

303. An Act Protecting Individual Personal Information in Information and Communications Systems in the Government and the Private Sector, Creating for this purpose a National Privacy Commission, and For Other Purposes [Data Privacy Act of 2012], Republic Act No. 10173 §3(b).

304. In re: FLI Operating ABC Online Lending Application, NPC Case No. 19-910, 17 Dec. 2020, at 22, *available at* https://www.privacy.gov.ph/wp-content/uploads/2021/02/NPC-19-910-In-re-FLI-Decision-LYA-Final-pseudonymized-17Dec2020-.pdf (last accessed 24 Apr. 2022).

305. An Act Protecting Individual Personal Information in Information and Communications Systems in the Government and the Private Sector, Creating for this purpose a National Privacy Commission, and For Other Purposes [Data Privacy Act of 2012], Republic Act No. 10173 §3(b).

306. *See* NPC Case No. 19-498, 9 Jun. 2020, at 6 (NPC 2020) (unreported).

307. *See* In re: FLI Operating ABC Online Lending Application, NPC Case No. 19-910, 17 Dec. 2020, at 22, *available at* https://www.privacy.gov.ph/wp-content/uploads/2021/02/NPC-19-910-In-re-FLI-Decision-LYA-Final-pseudonymized-17Dec2020-.pdf (last accessed 24 Apr. 2022).

platform does not equate to obtaining the consent of the data subject for purposes of processing his or her personal information as required under the law'.[308]

141. Meaningful and effective consent requires that the data subject has freely given consent, which is specific, an informed indication of will, and is evidenced by written, electronic or recorded means.[309] Absent any of these requirements, the consent given cannot be considered valid:

> To determine whether the consent given by the data subject is proper, an examination must be made whether such consent was freely given, specific, informed, and an indication of will. Respondent points to the fact that it was Complainant himself who provided his personal information to [the PIC] as proof of consent. While this may show that there was a positive act showing an indication of will on the part of the Complainant and that such act was freely given, it is not enough to show that the given consent was specific or informed. These two (2) requirements relate to the obligation of personal information controllers such as [the PIC] to comply with the general privacy principle of transparency.[310]

142. The Commission, however, held that even if the data subject manifests his or her consent through a positive act, it is not sufficient to warrant valid consent. As held in NPC 19-910, 'the mere posting of a PIC's privacy policy or notice and requiring the consumers to agree thereon via the online platform does not equate to obtaining the consent of the data subject for purposes of processing his or her personal information as required under the law'[311] because the PIC required the data subject to agree to both a Privacy Notice and a Credit Agreement without giving the data subject a meaningful choice.[312] Thus, valid consent requires the fulfilment of all its requisites – freely given, specific, informed indication of will, and evidenced by a positive act.

143. Consent remains valid 'as long as the purpose, scope, method and extent of the processing remain to be the same as that disclosed to the data subject when consent was given'.[313] Corollary to this, the consent sought from the data subject should

---

308. *Ibid.*
309. *See ibid.*, at 24.
310. NPC Case No. 19-498, 9 Jun. 2020, at 6 (NPC 2020) (unreported).
311. In re: FLI Operating ABC Online Lending Application, NPC Case No. 19-910, 17 Dec. 2020, at 22, available at https://www.privacy.gov.ph/wp-content/uploads/2021/02/NPC-19-910-In-re-FLI-Decision-LYA-Final-pseudonymized-17Dec2020-.pdf (last accessed 24 Apr. 2022) (citing National Privacy Commission, Re: Privacy Policy and Consent of Data Subjects, Advisory Opinion No. 13, Series of 2018, at 2 (8 Apr. 2018)).
312. *Ibid.*
313. National Privacy Commission, Re: Ayala Rewards Circle, Advisory Opinion No. 58, Series of 2018, at 4 (26 Oct. 2018).

be limited to personal information that is relevant and necessary for the specific processing activity.[314] Following the idea of 'just in time consent', the PIC may request the data subject's consent for specific types of processing only when the need to do so arises.

144. Consent is not invalidated by the mere fact that the data subject agrees to a contract of adhesion.[315] A contract of adhesion was defined by the Supreme Court as follows:

> A contract of adhesion, wherein one party imposes a ready-made form of contract on the other, is not strictly against the law. *A contract of adhesion is as binding as ordinary contracts, the reason being that the party who adheres to the contract is free to reject it entirely*. Contrary to petitioner's contention, not every contract of adhesion is an invalid agreement. As we had the occasion to state in Development Bank of the *Philippines v. Perez*:
> ... In discussing the consequences of a contract of adhesion, we held in *Rizal Commercial Banking Corporation v. Court of Appeals:*
> It bears stressing that a contract of adhesion is just as binding as ordinary contracts. It is true that we have, on occasion, struck down such contracts as void when the weaker party is imposed upon in dealing with the dominant bargaining party and is reduced to the alternative of taking it or leaving it, completely deprived of the opportunity to bargain on equal footing, *Nevertheless, contracts of adhesion are not invalid per se; they are not entirely prohibited. The one who adheres to the contract is in reality free to reject it entirely; if he adheres, he gives his consent.*[316]

145. In NPC 19-134, the Commission held that the data subject's consent to the processing of his personal and sensitive personal information 'is not invalidated by the mere fact that the [Personal Data Sheet] is a contract of adhesion'.[317] A Personal Data Sheet (PDS) is an official document that contains the personal background, qualifications, and eligibility of a government employee.[318] As such, it contains personal and sensitive personal information.[319] It specifically states that the data subject allows the agency head or authorized representative to verify or validate the contents:

---

314. *See* National Privacy Commission, Rules and Regulations Implementing the Data Privacy Act of 2012, Republic Act No. 10173, §18(c) (2016).
315. *VVC v. CJB*, NPC Case No. 19-134, 10 Dec. 2021, at 10, *available at* https://www.privacy.gov.ph/wp-content/uploads/2022/04/NPC-19-134-VVC-v.-CJB-Decision-2021.12.10.pdf (last accessed 25 Apr. 2022).
316. *Cabanting v. BPI Family Savings Bank, Inc.*, G.R. No. 201927 (2016). Emphasis supplied.
317. *VVC v. CJB*, NPC Case No. 19-134, 10 Dec. 2021, at 10, *available at* https://www.privacy.gov.ph/wp-content/uploads/2022/04/NPC-19-134-VVC-v.-CJB-Decision-2021.12.10.pdf (last accessed 25 Apr. 2022).
318. National Privacy Commission, Advisory on Access to Personal Data Sheets of Government Personnel, Advisory No. 02, Series of 2017 (3 Apr. 2017).
319. *VVC v. CJB*, NPC Case No. 19-134, 10 Dec. 2021, at 7, *available at* https://www.privacy.gov.ph/wp-content/uploads/2022/04/NPC-19-134-VVC-v.-CJB-Decision-2021.12.10.pdf (last accessed 25 Apr. 2022).

> I declare under oath that I have personally accomplished this Personal Data Sheet which is a true, correct and complete statement pursuant to the provisions of pertinent laws, rules and regulations of the Republic of the Philippines. *I authorize the agency head/authorized representative to verify/validate the contents stated herein.* I agree that any misrepresentation made in this document and its attachments shall cause the filing of administrative case/s against me.[320]

146. The Commission held that the statement 'shows that [the data subject] was informed of the purpose behind the processing of her personal and sensitive personal information'[321] and that the data subject indicated her consent to the processing by signing and agreeing to the conditions stated in the PDS:

> [The data subject] freely gave her consent despite the fact that the PDS is a condition for employment in the government. Such consent is not invalidated by the mere fact that the PDS is a contract of adhesion.
>
> . . .
>
> Indeed, [the data subject] always had the option to not sign the PDS and consequently, to not accept employment with the [government agency]. Thus, [the data subject] freely gave her consent to the processing of her personal and sensitive personal information stated in the PDS.[322]

147. Consent, as a lawful basis for processing personal information, is also manifested in the fulfilment of ordinary contracts. Section 12(b) of the DPA provides:

> Section 12. *Criteria for Lawful Processing of Personal Information.* The processing of personal information shall be permitted only if not otherwise prohibited by law, and when at least one of the following conditions exists:
>
> . . .
>
> (b) The processing of personal information is necessary and is related to the fulfillment of a contract with the data subject or in order to take steps at the request of the data subject prior to entering into a contract[.][323]

148. Consent of the parties is an essential requisite of a contract. The Civil Code provides:

> Art. 1318. There is no contract unless the following requisites concur:
>
> (1) *Consent of the contracting parties;*

320. *Ibid.*, at 8.
321. *Ibid.*, at 11.
322. *Ibid.*, at 10–11.
323. An Act Protecting Individual Personal Information in Information and Communications Systems in the Government and the Private Sector, Creating for this purpose a National Privacy Commission, and For Other Purposes [Data Privacy Act of 2012], Republic Act No. 10173 §12(b) (2012).

(2) Object certain which is the subject matter of the contract;
(3) Cause of the obligation which is established. (1261)[324]

149. As held by the Supreme Court, a contract is perfected by the consent of the parties:

> Under the law, *a contract is perfected by mere consent*, that is, from the moment that there is a meeting of the offer and the acceptance upon the thing and the cause that constitute the contract. The law requires that the offer must be certain and the acceptance absolute and unqualified. An acceptance of an offer may be express and implied; a qualified offer constitutes a counter-offer. Case law holds that an offer, to be considered certain, must be definite, while an acceptance is considered absolute and unqualified when it is identical in all respects with that of the offer so as to produce consent or a meeting of the minds. We have also previously held that the ascertainment of whether there is a meeting of minds on the offer and acceptance depends on the circumstances surrounding the case.[325]

150. Thus, consent is necessary to enter into or fulfil a contract. Contrary to the DPA, where consent must be an express indication of the data subjects' will, in contracts, consent may be implied from the actions or statements of the parties when entering into or fulfilling a contract.[326]

151. While the Commission has not had the opportunity to decide on the matter, the processing of personal information when entering into or fulfilling a contract must still comply with the DPA in relation to the requisites of consent. If the PIC or PIP claims to have processed personal information under section 12(b) of the DPA, then it has the burden of proving by substantial evidence (1) the existence and validity of the contract taking into consideration the essential requisites of a contract discussed above; (2) the terms of the contract especially in cases when the contract is not in writing; and (3) the processing is necessary and related to the fulfilment of the contract.[327]

---

324. An Act to Ordain and Institute the Civil Code of the Philippines [Civil Code], Republic Act No. 386, art. 1318 (1949). Emphasis supplied.
325. *Traders Royal Bank v. Cuison Lumber Co., Inc.*, and Josefa Jerodias Vda. De Cuison, G.R No. 174286 (2009). Emphasis supplied.
326. *See* An Act to Ordain and Institute the Civil Code of the Philippines [Civil Code], Republic Act No. 386, art. 1320 (1949).
327. *See* An Act Protecting Individual Personal Information in Information and Communications Systems in the Government and the Private Sector, Creating for this purpose a National Privacy Commission, and For Other Purposes [Data Privacy Act of 2012], Republic Act No. 10173 §12(b) (2012).

§2. Compliance with a Legal Obligation

152. Processing of personal information is permitted when it is necessary for compliance with a legal obligation. Section 12(c) of the DPA provides for compliance with a legal obligation as a basis for lawful processing:

> Section 12. *Criteria for Lawful Processing of Personal Information.* The processing of personal information shall be permitted only if not otherwise prohibited by law, and when at least one of the following conditions exists:
>
> . . .
>
> (c) The processing is necessary for compliance with a legal obligation to which the personal information controller is subject[.][328]

153. Lawful processing on the basis of a legal obligation is contingent on the law from which the legal obligation is derived.[329] As such, processing on the basis of compliance with a legal obligation requires the determination of whether: (1) the legal obligation the PIC cites as lawful criteria exists and applies to the PIC; (2) the processing that the PIC performs is necessary to comply with the legal obligation; and (3) all the conditions imposed by the legal obligation for the processing of the personal information have been complied.[330] It is incumbent upon the Commission to examine these factors as a means of strictly enforcing the DPA and its IRR and determining if the PIC's claim of processing is indeed necessary to comply with its claimed legal obligation.

154. First, the legal obligation which the PIC claims that it is subject to exists and applies to the PIC. It would be difficult for the PIC to claim that the legal obligation is hinged on the law without referring to a particular legal provision that specifically applies to the PIC. The law from which the legal obligation is derived serves as the basis for processing. It determines the purpose of the processing, categories of personal and sensitive personal information subject to processing, the data subject concerned, and other measures to ensure lawful and fair processing. The provision of the law where the processing is based should apply to the circumstances of the PIC.

155. Second, the processing that the PIC performs is necessary to comply with the legal obligation. There must be a clear showing that the processing of personal and sensitive personal information is necessary. 'Necessary' is determined based on the processing undertaken and the legal obligation claimed by the PIC.[331] The processing undertaken must be evaluated taking into consideration the general privacy

328. *Ibid.*, Republic Act No. 10173 §12(c).
329. *RLA v. PLDT Enterprise*, NPC Case No. 18-010, 10 Dec. 2021, at 24, *available at* https://www.privacy.gov.ph/wp-content/uploads/2022/03/02-NPC_18_010_RLA_v_PLDT_Enterprise_Resolution_w_Dissenting_Opinion.pdf (last accessed 25 Apr. 2022).
330. *Ibid.*
331. *Ibid.*

principle of proportionality. The PIC should only process as much personal and sensitive personal information as is proportional or necessary to achieve its clearly defined and stated purpose, which under this criterion is the legal obligation the PIC claims as its basis for lawful processing.[332] The personal and sensitive personal information that the PIC processes should be adequate and relevant to the fulfilment of or compliance with the legal obligation.

156. Third, the conditions imposed by the legal obligation for the processing of personal information, if any, must have been complied. There are instances where the provision of law on which the processing is based imposes obligations and conditions on the PIC. As such, the PIC must also comply with these conditions. If a PIC fails to comply with the conditions imposed by the law, then it cannot validly claim that it is processing personal or sensitive personal information in compliance with that legal obligation. Fulfilment of the criterion under section 12(c) requires that everything required by that legal obligation has been complied with.

157. In NPC 18-010, a telecommunications company asserted that it was acting as a PIP since the installation and the publication of the complainant's personal information in a telephone listing directory resulted from the instructions of a PIC.[333] The telecommunications company further argued that it was processing the complainant's personal information in compliance with a legal obligation imposed by the National Telecommunications Commission.[334] The Commission held that compliance with everything required by the claimed legal obligation as a condition for the processing is an essential element for any claim of valid processing under this criterion:

> Processing based on a legal obligation requires that all conditions imposed by the legal obligation have been complied with. Section 12(c) of the DPA requires not only that the processing is 'necessary' but also that it be in 'compliance with a legal obligation'. Compliance with everything required by the claimed legal obligation as a condition for the processing is an essential element for any claim of valid processing under this criterion.
>
> In this case, [the PIC's] compliance with a legal obligation as a valid criterion for lawful processing requires compliance with its legal obligation under both Section 149 of Revised Order 1 and Section 2.2 of NTC MC 05-06-2007. It, therefore, follows that determining the legal obligation that [the PIC] is required to comply with necessarily includes an examination of the obligations imposed by those two provisions. As previously discussed, for [the PIC] to say that it published the listing directory in compliance with a legal obligation under Section 149 of Revised Order 1 and Section 2.2 of NTC MC 05-06-2007, it must demonstrate that it also fulfilled the conditions under Section 2.2

332. *See* National Privacy Commission, Rules and Regulations Implementing the Data Privacy Act of 2012, Republic Act No. 10173, §18(c) (2016).

333. *RLA v. PLDT Enterprise*, NPC Case No. 18-010, 10 Dec. 2021, at 8, available at https://www.privacy.gov.ph/wp-content/uploads/2022/03/02-NPC_18_010_RLA_v_PLDT_Enterprise_Resolution_w_Dissenting_Opinion.pdf (last accessed 25 Apr. 2022).

334. *Ibid.*, at 4.

of NTC MC 05-06-2007, which includes securing the consent of its subscribers before publishing their personal information in the listing directory.[335]

§3. Legitimate Interest

158. Processing based on legitimate interest is provided under section 12 of the DPA:

> Section 12. *Criteria for Lawful Processing of Personal Information.* The processing of personal information shall be permitted only if not otherwise prohibited by law, and when at least one of the following conditions exists:
>
> . . .
>
> (f) The processing is necessary for the purposes of the legitimate interests pursued by the personal information controller or by a third party or parties to whom the data is disclosed, except where such interests are overridden by fundamental rights and freedoms of the data subject which require protection under the Philippine Constitution.[336]

159. Valid processing based on legitimate interest requires the fulfilment of the following conditions: (1) the legitimate interest is established; (2) the processing is necessary to fulfil the legitimate interest that is established; and (3) the interest is legitimate or lawful and it does not override fundamental rights and freedoms of data subjects.

160. First, the PIC must clearly establish the legitimate interest it seeks as a lawful basis to process personal data. It is incumbent upon the PIC to apprise the data subject of the 'nature, purpose, and extent of the processing of his or her personal data, including the risks and safeguards involved'[337] in line with the general privacy principle of transparency. Any further processing of personal data must be within the reasonable expectation of the data subject at the time and in the context of the collection of the personal information that further processing may take place. This is understood in relation to section 19(e) of the IRR. As such, when personal data is further processed, it requires the following adequate safeguards:

> Section 19. General principles in collection, processing and retention.
>
> . . .
>
> e. Any authorized further processing shall have adequate safeguards.

335. *Ibid.*, at 26–27.
336. An Act Protecting Individual Personal Information in Information and Communications Systems in the Government and the Private Sector, Creating for this purpose a National Privacy Commission, and For Other Purposes [Data Privacy Act of 2012], Republic Act No. 10173 §12(f) (2012).
337. National Privacy Commission, Rules and Regulations Implementing the Data Privacy Act of 2012, Republic Act No. 10173, §18(a) (2016).

1. Personal data originally collected for a declared, specified, or legitimate purpose may be processed further for historical, statistical, or scientific purposes, and, in cases laid down in law, may be stored for longer periods, subject to implementation of the appropriate organizational, physical, and technical security measures required by the Act in order to safeguard the rights and freedoms of the data subject.
2. Personal data which is aggregated or kept in a form which does not permit identification of data subjects may be kept longer than necessary for the declared, specified, and legitimate purpose.
3. Personal data shall not be retained in perpetuity in contemplation of a possible future use yet to be determined.[338]

161. In NPC 18-010, the Commission held that the publication of the data subject's personal information in a telephone listing directory is not something that he could have reasonably foreseen from the initial purpose of the processing:

> Although [the PIC] obtained [the data subject's] consent, the authority granted to [the PIC] was only for the purpose of providing the telephone and Corporate DSL subscription services. It does not extend to the publication of [the data subject's] personal information in the listing directory.[339]
>
> [The data subject] could not have reasonably foreseen that [the PIC] intended to process his personal information by publishing it in the listing directory. In fact, the statement in the Terms and Conditions stated in the Application Form that was presented to [the PIP] does not adequately declare and specify the purpose of publishing data subjects' personal information in the listing directory. Neither [the PIC's] Application Form nor its Terms and Conditions provided the necessary information that would have allowed its subscribers, like [the data subject], to reasonably foresee that their personal information would be published, much less allow them to exercise their right to be excluded from the listing directory or even know that such a right exists in the first place.[340]

162. Second, the processing must be necessary for the legitimate interest that was established by the PIC. 'Necessary' is determined in relation to the general privacy principle of proportionality. The PIC should process information that is adequate and reasonable to fulfil its established legitimate interest:

> It should be stressed, however, that having a legitimate purpose or some other lawful criteria to process does not result in the PIC granting all request to

---

338. *Ibid.*, §19(e).
339. *RLA v. PLDT Enterprise*, NPC Case No. 18-010, 10 Dec. 2021, at 27, available at https://www.privacy.gov.ph/wp-content/uploads/2022/03/02-NPC_18_010_RLA_v_PLDT_Enterprise_Resolution_w_Dissenting_Opinion.pdf (last accessed 25 Apr. 2022).
340. *Ibid.*, at 27 28.

access by the data subjects. Such requests should be evaluated on a case-by-case basis and must always be subject to the PIC's guidelines for the release of such information.

Aside from legitimate purpose, the qualifier 'necessary' also pertains to the general privacy principle of proportionality. Under the IRR, the processing of information shall be adequate, relevant, suitable, necessary, and not excessive in relation to a declared and specified purpose. Personal data shall be processed only if the purpose of the processing could not reasonably be fulfilled by other means. The proportionality principle, as manifested in the qualifier 'necessary' serves as a sufficient test in determining whether the processing is justified in relation to the declared purpose.[341]

163. Third, the interest of the PIC must be lawful or legitimate. The interest where the processing of personal data is rooted must be in accordance with the law. It must not override the fundamental rights and freedoms of data subjects. The Constitutionally protected rights and freedoms of the data subject prevail over the legitimate interest of the PIC.[342]

164. This determination is similar to the following tests:

1. Purpose test – The existence of a legitimate interest must be clearly established, including a determination of what the particular processing operation seeks to achieve;
2. Necessity test – The processing of personal information must be necessary for the purpose of the legitimate interest pursued by the PIC or third party to whom personal information is disclosed, where such purpose could not be reasonably fulfilled by other means; and
3. Balancing test – The fundamental rights and freedoms of data subjects must not be overridden by the legitimate interests of the PIC or third party, considering the likely impact of the processing on the data subjects.[343]

165. A PIC processing sensitive personal information cannot rely on legitimate interest as a criterion for lawful processing.

---

341. *BGM v. IPP*, NPC Case No. 19-653, 17 Dec. 2020, at 8, available at https://www.privacy.gov.ph/wp-content/uploads/2021/02/NPC-19-653-BGM-vs-IPP-Decision-FINAL-Pseudonymized-21Dec2020.pdf (last accessed 28 Apr. 2022).
342. *See* An Act Protecting Individual Personal Information in Information and Communications Systems in the Government and the Private Sector, Creating for this purpose a National Privacy Commission, and For Other Purposes [Data Privacy Act of 2012], Republic Act No. 10173 §12(f) (2012).
343. National Privacy Commission, Re: Private Detective Services, Advisory No. 10, Series of 2021, at 4 (22 Mar. 2021).

§4. Protection of Life and Health

166. The DPA considers certain criteria related to the protection of life and health as a basis for lawful processing. The criterion relates to the processing of health information. With regard to personal information, Section 12 of the DPA provides that processing is necessary to protect the life and health of the data subject:

> Section 12. *Criteria for Lawful Processing of Personal Information.* The processing of personal information shall be permitted only if not otherwise prohibited by law, and when at least one of the following conditions exists:
>
> ...
>
> (c) The processing is necessary to protect vitally important interests of the data subject, including life and health[.][344]

167. This criterion for lawful processing requires that: (1) the specific purpose enumerated in section 12(d) exists; and (2) the processing is necessary for fulfilling the specific purpose.

168. First, the specific purpose enumerated in section 12(d) exists. Section 12(d) is contingent on the existence of 'vitally important interests of the data subjects, including life and health'.[345]

169. Second, the processing must be necessary for the fulfilment of the specific purposes under section 12(d). As such, the processing must be relevant, adequate, and not excessive in relation to the specific purpose for which the personal data are collected and processed.[346]

170. In an Advisory Opinion, the Commission examined whether a hospital can disclose the fact that diagnostic exams or chemical tests have been performed on an individual in a hospital.[347] It categorized 'information about whether a diagnostic test has been performed' as information that relates to a patient's medical condition, which requires an examination of sections 12 and 13 of the DPA.[348]

171. The Commission advised that the processing does not fulfil sections 12 and 13 of the DPA:

344. An Act Protecting Individual Personal Information in Information and Communications Systems in the Government and the Private Sector, Creating for this purpose a National Privacy Commission, and For Other Purposes [Data Privacy Act of 2012], Republic Act No. 10173 §12(c) (2012).
345. *Ibid.*, Republic Act No. 10173 §12(d).
346. *Ibid.*, Republic Act No. 10173 §11.
347. National Privacy Commission, Re: Request for Information from Rizal Medical Center, Advisory No. 44, Series of 2018, at 3 (7 Aug. 2018).
348. *Ibid.*, at 3–5.

> Based on the information provided in this particular inquiry, the requested disclosure of personal information to a third party does not meet any of the criteria provided by the DPA in Sections 12 and 13. *It should be emphasized that the request for disclosure in this instance is from a third party, an individual other than a patient or a patient's authorized representative.* The request is also not being made by a public authority for the fulfillment of their functions, nor does it proceed from a duly issued subpoena or court order. *The information requested also pertains to a patient's health, with clinical value, and is considered sensitive and privileged in nature, the processing of which is prohibited except under specific circumstances.*[349]

172. Thus, absent any valid criteria for lawful processing, the Commission advised that 'the hospital is not obligated to release any health information to the requesting party, including the fact of whether any diagnostic or chemical tests have been done'.[350]

§5. Public Interest

173. Processing personal information for purposes related to the public interest is a valid criterion for lawful processing. The purposes enumerated under section 12(e) are:

> Section 12. *Criteria for Lawful Processing of Personal Information.* The processing of personal information shall be permitted only if not otherwise prohibited by law, and when at least one of the following conditions exists:
>
> . . .
>
> (e) The processing is necessary *in order to respond to national emergency, to comply with the requirements of public order and safety, or to fulfill functions of public authority which necessarily includes the processing of personal data for the fulfillment of its mandate*[.][351]

174. This criterion for lawful processing requires that: (1) a specific purpose enumerated in section 12(e), as applicable, exists; and (2) the processing is necessary for fulfilling the specific purpose.

175. First, any of the specific purposes for processing enumerated in section 12(e) exists. As such, the processing should be for the purpose of responding to a national emergency, complying with the requirements of public order and safety, or

349. *Ibid.*, at 5. Emphasis supplied.

350. *Ibid.*, at 7.

351. An Act Protecting Individual Personal Information in Information and Communications Systems in the Government and the Private Sector, Creating for this purpose a National Privacy Commission, and For Other Purposes [Data Privacy Act of 2012], Republic Act No. 10173 §12(e) (2012). Emphasis supplied.

the fulfilment of the functions of public authority, including its mandate.[352] These specific purposes pertain to information of public concern, which the Supreme Court has held:

> In determining whether or not a particular information is of public concern, there is no rigid test which can be applied. 'Public concern' like 'public interest' is a term that eludes exact definition. Both terms embrace a broad spectrum of subjects which the public may want to know, either because these directly affect their lives, or simply because such matters naturally arouse the interest of an ordinary citizen[.][353]

176. Second, the processing should be necessary for the fulfilment of any of the specific purposes enumerated under section 12(e). This means that the processing should be in line with the response to a national emergency, compliance with the requirements of public order and safety, or fulfilment of the functions of the public authority.

177. In an Advisory Opinion, the Commission opined that '[t]he DPA should not be an obstacle to the collection and further processing of personal data by [the Department of Health] as long as the same is necessary for the fulfillment of its mandate'.[354] It stated:

> The processing of personal data by DOH finds support in the DPA. The DOH is a public authority performing regulatory functions, and is permitted to process personal data to the extent necessary for the fulfillment of these functions. DOH also processes personal data for research purpose. Furthermore, DOH may also rely on the provisions of the DPA in Sections 12 and 13 providing the criteria for lawful processing of personal information and sensitive personal information, respectively.[355]

178. The function of a public authority stems from its mandate provided by law. In an Advisory Opinion, the Commission discussed the parameters in the exercise of a law enforcement authority's mandate as a lawful basis for processing:

> Thus, the disclosure of personal information of patients to law enforcement officers may be allowed under the DPA when it is pursuant to its mandate to investigate and prevent crimes, and strictly following the existing standard operating procedures in the conduct of an investigation and law enforcement operation as stated in the Revised PNP Operational Procedures, and other

352. *Ibid.*
353. *Akbayan v. Aquino*, GR. No. 170516 (2008).
354. National Privacy Commission, Re: Collection of Health Information by the Department of Health, Advisory No. 83, Series of 2018, at 2 (26 Nov. 2018).
355. *Ibid.*, at 3.

pertinent laws, rules, and regulations governing the same (i.e. criminal procedures on search and seizure, etc.) Only these contexts do the exercise of a mandate become[s] a lawful basis for processing.[356]

356. National Privacy Commission, Re: Disclosure of Personal Information to the Police and Media, Advisory No. 49, Series of 2018, at 2-3 (26 Nov. 2018).

Chapter 3. Special Categories of Personal Information

179. Special categories of personal data refer to sensitive personal information under the DPA. The processing of sensitive personal information is allowed under its own set of lawful criteria provided under Section 13 of the DPA:

> Section 13. *Sensitive Personal Information and Privileged Information.* The processing of sensitive personal information and privileged information shall be prohibited, except in the following cases:
>
> (a) The data subject has given his or her consent, specific to the purpose prior to the processing, or in the case of privileged information, all parties to the exchange have given their consent prior to processing;
> (b) The processing of the same is provided for by existing laws and regulations: *Provided*, That such regulatory enactments guarantee the protection of the sensitive personal information and the privileged information: *Provided, further*, That the consent of the data subjects are not required by law or regulation permitting the processing of the sensitive personal information or the privileged information;
> (c) The processing is necessary to protect the life and health of the data subject or another person, and the data subject is not legally or physically able to express his or her consent prior to the processing;
> (d) The processing is necessary to achieve the lawful and non-commercial objectives of public organizations and their associations: *Provided*, That such processing is only confined and related to the *bona fide* members of these organizations or their associations: *Provided, further*, That the sensitive personal information are not transferred to third parties: *Provided, finally*, That consent of the data subject was obtained prior to processing;
> (e) The processing is necessary for purposes of medical treatment, is carried out by a medical practitioner or a medical treatment institution, and an adequate level of protection of personal information is ensured; or
> (f) The processing concerns such personal information as is necessary for the protection of lawful rights and interests of natural or legal persons in court proceedings, or the establishment, exercise or defense of legal claims, or when provided to government or public authority.[357]

180. Similar to the criteria for lawful processing of personal information, the privacy principles of transparency, legitimate purpose, and proportionality apply when interpreting the criteria for lawful processing of sensitive personal information under Section 13 of the DPA.

357. An Act Protecting Individual Personal Information in Information and Communications Systems in the Government and the Private Sector, Creating for this purpose a National Privacy Commission, and For Other Purposes [Data Privacy Act of 2012], Republic Act No. 10173 §13 (2012).

181. Considering that several criteria for lawful processing under section 13 are similar to those under section 12, the discussion will refer to certain grounds of lawful processing in the previous chapter.

§1. Consent

182. Consent, as a lawful processing of sensitive personal information, is provided in section 13 of the DPA and section 22 of the IRR. Section 13 states:

> Section 13. *Sensitive Personal Information and Privileged Information.* The processing of sensitive personal information and privileged information shall be prohibited, except in the following cases:
>
> (c) The data subject has given his or her consent, specific to the purpose prior to the processing, or in the case of privileged information, all parties to the exchange have given their consent prior to processing[.][358]

183. Section 22 of the IRR provides:

> Section 22. *Sensitive Personal Information and Privileged Information.* The processing of sensitive personal and privileged information is prohibited, except in any of the following cases:
>
> a. Consent is given by data subject, or by the parties to the exchange of privileged information, *prior to the processing of the sensitive personal information or privileged information, which shall be undertaken pursuant to a declared, specified, and legitimate purpose[.]*[359]

184. The discussion on consent as lawful criteria for processing personal information under Chapter 2 is applicable to consent as lawful criteria for processing sensitive personal information.

185. The criteria for lawful processing of sensitive personal information under section 13(d) of the DPA is also based on consent. Although the specific processing activity is carved out under a separate subsection, a reading of section 13(d) shows that the consent of the data subject is a requirement for processing:

> Section 13. *Sensitive Personal Information and Privileged Information.* The processing of sensitive personal information and privileged information shall be prohibited, except in the following cases:
>
> . . .

358. *Ibid.*, Republic Act No. 10173 §13(c).
359. National Privacy Commission, Rules and Regulations Implementing the Data Privacy Act of 2012, Republic Act No. 10173, §22(a) (2016). Emphasis supplied.

(d) The processing is necessary to achieve the lawful and non-commercial objectives of public organizations and their associations: Provided, That such processing is only confined and related to the bona fide members of these organizations or their associations: Provided, further, That the sensitive personal information are not transferred to third parties: Provided, finally, *That consent of the data subject was obtained prior to processing*[.][360]

186. Sensitive personal information of members of public organizations and their associations may be processed if their consent were obtained prior to processing and if the processing is necessary to achieve the lawful and non-commercial objectives of the public organizations.

§2. Law and Regulation

187. A PIC or PIP may process sensitive personal information when the processing is provided for by existing laws and regulations:

> Section 13. *Sensitive Personal Information and Privileged Information.* The processing of sensitive personal information and privileged information shall be prohibited, except in the following cases:
>
> . . .
>
> (c) The processing of the same is provided for by existing laws and regulations: *Provided,* That such regulatory enactments guarantee the protection of the sensitive personal information and the privileged information: *Provided, further,* That the consent of the data subjects are not required by law or regulation permitting the processing of the sensitive personal information or the privileged information[.][361]

188. Section 13(b) refers to a criterion for the lawful processing of sensitive personal information. Nevertheless, the discussion under Chapter 2 on the processing of personal information in compliance with a legal obligation remains applicable.

189. In addition to the requisites discussed in Chapter 2, section 13(b) specifically provides that (1) the law or regulation does not require the consent of the data subject to process sensitive personal information; and (2) the law or regulation guarantees the protection of the sensitive personal information.

360. An Act Protecting Individual Personal Information in Information and Communications Systems in the Government and the Private Sector, Creating for this purpose a National Privacy Commission, and For Other Purposes [Data Privacy Act of 2012], Republic Act No. 10173 §13(d) (2012). Emphasis supplied.
361. *Ibid.*, Republic Act No. 10173 §13(b).

190. While cases have yet to be resolved in this area, the second requisite under section 13(b) will likely be interpreted to require PICs and PIPs to take measures that guarantee the protection of the data subjects' sensitive personal information. With the passage of the DPA, PICs or PIPs processing sensitive personal information, regardless of the lawful criteria they are relying upon, have to comply with the general privacy principles and their respective obligations under the DPA and other privacy regulations for the protection of the information that will be processed.

§3. Protection of Life and Health

191. In relation to sensitive personal information, section 13 allows the processing of such if it is necessary to protect the life and health of the data subject or another person and for the purpose of medical treatment, subject to the fulfilment of certain conditions:

> Section 13. *Sensitive Personal Information and Privileged Information.* The processing of sensitive personal information and privileged information shall be prohibited, except in the following cases:
>
> . . .
>
> (c) The processing is necessary to protect the life and health of the data subject or another person, and the data subject is not legally or physically able to express his or her consent prior to the processing;
>
> . . .
>
> (f) The processing is necessary for purposes of medical treatment, is carried out by a medical practitioner or a medical treatment institution, and an adequate level of protection of personal information is ensured[.][362]

192. Similar to the discussion under Chapter 2, the requisites are as follows: (1) the specific purpose enumerated in section 13(c) or (e), as applicable, exists; and (2) the processing is necessary for fulfilling the specific purpose. When processing sensitive personal information for a medical purpose under section 13(c) and (e), more protections are afforded because of its nature.

193. Section 13(c) is based on the protection of 'life and health of the data subject or another person'.[363] As such, there must be a purpose that calls for the protection of life and health. Section 13(c) also requires that the data subject is unable to express his or her consent prior to the processing of his or her sensitive personal information.[364] Section 13(e) requires the existence of a need for medical treatment that is performed by a medical practitioner or a medical treatment institution.[365] It

---

362. *Ibid.*, Republic Act No. 10173 §13(c) & (f).
363. *Ibid.*, Republic Act No. 10173 §13(c).
364. *Ibid.*
365. *Ibid.*

is also incumbent upon the PIC to show that an adequate level of protection in relation to the processing of sensitive personal information exists.[366]

§4. Exercise or Defence of Legal Claims

194. Sensitive personal information may be lawfully processed if it is necessary for the protection of the lawful rights and interests of persons in court proceedings, the establishment, exercise or defence of legal claims, or when provided to government or public authority:

> Section 13. *Sensitive Personal Information and Privileged Information.* The processing of sensitive personal information and privileged information shall be prohibited, except in the following cases:
>
> . . .
>
> (f) The processing concerns such personal information as is necessary for the protection of lawful rights and interests of natural or legal persons in court proceedings, or the establishment, exercise or defense of legal claims, or when provided to government or public authority.[367]

195. Lawful processing on the basis of legal claims requires a determination of the following: (1) the processing is necessary for the protection of lawful rights and interests of natural or legal persons in court proceedings, establishment, exercise or defence of legal claims; or when provided to government or public authority; (2) the processing is lawful or within the limitations of the law; and (3) the conditions or the procedures set out by law or regulation, including those established by government agencies, for the release of such information have been met.[368]

196. First, the processing shall be necessary for the purposes enumerated in section 13 of the IRR. The Commission discussed 'necessary' in relation to the general privacy principle of proportionality in NPC Case No. 17-018:

> [T]he qualifier 'necessary' also pertains to the general privacy principle of proportionality. Under the IRR, the processing of information shall be adequate, relevant, suitable, necessary, and not excessive in relation to a declared and specified purpose. Personal data shall be processed only if the purpose of the processing could not reasonably be fulfilled by other means.[369]

---

366. *Ibid.*
367. *Ibid.*, Republic Act No. 10173 §13(c).
368. *See ibid.*, Republic Act No. 10173 §13.
369. National Privacy Commission, Rules and Regulations Implementing the Data Privacy Act of 2012, Republic Act No. 10173, §18(c) (2016).

> The proportionality principle, as manifested in the qualifier 'necessary'[,] serves as a sufficient test in determining whether the processing is justified in relation to the declared purpose.[370]

197. The processing should be necessary for the protection of lawful rights and interests of natural or legal persons in court proceedings or the establishment, exercise, or defence of legal claims. This requires a consideration of the relationship of the parties at the time of the processing. It, however, does not require the existence of a court or administrative proceeding as a pre-requisite.[371] To require an existing court proceeding will result in absurdity since it would render the purpose of processing to establish a legal claim impossible. Further, it does not require that the legal claim actually resulted in the filing of an actual case. As held by the Commission:

> The determination of a valid reliance on the second part of Section 13(f), i.e. 'the processing is necessary for the establishment, exercise or defense of legal claims,' requires a consideration of the relationship of the parties at the time of the processing taking into consideration the juridical ties between them. Whether the legal claim that is established, exercised, or defended, resulted in the filing of an actual case is immaterial since the exercise of these remedies is a decision independent from the existence of a cause of action.[372]

198. Second, the processing shall be lawful or within the limitations of the law, including processing under a constitutional or statutory mandate. This is in consonance with the general privacy principle of legitimate purpose where the declared and specified purpose of the processing must not be contrary to law, morals, or public policy. The Commission held:

> The DPA should not be seen as curtailing the practice of law in litigation. Considering that it is almost impossible for Congress to determine beforehand what specific data is 'necessary' or may or may not be collected by lawyers for purposes of building a case, applying the qualifier 'necessary' to the second instance in Section 13(f) therefore, serves to limit the potentially broad concept of 'establishment of legal claims' consistent with the general principles of legitimate purpose and proportionality.
>
> As regards legitimate purpose, the Implementing Rules and Regulations (IRR) of the Data Privacy Act provides that the processing of information shall

---

370. *EA and TA v. EJ*, NPC Case No. 17-018, 15 Jul. 2019, at 10, available at https://www.privacy.gov.ph/wp-content/uploads/2022/04/NPC-17-018-EA-and-TA-v-EJ-Decision-2019.07.15-.pdf (last accessed 28 Apr. 2022).
371. *Ibid.*, at 8.
372. NPC Case No. 17-018, 05 Nov. 2020 at 3 (NPC 2020) (unreported).

> be compatible with a declared and specified purpose which must not be contrary to law, morals, or public policy.[373] This means that the processing done for the establishment of a legal claim should not in any manner be outside the limitations provided by law.[374]

199. Third, the conditions and the procedures set out by law or regulation, including those established by government agencies, for the release of such information have been met. Lawful processing also requires compliance with the conditions or procedures set out by law:

> Aside from this, Section 13(f) also requires compliance with the general principles particularly, transparency, legitimate purpose, and proportionality, as well as compliance with the limitations provided by law. This involves, among others, compliance with the procedures set out by law, including those established by government agencies such as the Philippine Statistics Authority in this case for the release of documents in their possession.[375]

200. It is not sufficient to process personal or sensitive personal information based on lawful criteria without fulfilling the obligation to comply with the necessary procedural requirements for the release of such information.[376]

201. Certain obligations to protect the data subjects' rights and freedoms are imposed upon PICs relying on this criterion for lawful processing:

> If the controller decides to pursue and exercise their legal claim/s by availing of the appropriate remedy provided by law, such as filing a case in court or a quasi-judicial body, the existing requirements of due process during the course of the proceedings should cause the controller to comply with the declaration required under Section 11 of the DPA.
>
> If, after going through the initial processing to establish their claim, the controller decides not to pursue their legal remedy for whatever reason, the controller is bound to comply with their obligations under the Data Privacy Act, including the disposal of the personal information processed.[377]

202. While the criteria for lawful processing based on the establishment of legal claims are only enumerated as a criterion for lawful processing of sensitive personal information under section 13(f) of the DPA, the same criterion also applies to the processing of personal information under section 12(f) of the DPA on legitimate

---

373. National Privacy Commission, Rules and Regulations Implementing the Data Privacy Act of 2012, Republic Act No. 10173, §18(b) (2016).
374. NPC Case No. 17-018, 05 Nov. 2020 at 4 (NPC 2020) (unreported).
375. *Ibid.*, at 3.
376. *EA and TA v. EJ*, NPC Case No. 17-018, 15 Jul. 2019, at 10, available at https://www.privacy.gov.ph/wp-content/uploads/2022/04/NPC-17-018-EA-and-TA-v-EJ-Decision-2019.07.15-.pdf (last accessed 28 Apr. 2022).
377. NPC Case No. 17-018, 05 Nov. 2020 at 5 (NPC 2020) (unreported).

interest since the processing of personal information for the protection of lawful rights and interests is considered a legitimate interest.[378] For reference, section 12(f) of the DPA provides:

> Section 12. *Criteria for Lawful Processing of Personal Information.* – The processing of personal information shall be permitted only if not otherwise prohibited by law, and when at least one of the following conditions exists:
>
> . . .
>
> (f) The processing is necessary for the purposes of the legitimate interests pursued by the personal information controller or by a third party or parties to whom the data is disclosed, except where such interests are overridden by fundamental rights and freedoms of the data subject which require protection under the Philippine Constitution.[379]

203. Thus, personal and sensitive personal information may be processed on the basis of establishing legal claims following section 12(f) and section 13(f), respectively.

---

378. *KRL v. University*, AA, MC, NCB, RG GV, GCT, RR, MR, PB, CID 17-K-003, 19 Nov. 2019, at 13, *available at* https://www.privacy.gov.ph/wp-content/uploads/2022/04/CID-17-K-003-KRL-v.-University-Decision-2019.11.19-.pdf (last accessed 28 Apr. 2022).
379. An Act Protecting Individual Personal Information in Information and Communications Systems in the Government and the Private Sector, Creating for this purpose a National Privacy Commission, and For Other Purposes [Data Privacy Act of 2012], Republic Act No. 10173 §12(f) (2012).

Part IV. Data Subject Rights

204. The DPA seeks to protect the rights of data subjects or individuals whose personal information are processed.[380] Recognizing the character of data privacy as a fundamental human right,[381] the protection of data subjects is paramount, as provided in section 6 of the IRR:

Section 6. *Protection afforded to Data Subjects.*

a. Unless directly incompatible or inconsistent with the preceding sections in relation to the purpose, function, or activities the non-applicability concerns,[382] the personal information controller or personal information processor shall uphold the rights of data subjects, and adhere to general data privacy principles and the requirements of lawful processing.

380. *Ibid.*, Republic Act No. 10173 §3(c).
381. *Ibid.*, Republic Act No. 10173 §2.
382. *See* National Privacy Commission, Rules and Regulations Implementing the Data Privacy Act of 2012, Republic Act No. 10173, §5 (2016).

Section 5. *Special Cases.* The Act and these Rules shall not apply to the following specified information, only to the minimum extent of collection, access, use, disclosure or other processing necessary to the purpose, function, or activity concerned:

a. Information processed for purpose of allowing public access to information that fall within matters of public concern, pertaining to:
   1. Information about any individual who is or was an officer or employee of government that relates to his or her position or functions, including:
      (a) The fact that the individual is or was an officer or employee of the government;
      (b) The title, office address, and office telephone number of the individual;
      (c) The classification, salary range, and responsibilities of the position held by the individual; and
      (d) The name of the individual on a document he or she prepared in the course of his or her employment with the government;
   2. Information about an individual who is or was performing a service under contract for a government institution, but only in so far as it relates to such service, including the name of the individual and the terms of his or her contract;
   3. Information relating to a benefit of a financial nature conferred on an individual upon the discretion of the government, such as the granting of a license or permit, including the name of the individual and the exact nature of the benefit: Provided, that they do not include benefits given in the course of an ordinary transaction or as a matter of right;

b. The burden of proving that the Act and these Rules are not applicable to a particular information falls on those involved in the processing of personal data or the party claiming the non-applicability.
c. In all cases, the determination of any exemption shall be liberally interpreted in favor of the rights and interests of the data subject.[383]

205. PICs and PIPs are duty-bound to uphold data subject rights subject to limitations as may be provided for by law.[384] Pursuant to this obligation, they shall 'implement mechanisms which enable the free exercise of the same through procedures which are clear, simple, straightforward, and convenient'.[385]

206. The DPA further provides that when doubt exists in the interpretation of the provisions of law, PICs and PIPs shall be mindful of the rights and interests of data subjects:

---

b. Personal information processed for journalistic, artistic or literary purpose, in order to uphold freedom of speech, of expression, or of the press, subject to requirements of other applicable law or regulations;
c. Personal information that will be processed for research purpose, intended for a public benefit, subject to the requirements of applicable laws, regulations, or ethical standards;
d. Information necessary in order to carry out the functions of public authority, in accordance with a constitutionally or statutorily mandated function pertaining to law enforcement or regulatory function, including the performance of the functions of the independent, central monetary authority, subject to restrictions provided by law. Nothing in this Act shall be construed as having amended or repealed Republic Act No. 1405, otherwise known as the Secrecy of Bank Deposits Act; Republic Act No. 6426, otherwise known as the Foreign Currency Deposit Act; and Republic Act No. 9510, otherwise known as the Credit Information System Act (CISA);
e. Information necessary for banks, other financial institutions under the jurisdiction of the independent, central monetary authority or Bangko Sentral ng Pilipinas, and other bodies authorized by law, to the extent necessary to comply with Republic Act No. 9510 (CISA), Republic Act No. 9160, as amended, otherwise known as the Anti-Money Laundering Act, and other applicable laws;
f. Personal information originally collected from residents of foreign jurisdictions in accordance with the laws of those foreign jurisdictions, including any applicable data privacy laws, which is being processed in the Philippines. The burden of proving the law of the foreign jurisdiction falls on the person or body seeking exemption. In the absence of proof, the applicable law shall be presumed to be the Act and these Rules:

Provided, that the non-applicability of the Act or these Rules do not extend to personal information controllers or personal information processors, who remain subject to the requirements of implementing security measures for personal data protection: Provided further, that the processing of the information provided in the preceding paragraphs shall be exempted from the requirements of the Act only to the minimum extent necessary to achieve the specific purpose, function, or activity.

383. National Privacy Commission, Rules and Regulations Implementing the Data Privacy Act of 2012, Republic Act No. 10173, §6 (2016).
384. National Privacy Commission, Data Subject Rights, Advisory No. 01, Series of 2021 [NPC Advisory No. 21-01], §2(C) (29 Jan. 2021).
385. *Ibid.*

Section. 38. *Interpretation.* – Any doubt in the interpretation of any provision of this Act shall be liberally interpreted in a manner mindful of the rights and interests of the individual about whom personal information is processed.[386]

207. The rights afforded to data subjects are the right to be informed, right to access, right to object, right to erasure and blocking, right to rectify, right to file a complaint, right to damages, and right to data portability. These are enumerated in sections 16 and 18 of the DPA:

Section 16. *Rights of the Data Subject.* The data subject is entitled to:

(a) Be informed whether personal information pertaining to him or her shall be, are being or have been processed;
(b) Be furnished the information indicated hereunder before the entry of his or her personal information into the processing system of the personal information controller, or at the next practical opportunity:
  (1) Description of the personal information to be entered into the system;
  (2) Purposes for which they are being or are to be processed;
  (3) Scope and method of the personal information processing;
  (4) The recipients or classes of recipients to whom they are or may be disclosed;
  (5) Methods utilized for automated access, if the same is allowed by the data subject, and the extent to which such access is authorized;
  (6) The identity and contact details of the personal information controller or its representative;
  (7) The period for which the information will be stored; and
  (8) The existence of their rights, i.e., to access, correction, as well as the right to lodge a complaint before the Commission.

  Any information supplied or declaration made to the data subject on these matters shall not be amended without prior notification of data subject: *Provided*, That the notification under subsection (b) shall not apply should the personal information be needed pursuant to a *subpoena* or when the collection and processing are for obvious purposes, including when it is necessary for the performance of or in relation to a contract or service or when necessary or desirable in the context of an employer-employee relationship, between the collector and the data subject, or when the information is being collected and processed as a result of legal obligation;
(c) Reasonable access to, upon demand, the following:
  (1) Contents of his or her personal information that were processed;
  (2) Sources from which personal information were obtained;
  (3) Names and addresses of recipients of the personal information;
  (4) Manner by which such data were processed;

386. National Privacy Commission, Rules and Regulations Implementing the Data Privacy Act of 2012, Republic Act No. 10173, §38 (2016).

(5) Reasons for the disclosure of the personal information to recipients;
(6) Information on automated processes where the data will or likely to be made as the sole basis for any decision significantly affecting or will affect the data subject;
(7) Date when his or her personal information concerning the data subject were last accessed and modified; and
(8) The designation, or name or identity and address of the personal information controller;

(d) Dispute the inaccuracy or error in the personal information and have the personal information controller correct it immediately and accordingly, unless the request is vexatious or otherwise unreasonable. If the personal information have been corrected, the personal information controller shall ensure the accessibility of both the new and the retracted information and the simultaneous receipt of the new and the retracted information by recipients thereof: *Provided*, That the third parties who have previously received such processed personal information shall he informed of its inaccuracy and its rectification upon reasonable request of the data subject;
(e) Suspend, withdraw or order the blocking, removal or destruction of his or her personal information from the personal information controller's filing system upon discovery and substantial proof that the personal information are incomplete, outdated, false, unlawfully obtained, used for unauthorized purposes or are no longer necessary for the purposes for which they were collected. In this case, the personal information controller may notify third parties who have previously received such processed personal information; and
(f) Be indemnified for any damages sustained due to such inaccurate, incomplete, outdated, false, unlawfully obtained or unauthorized use of personal information.[387]

Section 18. *Right to Data Portability*. The data subject shall have the right, where personal information is processed by electronic means and in a structured and commonly used format, to obtain from the personal information controller a copy of data undergoing processing in an electronic or structured format, which is commonly used and allows for further use by the data subject. The Commission may specify the electronic format referred to above, as well as the technical standards, modalities and procedures for their transfer.[388]

387. An Act Protecting Individual Personal Information in Information and Communications Systems in the Government and the Private Sector, Creating for this purpose a National Privacy Commission, and For Other Purposes [Data Privacy Act of 2012], Republic Act No. 10173 §16 (2012).
388. *Ibid.*, Republic Act No. 10173 §18.

208. These rights may be exercised by the data subjects themselves or they may authorize another person to exercise such rights on their behalf.[389] Such authorization must be specific and supported by appropriate documents, such as a Special Power of Attorney.[390]

209. The transmissibility of data subject rights is also recognized. If a data subject passes away, is incapacitated, or is incapable of exercising his or her rights, his or her lawful heirs and assignees may invoke the data subject's rights, as provided in section 17 of the DPA:

> Section 17. *Transmissibility of Rights of the Data Subject.* The lawful heirs and assigns of the data subject may invoke the rights of the data subject for, which he or she is an heir or assignee at any time after the death of the data subject or when the data subject is incapacitated or incapable of exercising the rights as enumerated in the immediately preceding section.[391]

210. The Commission issued Advisory No. 2021-01 (Advisory 21-01) specifically on data subject rights.[392] Advisory 21-01 seeks to guide PICs and PIPs in fulfilling their obligations in relation to upholding the rights of their data subjects.[393]

211. It provides that PICs shall establish policies and procedures to allow data subjects to exercise their rights under the DPA:[394]

> Section 5. *Policies and procedures.* PICs shall establish policies and procedures allowing for the exercise of data subjects of their rights. The following shall be considered:
>
> A. *Request form.* There is no standard form or template. PICs shall, however, ensure that the process is clear, simple, straightforward, and convenient, and should be sufficiently communicated to the data subjects. PICs may adopt a standard form: *provided,* that any request containing information sufficient to process such request should be acted upon even if a standard form is not used.
>
> . . .
>
> B. *Verification of the identity of the requesting party.* The PIC shall use reasonable measures to verify the identity of the requesting data subject. For

389. National Privacy Commission, Data Subject Rights, Advisory No. 01, Series of 2021 [NPC Advisory No. 21-01], §3 (29 Jan. 2021).
390. *Ibid.*
391. An Act Protecting Individual Personal Information in Information and Communications Systems in the Government and the Private Sector, Creating for this purpose a National Privacy Commission, and For Other Purposes [Data Privacy Act of 2012], Republic Act No. 10173 §17 (2012).
392. National Privacy Commission, Data Subject Rights, Advisory No. 01, Series of 2021 [NPC Advisory No. 21-01] (29 Jan. 2021).
393. *See ibid.*
394. *Ibid.*, §5.

this purpose, the PIC may require the presentation of supporting documents to verify the identity of the requesting party, ensuring that the requested information is only to the extent necessary to confirm such identity.

. . .

C. *Assistance of PIPs.* PICs shall ensure, by contractual or other reasonable means, that the PIPs it has engaged to process personal data on its behalf shall cooperate and coordinate with the PIC in addressing any requests for the exercise of data subject rights.

D. *Fees and charges.* Generally, PICs shall not charge any fee to fulfil the exercise of data subject rights. As an exception, where data subjects request copies of their personal data and the other information in exercising their right to access, the PIC may require reasonable fees to cover administrative costs: *provided,* that fees imposed shall not be so exorbitant or excessive as to have the effect of discouraging such requests.

E. *Reasonable period for complying with the request.* The PIC must comply with requests without undue delay: *provided,* that the period will not exceed thirty (30) working days after receipt of the request and/or the necessary supporting or additional documentation: *provided further*, that if a request is complex or numerous, compliance with such request may be extended for a period not exceeding another fifteen (15) working days: *provided finally,* that the data subject or his or her authorized representative is notified of the reason for the extension.

   For government agencies, the pertinent provisions of Republic Act No. 11032 or the Ease of Doing Business and Efficient Government Service Delivery Act of 2018 and its Implementing Rules and Regulations shall apply in responding and complying with requests of data subjects.

F. *Retention.* PICs shall not retain personal data for the sole purpose of making it available for potential future requests for the right to access or data portability. Personal data shall be retained only for as long as necessary for the fulfillment of the purposes for which the data was obtained.[395]

212. The exercise of data subject rights, however, is not absolute. It must be reasonable.[396] PICs and PIPs may deny or limit the exercise of data subject rights if such denial or limitation is necessary for public interest, protection of other fundamental rights, or when the processing of personal data is for the following purposes: scientific and statistical research; criminal, administrative, or tax liabilities investigations of the data subject; for the interest of national security; or other analogous cases:[397]

---

395. *Ibid.*
396. *Ibid.*, §13.
397. *Ibid.*

Section 13. *Limitations.* The exercise of the rights of data subjects shall be reasonable. The same may be limited when necessary for public interest, protection of other fundamental rights, or when the processing of personal data is for the following purposes:

A. Scientific and statistical research: *provided*, that:
   1. No activities are carried out and no decisions are taken regarding the data subject;
   2. The personal data shall be held under strict confidentiality and shall be used only for research purpose; and
   3. Any research undertaken shall be subject to the applicable ethical and legal standards and processes, including but not limited to the submission of the research protocol to a recognized research ethics committee or ethics review board to ensure that ethical standards are observed.

B. Investigations in relation to any criminal, administrative, or tax liabilities of a data subject: *provided*, that:
   1. The investigation is being conducted by persons or entities duly authorized by law or regulation;
   2. The investigation or any stage thereof relates to any criminal, administrative, or tax liabilities of a data subject as may be defined under existing laws and regulations; and
   3. The limitation applies to the extent that complying with the requirements of upholding data subject rights would prevent, impair, or otherwise prejudice the investigation.

C. In the interest of national security, rights of data subjects may be limited pursuant to laws, rules and regulations, or order of a competent court.

D. Limitations on the exercise of data subject rights may be applied to analogous cases where the PIC has a legitimate purpose justifying such limitation. In all cases, limitations shall be proportional to the purpose of such limitation.[398]

213. PICs must take these into consideration when denying or limiting the exercise of data subject rights. It must also ensure that the data subject is 'clearly and fully informed of the reason for the limitation or denial'.[399] If the data subject disagrees with the PIC's denial or limitation of the exercise of his or her right, he or she may file a complaint before the Commission.[400] The Commission may then proceed to determine if such denial or limitation was reasonable based on the law and the factual circumstances surrounding the matter.

398. *Ibid.*
399. *Ibid.*, §14.
400. *Ibid.*, §15.

Chapter 1. Right to Be Informed

214. A PIC has an obligation to inform or notify its data subjects about the processing of their personal information. Section 16 of the DPA on the right to information provides:

> Section 16. *Rights of the Data Subject.* The data subject is entitled to:
>
> (a) Be informed whether personal information pertaining to him or her shall be, are being or have been processed[.][401]

215. A PIC must also furnish the data subject before or at the next practical opportunity with the following information:

> Section 16. *Rights of the Data Subject.* The data subject is entitled to:
>
> . . .
>
> (b) Be furnished the information indicated hereunder before the entry of his or her personal information into the processing system of the personal information controller, or at the next practical opportunity:
> (1) Description of the personal information to be entered into the system;
> (2) Purposes for which they are being or are to be processed;
> (3) Scope and method of the personal information processing;
> (4) The recipients or classes of recipients to whom they are or may be disclosed;
> (5) Methods utilized for automated access, if the same is allowed by the data subject, and the extent to which such access is authorized;
> (6) The identity and contact details of the personal information controller or its representative;
> (7) The period for which the information will be stored; and
> (8) The existence of their rights, i.e., to access, correction, as well as the right to lodge a complaint before the Commission.
>
> Any information supplied or declaration made to the data subject on these matters shall not be amended without prior notification of data subject: *Provided*, That the notification under subsection (b) shall not apply should the personal information be needed pursuant to a *subpoena* or when the collection and processing are for obvious purposes, including when it is necessary for the performance of or in relation to a contract or service or when necessary or desirable in the context of

401. An Act Protecting Individual Personal Information in Information and Communications Systems in the Government and the Private Sector, Creating for this purpose a National Privacy Commission, and For Other Purposes [Data Privacy Act of 2012], Republic Act No. 10173 §16(a) (2012).

> an employer-employee relationship, between the collector and the data subject, or when the information is being collected and processed as a result of legal obligation[.][402]

216. Additionally, Advisory 21-01 explains that the concept of 'next practical opportunity' is dependent 'upon the surrounding circumstance of the case. However, the timing of the provision of information must always be within a reasonable period to give effect to the data subject's right to be informed'.[403]

217. It further sets out the manner by which a PIC should communicate these types of information to the data subjects in line with the general privacy principle of transparency.[404] A PIC furnishes its data subjects with information on the processing of their data through a privacy notice, which is 'a statement made to data subjects that describes how the [PIC] collects, uses, retains, and discloses personal information'.[405]

218. To properly achieve its purpose, the information provided must be 'in clear and plain language'.[406] The Commission, in several cases, explained how this requirement relates to the principle of transparency.

219. In NPC Case No. 19-450, the Commission discussed that:

> [T]he requirement to use clear and plain language does not mean using layman's terms to substitute technical words at the risk of not capturing the complex concepts they represent. Rather, this requirement means that information should be provided in as simple a manner as possible, avoiding sentence or language structures that are complex. The information provided should be concrete and definitive; it should not be phrased in abstract or ambivalent terms or leave room for different interpretations such as in the above-cited provision which uses the word 'any' several times, as well as wordings like 'including but not limited to'.[407]

220. In another case, NPC Case No. 19-498, the Commission held that the 'test to determine if the PIC has complied with the general privacy principle of transparency is to examine whether an average member of the target audience could have

402. *Ibid.*, Republic Act No. 10173 §16(b).
403. National Privacy Commission, Data Subject Rights, Advisory No. 01, Series of 2021 [NPC Advisory No. 21-01], §6(B) (29 Jan. 2021).
404. *Ibid.*, §6.
405. *Ibid.*, §6(C).
406. *Ibid.*
407. *JRG v. CXXX Lending Corporation*, NPC Case No. 19-450, 9 Jun. 2020, at 6, *available at* https://www.privacy.gov.ph/wp-content/uploads/2022/01/Decision_NPC-19-450-JRG-v.-CXXX.pdf (last accessed 6 Apr. 2022).

understood the information provided to them'.[408] Thus, a PIC should determine the best way to present the required information to its target data subjects, even if it means translating the information to a language that is more familiar to the target audience.

221. Advisory 21-01 also specifically provides that 'a privacy notice is not equivalent to consent'.[409] A privacy notice should provide a data subject with all the necessary information related to a specific type of processing.[410] While consent may not be required in instances when it is not the basis for the processing of personal data, a privacy notice is always required to ensure that data subjects are informed of the purpose, scope, nature, and extent of the processing of their personal data by PICs.[411]

---

408. *JVA v. UXXX Lending Corporation*, NPC Case No. 19-498, 9 Jun. 2020, at 7, *available at* https://www.privacy.gov.ph/wp-content/uploads/2022/01/Decision-NPC-Case-No.-19-498-JVA-v.-UXXX.pdf (last accessed 6 Apr. 2022).
409. National Privacy Commission, Data Subject Rights, Advisory No. 01, Series of 2021 [NPC Advisory No. 21-01], §6(D) (29 Jan. 2021).
410. *Ibid.*
411. *Ibid.*

Chapter 2. Right to Access

222. A data subject has the right to access his or her personal information:

> Section 16. *Rights of the Data Subject.* The data subject is entitled to:
>
> . . .
>
> (c) Reasonable access to, upon demand, the following:
> (1) Contents of his or her personal information that were processed;
> (2) Sources from which personal information were obtained;
> (3) Names and addresses of recipients of the personal information;
> (4) Manner by which such data were processed;
> (5) Reasons for the disclosure of the personal information to recipients;
> (6) Information on automated processes where the data will or likely to be made as the sole basis for any decision significantly affecting or will affect the data subject;
> (7) Date when his or her personal information concerning the data subject were last accessed and modified; and
> (8) The designation, or name or identity and address of the personal information controller[.][412]

223. Advisory 21-01 further clarifies that the right to access personal information includes the right to obtain information for the purposes of the processing and the period for which particular categories of information will be stored:

> Section 8. *Right to Access.* The right of data subjects to access information on the processing of their personal data shall be subject to the following guidelines:
> A. A data subject has the right to obtain confirmation on whether or not data relating to him or her are being processed, as well as information about any of the following:
>
> . . .
>
> 3. Purposes of processing;
>
> . . .
>
> 9. Period for which particular categories of information will be stored[.][413]

224. A data subject may only request access to his or her own personal information.[414] Advisory 21-01 particularly excludes access to information relating to any other individual, as well as any analysis made by the PIC with respect to a data

412. An Act Protecting Individual Personal Information in Information and Communications Systems in the Government and the Private Sector, Creating for this purpose a National Privacy Commission, and For Other Purposes [Data Privacy Act of 2012], Republic Act No. 10173 §16(c) (2012).
413. National Privacy Commission, Data Subject Rights, Advisory No. 01, Series of 2021 [NPC Advisory No. 21-01], §8(A) (29 Jan. 2021).
414. *Ibid.*, §8(B).

subject's personal data, including specifically inferred, derived, modelled, or business-generated data.[415] This means that information relating to the individual resulting from the processing done by the PIC, such as credit rating and other similar processing using proprietary information of a company, is not covered by the right to access:

> Section 8. *Right to Access.* The right of data subjects to access information on the processing of their personal data shall be subject to the following guidelines:
>
> . . .
>
> B. A data subject may only request to have access to his or her own personal data and the other information in the immediately preceding paragraph and not to the information relating to any another individual.
>
> This would likewise exclude any analysis made by the PIC with respect to a data subject's personal data, i.e.[,] inferred, derived, modeled, or business-generated data.[416]

225. The exercise of the right to access must be reasonable. It may be limited to the following circumstances:

> Section 8. *Right to Access.* The right of data subjects to access information on the processing of their personal data shall be subject to the following guidelines:
>
> . . .
>
> C. The following instances, where applicable, may limit the right to access:
> a) Publicly available information. If an existing law or regulation requires PICs to make the personal data available to the public, *the PIC has the discretion on whether to comply with the request or to direct the requesting party to where such information may be found or accessed.* However, access to the other information in Section 8(A) should still be provided to the data subject where that specific information is not publicly available.
> b) Repeated requests. The PIC may decide not to comply with repeated, identical, or similar requests if such request for access has been previously granted unless a reasonable interval of time from the previous request has elapsed. The determination of what constitutes a reasonable interval of time shall depend on the nature of the request, considering any changes or updates in the personal data and/or the other information in Section 8(A) from the time of the previous request.
> c) Requests which will entail disproportionate effort. After reasonable evaluation, if the request for access would result in a disproportionate amount of effort or resources, the PIC may refuse to comply with the

415. *Ibid.*
416. *Ibid.*

request. The determination of what constitutes disproportionate effort may be made on the basis of the particular circumstances of the request. Factors to consider may include the availability of the information, the purpose of the request, and the necessity and benefit of the requested information to the data subject.

d) Consideration of the safety of the data subject. In exceptional cases and subject to any applicable ethical guidelines, limitations on the right to access may apply if in the professional evaluation and determination of the PIC, providing access to the requested information may cause serious harm to the physical, mental, or emotional health of the data subject.[417]

226. Further, in the case of NPC 19-653, the Commission held that 'having a legitimate purpose or some other lawful criteria to process does not result in the PIC granting all requests to access by the data subjects. Such requests should be evaluated on a case-by-case basis and must always be subject to the PIC's guidelines for the release of such information'.[418] In the event where a request to access information is denied, PICs should already have documented policies and guidelines on the basis and process of the denial in terms of communicating with the data subject the reasons why such a request cannot be permitted.[419]

227. The Commission has also held that excessive or stringent requirements established by the PIC violate the data subject's right to access his or her personal information.[420] After all, the DPA should not be used as a tool to deprive data subjects of the very rights guaranteed by the DPA without proper justification and notice to the data subjects.[421]

---

417. *Ibid.*, §8(C). Emphasis supplied.
418. *BGM v. IPP*, NPC Case No. 19-653, 17 Dec. 2020, at 8, *available at* https://www.privacy.gov.ph/wp-content/uploads/2021/02/NPC-19-653-BGM-vs-IPP-Decision-FINAL-Pseudonymized-21Dec2020.pdf (last accessed 6 Apr. 2022).
419. *Ibid.*
420. NPC Case No. 19-653, 24 Jun. 2021, at 5 (NPC 2021) (unreported).
421. *D.N.T. v K.K. and X.F.*, NPC Case No. 19-1201, 18 Mar. 2021, at 3, *available at* https://www.privacy.gov.ph/wp-content/uploads/2022/03/NPC-19-1201-D.N.T.-v.-K.K.-et.-al.-Resolution-2021.03.18.pdf (last accessed 29 Apr. 2022).

Chapter 3. Right to Rectification

228. A data subject enjoys the right to rectify his or her personal data.[422] The right to rectification allows the data subject to dispute the inaccuracy or error in his personal information and requires the PIC to correct such error in its records:

> Section 16. *Rights of the Data Subject.* – The data subject is entitled to:
>
> . . .
>
> (d) Dispute the inaccuracy or error in the personal information and have the personal information controller correct it immediately and accordingly, unless the request is vexatious or otherwise unreasonable. If the personal information have been corrected, the personal information controller shall ensure the accessibility of both the new and the retracted information and the simultaneous receipt of the new and the retracted information by recipients thereof: *Provided,* That the third parties who have previously received such processed personal information shall be informed of its inaccuracy and its rectification upon reasonable request of the data subject[.][423]

229. The right to rectify also includes the right to have incomplete personal data completed, as provided in Advisory 21-01:

> Section 9. *Right to Rectification.* The data subject has the right to dispute the inaccuracy or error in his or her personal data and have the PIC correct the same within a reasonable period of time.
>
> . . .
>
> C. Considering the purpose/s of the processing, *the data subject shall have the right to have incomplete personal data completed, including means of providing a supplementary statement.*[424]

230. The data subjects must be permitted to access both the retracted and rectified pieces of personal information.[425] Upon his or her request, the PIC must also inform any third parties who have received the retracted personal information of the inaccuracy and the subsequent rectification.[426] Advisory 21-01 reiterates these obligations:

---

422. An Act Protecting Individual Personal Information in Information and Communications Systems in the Government and the Private Sector, Creating for this purpose a National Privacy Commission, and For Other Purposes [Data Privacy Act of 2012], Republic Act No. 10173 §16(d) (2012).
423. *Ibid.*
424. National Privacy Commission, Data Subject Rights, Advisory No. 01, Series of 2021 [NPC Advisory No. 21-01], §9(C) (29 Jan. 2021). Emphasis supplied.
425. National Privacy Commission, Rules and Regulations Implementing the Data Privacy Act of 2012, Republic Act No. 10173, §34(d) (2016).
426. *Ibid.*

> Section 9. *Right to Rectification.* The data subject has the right to dispute the inaccuracy or error in his or her personal data and have the PIC correct the same within a reasonable period of time.
>
> A. If the personal data has been corrected, the PIC shall:
>
> 1. Ensure the accessibility of both the new and the retracted information, and the simultaneous receipt of the new and the retracted information by the intended recipients; and
> 2. Inform the recipients or third parties who have previously received such personal data of its inaccuracy and its subsequent rectification, upon reasonable request of the data subject.[427]

231. The DPA provides that the inaccurate piece of personal information shall be rectified 'immediately and accordingly'.[428] In NPC 18-038, the Commission explained this further:

> While the provision states that the information must be corrected 'immediately and accordingly,' the Commission looks at the circumstances surrounding the request. This may include, among others, the volume of information involved and the time that has lapsed since the time the information was processed. Hence, there is no uniform timeframe for all the personal information controllers to comply with the obligation to correct inaccurate information, as long as there is no undue or excessive delay.[429]

232. The exercise of the right to rectify must be reasonable. Otherwise, the PIC may deny this right if the request for rectification is manifestly unfounded, vexatious, or otherwise unreasonable:

> Section 9. *Right to Rectification.*
>
> . . .
>
> D. The request for rectification may be denied if the same is *manifestly unfounded, vexatious, or otherwise unreasonable*. The determination of whether the request is manifestly unfounded, vexatious, or unreasonable may be made on the basis of the particular circumstances of the request. A request may be considered as such when it is made with *no real purpose other than to harass, cause annoyance, or hamper the delivery and performance of service.*[430]

---

427. National Privacy Commission, Data Subject Rights, Advisory No. 01, Series of 2021 [NPC Advisory No. 21-01], §9(A) (29 Jan. 2021). Emphasis supplied.
428. An Act Protecting Individual Personal Information in Information and Communications Systems in the Government and the Private Sector, Creating for this purpose a National Privacy Commission, and For Other Purposes [Data Privacy Act of 2012], Republic Act No. 10173 §16(d) (2012).
429. NPC 18-038, 21 May 2020, at 9 (NPC 2020) (unreported).
430. National Privacy Commission, Data Subject Rights, Advisory No. 01, Series of 2021 [NPC Advisory No. 21-01], §9(D) (29 Jan. 2021). Emphasis supplied.

233. The right to rectify also excludes instances where the rectification requires an order from government bodies, such as 'a competent court, other pertinent government agencies, or otherwise covered by an official process under other applicable laws and regulations'.[431]

431. *Ibid.*

Chapter 4. Right to Object

234. The data subject has the right to object to the processing of his or her personal data:

> Section 34. *Rights of the Data Subject.* The data subject is entitled to the following rights:
>
> . . .
>
> b. Right to object. The data subject shall have the right to object to the processing of his or her personal data, including processing for direct marketing, automated processing or profiling. The data subject shall also be notified and given an opportunity to withhold consent to the processing in case of changes or any amendment to the information supplied or declared to the data subject in the preceding paragraph.[432]

235. The Commission interpreted that the right to object can only be exercised when the processing is based on consent or legitimate interest.[433] Advisory 21-01 states:

> Section 7. *Right to Object.* The data subject shall have the right to object to the processing of his or her personal data where such processing is based on consent or legitimate interest.[434]

236. The reason for this limitation can be gleaned from the exceptions on the exercise of the right to object detailed in section 34(b) of the IRR:

> Section 34. *Rights of the Data Subject.* The data subject is entitled to the following rights:
>
> . . .
>
> (b) Right to object.
>
> . . .
>
> When a data subject objects or withholds consent, the personal information controller shall no longer process the personal data, unless:
>
> 1. The personal data is needed pursuant to a subpoena;
> 2. The collection and processing are for obvious purposes, including, when it is necessary for the performance of or in relation to a contract or service to which the data subject is a party, or when necessary or desirable in the context of an employer-employee relationship between the collector and the data subject; or

432. National Privacy Commission, Rules and Regulations Implementing the Data Privacy Act of 2012, Republic Act No. 10173, §34(b) (2016).
433. National Privacy Commission, Data Subject Rights, Advisory No. 01, Series of 2021 [NPC Advisory No. 21-01], §7 (29 Jan. 2021).
434. *Ibid.*

3. The information is being collected and processed as a result of a legal obligation.[435]

237. The first and third exceptions enumerated in the IRR refer to a legal obligation or a requirement of law under section 12(c),[436] section 13(b),[437] and section 13(f)[438] of the DPA. The processing of personal data pursuant to a subpoena is necessarily related to the fulfilment of a legal obligation. The second exception enumerated in the IRR refers to a contract where the exercise of the right has to be pursuant to the terms of the contract under section 12(b) of the DPA.

238. In relation to the exercise of the right to object, however, the enumeration in the IRR failed to account for all the lawful criteria to process under sections 12 and 13 of the DPA. While not expressly included in the enumeration in the IRR, the right to object cannot be exercised when the processing is based on section 12(d)[439] and section 13(c) and (e)[440] of the DPA.

---

435. National Privacy Commission, Rules and Regulations Implementing the Data Privacy Act of 2012, Republic Act No. 10173, §34(b) (2016).
436. Section 12. Criteria for Lawful Processing of Personal Information. – The processing of personal information shall be permitted only if not otherwise prohibited by law, and when at least one of the following conditions exists: (c) The processing is necessary for compliance with a legal obligation to which the personal information controller is subject.
437. Section 13. Sensitive Personal Information and Privileged Information. – The processing of sensitive personal information and privileged information shall be prohibited, except in the following cases: (b) The processing of the same is provided for by existing laws and regulations: Provided, That such regulatory enactments guarantee the protection of the sensitive personal information and the privileged information: Provided, further, That the consent of the data subjects are not required by law or regulation permitting the processing of the sensitive personal information or the privileged information.
438. Section 13. Sensitive Personal Information and Privileged Information. – The processing of sensitive personal information and privileged information shall be prohibited, except in the following cases: (f) The processing concerns such personal information as is necessary for the protection of lawful rights and interests of natural or legal persons in court proceedings, or the establishment, exercise or defence of legal claims, or when provided to government or public authority.
439. Section 12. *Criteria for Lawful Processing of Personal Information.* – The processing of personal information shall be permitted only if not otherwise prohibited by law, and when at least one of the following conditions exists:

    (d) The processing is necessary to protect vitally important interests of the data subject, including life and health.

440. Section 13. *Sensitive Personal Information and Privileged Information.* – The processing of sensitive personal information and privileged information shall be prohibited, except in the following cases:

    (c) The processing is necessary to protect the life and health of the data subject or another person, and the data subject is not legally or physically able to express his or her consent prior to the processing;
    (e) The processing is necessary for purposes of medical treatment, is carried out by a medical practitioner or a medical treatment institution, and an adequate level of protection of personal information is ensured.

239. The right to object cannot be exercised if the processing is based on the lawful criteria of consent and legitimate interests since the processing will be rendered futile if the absolute exercise of the right to object is allowed.[441] The limitation recognizes that the exercise of the right to object does not preclude the PIC from processing the data subject's personal data if its processing is based on some other lawful criteria to process under sections 12 and 13 of the DPA.[442] In such cases, the PIC has the burden to determine and communicate to the data subject the specific lawful basis for processing the data subject's personal information:

> Section 7. *Right to Object.*
>
> . . .
>
> C. When a data subject objects, the PIC shall cease the processing of personal data and comply with the objection, unless the processing falls under any other allowable instances pursuant to in Sections 12 or 13, other than consent and legitimate interest.
>
> Should there be other grounds to continue processing the personal data, the PIC shall have the burden of determining and proving the appropriate lawful basis or compelling reason to continue such processing. The PIC shall communicate and inform the data subject of said lawful basis or compelling reason to continue processing.[443]

240. The right to object can also be exercised if there is a significant change in the scope, purpose, or extent of the processing activity and the lawful criteria used for the processing is consent.[444] If the data subject has previously given his or her consent to the processing of personal information, it is incumbent upon the PIC to notify and give the data subject an opportunity to object or to withdraw the consent given:

> Section 7. *Right to Object.*
>
> . . .
>
> A. In case of any significant change or amendment to the information provided to the data subject in a consent form, privacy notice, or similar communication, the data subject shall be notified and given an opportunity to object and/or withdraw consent, if consent was previously given for such personal data processing.
>
> For this purpose, a significant change or amendment shall include changes in the identity of the PIC, the purpose/s of processing, scope and method of processing, and other analogous instances.[445]

441. National Privacy Commission, Data Subject Rights, Advisory No. 01, Series of 2021 [NPC Advisory No. 21-01], §7(C) (29 Jan. 2021).
442. *Ibid.*
443. *Ibid.*
444. *Ibid.*, §7(A).
445. *Ibid.*

Chapter 5. Right to Erasure

241. The data subject may also exercise his right to the erasure of his personal data in particular circumstances.[446] The right to erasure and the right to blocking are both discussed in Section 16 of the DPA:

> Section 16. *Rights of the Data Subject.* The data subject is entitled to:
>
> . . .
>
> (e) Suspend, withdraw or order the blocking, removal or destruction of his or her personal information from the personal information controller's filing system upon discovery and substantial proof that the personal information are incomplete, outdated, false, unlawfully obtained, used for unauthorized purposes or are no longer necessary for the purposes for which they were collected. In this case, the personal information controller may notify third parties who have previously received such processed personal information[.][447]

242. Section 34 of the IRR explains when these rights may be exercised:

> Section 34. *Rights of the Data Subject.* The data subject is entitled to the following rights:
>
> . . .
>
> e. Right to Erasure or Blocking. The data subject shall have the right to suspend, withdraw or order the blocking, removal or destruction of his or her personal data from the personal information controller's filing system.
>   1. This right may be exercised upon discovery and substantial proof of any of the following:
>   (a) The personal data is incomplete, outdated, false, or unlawfully obtained;
>   (b) The personal data is being used for purpose not authorized by the data subject;
>   (c) The personal data is no longer necessary for the purposes for which they were collected;
>   (d) The data subject withdraws consent or objects to the processing, and there is no other legal ground or overriding legitimate interest for the processing;
>   (e) The personal data concerns private information that is prejudicial to data subject, unless justified by freedom of speech, of expression, or of the press or otherwise authorized;

446. *See* An Act Protecting Individual Personal Information in Information and Communications Systems in the Government and the Private Sector, Creating for this purpose a National Privacy Commission, and For Other Purposes [Data Privacy Act of 2012], Republic Act No. 10173 §16(e) (2012).

447. *Ibid.*

(f) The processing is unlawful;
(g) The personal information controller or personal information processor violated the rights of the data subject.

2. The personal information controller may notify third parties who have previously received such processed personal information.[448]

243. Section 10 of Advisory 21-01 similarly provides that the right to erasure and blocking may also be exercised as follows:

> Section 10. *Right to Erasure or Blocking.* A data subject has the right to request for the suspension, withdrawal, blocking, removal, or destruction of his or her personal data from the PIC's filing system, in both live and back-up systems.
> A. This right may be exercised upon discovery and substantial proof of any of the following:
> 1. The personal data is: a) incomplete, outdated, false, or unlawfully obtained; b) used for an unauthorized purpose; c) no longer necessary for the purpose/s for which they were collected; or d) concerns private information that is prejudicial to the data subject, unless justified by freedom of speech, of expression, or of the press, or otherwise authorized;
> 2. The data subject objects to the processing, and there are no other applicable lawful criteria for processing;
> 3. The processing is unlawful; or
> 4. The PIC or PIP violated the rights of the data subject.[449]

244. Certain obligations are imposed upon the PIC in relation to the right to erasure or blocking:

> Section 10. *Right to Erasure or Blocking.*
>
> . . .
>
> c) PICs shall *inform the recipients or third parties who have previously received such personal data of the fact of erasure. PICs shall likewise inform the data subject about such recipients of his or her personal data.*
> d) Where personal data that is the subject of a request for erasure is publicly available, i.e. online, reasonable and appropriate measures shall be taken by the PIC to *communicate with other PICs, including third party indexes, and request them to erase copies or remove or de-list search results or links to the pertinent personal data.* In determining what is reasonable and appropriate, the available technology and the cost of implementation shall be considered.

448. National Privacy Commission, Rules and Regulations Implementing the Data Privacy Act of 2012, Republic Act No. 10173, §34(e) (2016).
449. National Privacy Commission, Data Subject Rights, Advisory No. 01, Series of 2021 [NPC Advisory No. 21-01], §10(A) (29 Jan. 2021). Emphasis supplied.

e) Data subjects must be adequately informed of the consequences of the erasure of their personal data.[450]

245. The PIC also has an obligation to judiciously evaluate requests for the right to erasure or blocking.[451] The PIC shall approve the request for erasure or blocking if personal information involved has been unlawfully processed, used for unauthorized purposes, or resulted from a violation of data subject rights:

Section 10. *Right to Erasure or Blocking.*

. . .

B. PICs should judiciously evaluate requests for the exercise of the right to erasure or blocking.
   1. Approval of Request. When a request for erasure or blocking is made on any of the following grounds, the PIC is directed to grant such request: a) Unlawful processing; b) Used for unauthorized purposes; or c) Violation of data subject rights.[452]

246. The PIC, however, may deny the request for erasure or blocking, wholly or partly, when the personal data is still necessary for any of the following:

Section 10. *Right to Erasure or Blocking.*

. . .

c) Fulfillment of the purpose/s for which the data was obtained;
d) Compliance with a legal obligation which requires personal data processing;
e) Establishment, exercise, or defense of any legal claim;
f) Legitimate business purposes of the PIC, consistent with the applicable industry standard for personal data retention;
g) To apprise the public on matters that have an overriding public interest or concern, taking into consideration the following factors: i. constitutionally guaranteed rights and freedoms of speech, of expression, or of the press; ii. whether or not the personal data pertains to a data subject who is a public figure; and iii. other analogous considerations where personal data are processed in circumstances where data subjects can reasonably expect further processing.
h) As may be provided by any existing law, rules, and regulations.[453]

450. *Ibid.*, §10(C). Emphasis supplied.
451. *Ibid.*, §10(B).
452. *Ibid.*
453. *Ibid.*, §10(B) (2).

Chapter 6. Right to Restriction

247. The DPA and other privacy regulations do not categorically provide for a right to restriction. They, however, discuss the components of the right to restriction in relation to the right to rectification, right to object, and right of erasure. The discussion on these rights can be found in the appropriate chapters.

Chapter 7. Profiling

248. In relation to the right to be informed, a data subject is entitled to be informed of the 'existence of automated decision-making and profiling':

> Section 34. *Rights of the Data Subject.* The data subject is entitled to the following rights:
>
> 1. Right to be informed.
>   a. The data subject has a right to be informed whether personal data pertaining to him or her shall be, are being, or have been processed, including the existence of automated decision-making and profiling.[454]

249. The IRR defines 'profiling' as:

> 'Profiling' refers to *any form of automated processing of personal data consisting of the use of personal data to evaluate certain personal aspects relating to a natural person*, in particular to analyze or predict aspects concerning that natural person's performance at work, economic situation, health, personal preferences, interests, reliability, behavior, location or movements[.][455]

250. The PIC has an obligation to notify the Commission of its automated processing operations. When a PIC engages in automated processing operations, whether wholly or partly automated, the automated processing operations become the sole basis for making decisions about a data subject and when the decision would significantly affect the data subject.[456] The notification should include the following information:

a. The notification shall include the following information:
   1. Purpose of processing;
   2. Categories of personal data to undergo processing;
   3. Category or categories of data subject;
   4. Consent forms or manner of obtaining consent;
   5. The recipients or categories of recipients to whom the data are to be disclosed;
   6. The length of time the data are to be stored;
   7. Methods and logic utilized for automated processing;
   8. Decisions relating to the data subject that would be made on the basis of processed data or that would significantly affect the rights and freedoms of data subject; and
   9. Names and contact details of the compliance or data protection officer.[457]

---

454. National Privacy Commission, Rules and Regulations Implementing the Data Privacy Act of 2012, Republic Act No. 10173, §34(a) (1) (2016).
455. *Ibid.*, §3(p). Emphasis supplied.
456. *Ibid.*, §48 (2016).
457. *Ibid.*, §48(a).

251. The data subject, however, has the right to object and withhold consent in relation to automated processing if automated processing is the sole basis of a decision with legal effects on the data subject:[458]

> Section 48. *Notification of Automated Processing Operations.*
>
> . . .
>
> b. No decision with legal effects concerning a data subject shall be made solely on the basis of automated processing without the consent of the data subject.[459]

252. In such cases, the PIC shall provide data subjects with adequate information, in clear and plain language, on the exercise of the right to object and the provision of goods and services to the data subject:

> Section 7. *Right to Object.*
>
> . . .
>
> B. Data subjects have the right to object to the processing of his or her personal data for direct marketing, profiling, or in cases of automated processing where the personal data will, or is likely to, be made as the sole basis for any decision that significantly affects or will affect him or her.
>
> For this purpose, data subjects shall be provided by PICs in clear and easy to understand language with adequate information on the effect of the exercise of this right vis-à-vis the provision of goods and/or services by the PIC to the data subject. Said information that will be communicated to the data subjects should indicate the scope of the withdrawal of consent or objection and its consequences. This could mean removal of the personal data from the PIC's automated processing systems or its suppression in mailing/profiling lists in a way that it would not be processed for purposes that the data subject has objected to.[460]

458. National Privacy Commission, Profiling of Individuals and Collection of Personal Information Based on Publicly Available Data, Advisory Opinion No. 41, Series of 2017, at 3 (14 Aug. 2017).
459. National Privacy Commission, Rules and Regulations Implementing the Data Privacy Act of 2012, Republic Act No. 10173, §48(b) (2016).
460. National Privacy Commission, Data Subject Rights, Advisory No. 01, Series of 2021 [NPC Advisory No. 21-01], §7(B) (29 Jan. 2021).

Chapter 8. Other Data Subject Rights

§1. Right to Damages

253. The data subject may exercise his right to be indemnified for damages.[461] Section 16 of the DPA provides the situation when the data subject may be indemnified for damages:

> Section 16. *Rights of the Data Subject.* The data subject is entitled to:
>
> . . .
>
> (f) Be indemnified for any damages sustained due to such inaccurate, incomplete, outdated, false, unlawfully obtained or unauthorized use of personal information.[462]

254. The exercise of the right to damages is hinged on the violation of the data subject's rights and freedoms. In relation to the data subject's right to file a complaint, this may be exercised when the data subject perceives that his or her rights have been violated.[463] If the Commission finds that the data subject's rights have indeed been violated, then the Commission may award damages:

> Section 12. *Right to Damages.* The data subjects have the right to be indemnified for any damages sustained due to inaccurate, incomplete, outdated, false, unlawfully obtained, or unauthorized use of their personal data, taking into account any violation of his or her rights and freedoms as data subject.
> A. When there is a perceived violation of his or her rights, the data subject may file a complaint with the NPC, in accordance with its Rules of Procedure governing all complaints filed before the Commission.
> B. In cases where a data subject files a complaint for violation of his or her rights, and for any injury suffered as a result of the processing of his or her personal data, the Commission may award indemnity on the basis of the applicable provisions of the New Civil Code.[464]

255. The DPA gives individuals the right to receive indemnification from PICs or PIPs for both material and non-material damages.[465] Section 16 of the DPA refers

---

461. An Act Protecting Individual Personal Information in Information and Communications Systems in the Government and the Private Sector, Creating for this purpose a National Privacy Commission, and For Other Purposes [Data Privacy Act of 2012], Republic Act No. 10173 §16 (2012).
462. *Ibid.*, Republic Act No. 10173 §16(f).
463. National Privacy Commission, Data Subject Rights, Advisory No. 01, Series of 2021 [NPC Advisory No. 21-01], §12(A) (29 Jan. 2021).
464. *Ibid.*, §12.
465. *See* An Act Protecting Individual Personal Information in Information and Communications Systems in the Government and the Private Sector, Creating for this purpose a National Privacy Commission, and For Other Purposes [Data Privacy Act of 2012], Republic Act No. 10173 §16(f) (2012).

to provisions of the Civil Code on actual damages,[466] moral damages,[467] exemplary damages,[468] temperate damages,[469] liquidated damages,[470] and nominal damages.[471]

256. In NPC 19-528, the Commission held that the DPA does not require actual or monetary damages for data subjects to exercise the right to damages.[472] Section 37 of the DPA also provides that restitution is governed by the Civil Code:

> Section 37. *Restitution.* Restitution for any aggrieved party shall be governed by the provisions of the New Civil Code.[473]

257. In its Decision on the appeal of the same case, the Court of Appeals stated:

> Article 2221 of the [Civil Code] provides that nominal damages are adjudicated in order that a right of the plaintiff, which has been violated or invaded by the defendant, may be vindicated or recognized. Jurisprudence teaches us that nominal damages may be recovered where a legal right is technically violated and must be vindicated against an invasion that has produced no actual present loss quantified and proved. So long as there is a showing of a violation of the plaintiff's right an award of nominal damages is proper. Simply stated, nominal damages is awarded when injury has been done, but the pecuniary value of the damage is not shown by evidence and is thus subject to the discretion of the court according to the circumstances of the case.

---

466. Art. 2199. Except as provided by law or by stipulation, one is entitled to an adequate compensation only for such pecuniary loss suffered by him as he has duly proved. Such compensation is referred to as actual or compensatory damages.
467. Art. 2217. Moral damages include physical suffering, mental anguish, fright, serious anxiety, besmirched reputation, wounded feelings, moral shock, social humiliation, and similar injury. Though incapable of pecuniary computation, moral damages may be recovered if they are the proximate result of the defendant's wrongful act for omission.
468. Art. 2229. Exemplary or corrective damages are imposed, by way of example or correction for the public good, in addition to the moral, temperate, liquidated or compensatory damages.
469. Art. 2224. Temperate or moderate damages, which are more than nominal but less than compensatory damages, may be recovered when the court finds that some pecuniary loss has been suffered but its amount cannot, from the nature of the case, be provided with certainty.
470. Art. 2226. Liquidated damages are those agreed upon by the parties to a contract, to be paid in case of breach thereof.
471. Art. 2221. Nominal damages are adjudicated in order that a right of the plaintiff, which has been violated or invaded by the defendant, may be vindicated or recognized, and not for the purpose of indemnifying the plaintiff for any loss suffered by him.
472. *See MNLC v. PXXX Corporation*, NPC 19-528, 23 Feb. 2021, at 9, *available at* https://www.privacy.gov.ph/wp-content/uploads/2022/01/Resolution-02.23.2021-NPC-19-528-MNLC-vs-PXXX-Corporation.pdf (last accessed 6 Apr. 2022).
473. An Act Protecting Individual Personal Information in Information and Communications Systems in the Government and the Private Sector, Creating for this purpose a National Privacy Commission, and For Other Purposes [Data Privacy Act of 2012], Republic Act No. 10173 §37 (2012).

> [Petitioner]'s disregard of its responsibilities under the Data Privacy Act and the unauthorized processing of [the Respondent's] members' [Sensitive Personal Information] clearly violated their rights.[474]

258. Further, the consequences of processing inaccurate information are enough for the right to arise.[475] The Supreme Court has also clarified that no actual present loss is required to warrant the award of nominal damages; thus, 'nominal damages are recoverable where a legal right is technically violated and must be vindicated against an invasion that has produced no actual present loss of any kind or where there has been a breach of contract and no substantial injury or actual damages whatsoever have been or can be shown'.[476]

§2. Right to Data Portability

259. The data subject also enjoys the right to data portability, which allows the data subject to obtain a copy of his or her personal information undergoing processing in an electronic or structured format:

> Section 18. *Right to Data Portability*. The data subject shall have the right, where personal information is processed by electronic means and in a structured and commonly used format, to obtain from the personal information controller a copy of data undergoing processing in an electronic or structured format, which is commonly used and allows for further use by the data subject. The Commission may specify the electronic format referred to above, as well as the technical standards, modalities and procedures for their transfer.[477]

260. As provided in the IRR, the exercise of the right to data portability is related to the fact that the data subject has the right to control his or her personal data if the processing is based on consent or contract, for commercial purposes, or through automated means:

> Section 36. *Right to Data Portability*. Where his or her personal data is processed by electronic means and in a structured and commonly used format, the data subject shall have the right to obtain from the personal information controller a copy of such data in an electronic or structured format that is commonly used and allows for further use by the data subject. *The exercise of this*

474. *PXXX v. MNLC, Inc.*, CA-G.R. SP No. 168952, 14 Dec. 2021, at 26, *available at* https://services.ca.judiciary.gov.ph/csisver3-war/faces/pages/ResultInformation.xhtml (last accessed 28 Apr. 2022).
475. *MNLC v. PXXX Corporation*, NPC 19-528, 23 Feb. 2021, at 8, *available at* https://www.privacy.gov.ph/wp-content/uploads/2022/01/Resolution-02.23.2021-NPC-19-528-MNLC-vs-PXXX-Corporation.pdf (last accessed 6 Apr. 2022).
476. *Seven Brothers Shipping Corporation v. DMC-Construction Resources, Inc.*, G.R. No. 193914 (2014).
477. An Act Protecting Individual Personal Information in Information and Communications Systems in the Government and the Private Sector, Creating for this purpose a National Privacy Commission, and For Other Purposes [Data Privacy Act of 2012], Republic Act No. 10173 §18 (2012).

> *right shall primarily take into account the right of data subject to have control over his or her personal data being processed based on consent or contract, for commercial purpose, or through automated means.* The Commission may specify the electronic format referred to above, as well as the technical standards, modalities, procedures and other rules for their transfer.[478]

261. The right to data portability applies when processing is based on consent or contract and is done by electronic means and in a structured, commonly used format:

> Section 11. *Right to Data Portability.* The data subject shall have the right to obtain from the PIC a copy of his or her personal data and/or have the same transmitted from one PIC to another, in an electronic or structured format that is commonly used and allows further use by the data subject.
>
> A. For the exercise of this right, the following conditions must concur:
>
> 1. Processing is based on consent or contract; and 2. Personal data is processed by electronic means and in a structured and commonly used format.[479]

262. The right to data portability only covers the personal data and the data provided by the data subject to the PIC:

> Section 11. *Right to Data Portability.*
>
> . . .
>
> B. Data portability shall be limited to the personal data concerning the data subject, and which he or she has provided to the PIC:
>
> 1. Data actively and knowingly provided by the data subject, i.e. name, address, age, username, etc.; and
> 2. Observed data provided by the data subject by virtue of the use of the service or the device, i.e. access logs, transaction history, location data, etc.[480]

263. The exercise of the right to data portability is not absolute:

> Section 11. *Right to Data Portability.*
>
> . . .
>
> C The exercise of this right shall not adversely affect the rights and freedom of others. PICs, whether sending or receiving, should consider implementing security measures to reduce the risk for personal data of third parties to be included in the porting request. When ported data includes the data of

---

478. National Privacy Commission, Rules and Regulations Implementing the Data Privacy Act of 2012, Republic Act No. 10173, §36 (2016). Emphasis supplied.
479. National Privacy Commission, Data Subject Rights, Advisory No. 01, Series of 2021 [NPC Advisory No. 21-01], §11(A)(1) (29 Jan. 2021).
480. *Ibid.*, §11(B).

other individuals, i.e. names and contact details within the contact directory of the requesting party, receiving PICs are prohibited from further proceeding such data for its own purpose, i.e.[,] marketing, etc.[481]

§3. Right to File a Complaint

264. A data subject has the right to file a complaint before the Commission if he or she perceives that his or her data privacy rights have been violated.[482] Section 12 of Advisory 21-01 provides:

> Section 12. *Right to Damages.*
>
> . . .
>
> A. When there is a perceived violation of his or her rights, the data subject may file a complaint with the NPC, in accordance with its Rules of Procedure governing all complaints filed before the Commission.[483]

265. The filing of a complaint shall be according to the Rules of Procedure of the NPC. The process of filing a complaint following the Rules of Procedure of the NPC shall be discussed in Part VIII.

481. *Ibid.*, §11(C).
482. *Ibid.*, §12(A).
483. *Ibid.*

Part V. Duties of Controllers and Processors

Chapter 1. National Rules Regarding Duties of Controllers

266. A PIC is a natural or juridical person who controls the processing of personal data.[484] It also includes those who instruct another person or entity to process personal information on its behalf.[485] Section 3 of the DPA provides:

> Section 3. *Definition of Terms.*
>
> . . .
>
> (h) Personal information controller refers to a person or organization who controls the collection, holding, processing or use of personal information, including a person or organization who instructs another person or organization to collect, hold, process, use, transfer or disclose personal information on his or her behalf.[486]

267. A PIC does not include those who perform functions as instructed by another person or entity (i.e., PIPs).[487] It also excludes an individual who processes personal information for his or her personal, family or household affairs:

> Section 3. *Definition of Terms.*
>
> . . .
>
> The term excludes:
>
> (1) A person or organization who performs such functions as instructed by another person or organization; and
> (2) An individual who collects, holds, processes or uses personal information in connection with the individual's personal, family or household affairs.[488]

484. An Act Protecting Individual Personal Information in Information and Communications Systems in the Government and the Private Sector, Creating for this purpose a National Privacy Commission, and For Other Purposes [Data Privacy Act of 2012], Republic Act No. 10173 §3(h) (2012).
485. *Ibid.*
486. *Ibid.*
487. National Privacy Commission, Rules and Regulations Implementing the Data Privacy Act of 2012, Republic Act No. 10173, §3(m) (2016).
488. An Act Protecting Individual Personal Information in Information and Communications Systems in the Government and the Private Sector, Creating for this purpose a National Privacy Commission, and For Other Purposes [Data Privacy Act of 2012], Republic Act No. 10173 §3(h) (2012).

268. The test to determine if a person or entity acts as a PIC is if such person or entity controls the processing of personal information.[489] Control exists when a natural or juridical person decides on the information to be collected or on the purpose or extent of the processing:

> Section 3. *Definitions.* Whenever used in these Rules, the following terms shall have the respective meanings hereafter set forth:
>
> . . .
>
> m. 'Personal information controller' refers to a natural or juridical person, or any other body who controls the processing of personal data, or instructs another to process personal data on its behalf.
>
> . . .
>
> There is control if the natural or juridical person or any other body decides on what information is collected, or the purpose or extent of its processing[.][490]

269. The existence of control is the determining factor on whether a person or an entity is considered a PIC:

> There is nothing in the law that requires entities to be engaged in the primary business of processing information before they are considered personal information controllers. *By having the control of and discretion in the use of personal information of individuals, they are already considered the controller.* They are thus accountable for the protection of the information and for the observation of the obligations under the law. These persons and entities must be able to justify their processing of personal data under any of the lawful criteria provided in the law.[491]

270. In NPC 18-010, the Commission held that if the entity 'determines the purposes and means of processing personal information, the categories to be processed, and access to such personal information' through its decision-making power, then such entity is considered a PIC:

> In this case, [the PIC] maintains that 'the information collected from [the data subject] are standard information necessary for the purpose of providing the services under the [Corporate Individual] DSL subscription' and that it was [the employer of the data subject] who provided the required information to [the PIC]. Although it was [the employer of the data subject] who submitted

---

489. *RLA v. PLDT Enterprise*, NPC Case No. 18-010, 10 Dec. 2021, at 9, *available at* https://www.privacy.gov.ph/wp-content/uploads/2022/03/02-NPC_18_010_RLA_v_PLDT_Enterprise_Resolution_w_Dissenting_Opinion.pdf (last accessed 26 Apr. 2022).

490. National Privacy Commission, Rules and Regulations Implementing the Data Privacy Act of 2012, Republic Act No. 10173, §3(m) (2016).

491. *KGR v. BB, et al.*, CID 18-E-040, 12 May 2020, at 4, *available at* https://www.privacy.gov.ph/wp-content/uploads/2022/04/CID-18-E-040-KGR-v.-BB-et-al.-Decision-2020.05.12.pdf (last accessed 26 Apr. 2022). Emphasis supplied.

[the data subject's] personal information to [the PIC] to facilitate the installation of the Corporate Individual DSL account, [the employer of the data subject] and [the data subject] would not have known what categories of personal information they needed to submit without [the PIC's] instructions. Aside from this, it was [the PIC] that determined what 'standard information' it will require from its prospective subscribers and the purpose for each category of personal information it collects.[492]

271. In the same case, the PIC's Terms and Conditions expressly show that it undertakes certain processing activities, such as monitoring the usage and the content that its subscribers access for its own purposes and benefits and '[taking] any action deemed appropriate' at its 'sole discretion'.[493] It also claims for itself the authority to amend any provision in the Terms and Conditions without any need to consult, much less secure the consent of anyone, including its Enterprise clients that are supposed to be its PICs.[494] These acts clearly identify the PIC as such.

§1. The Obligations of a PIC

272. The PIC is imbued with several obligations under the DPA and other privacy regulations. At the core of these obligations are the general data privacy principles of transparency, legitimate purpose, and proportionality:[495]

(1) The PIC should collect personal information for specified and legitimate purposes determined and declared before, or as soon as reasonably practicable after collection.[496]
(2) The PIC should collect and process personal information adequately and not excessively.[497]
(3) The PIC should process personal information fairly and lawfully, and in accordance with the rights of a data subject.[498]
(4) The PIC should process accurate, relevant and up to date personal information.[499]

---

492. *RLA v. PLDT Enterprise*, NPC Case No. 18-010, 10 Dec. 2021, at 10, *available at* https://www.privacy.gov.ph/wp-content/uploads/2022/03/02-NPC_18_010_RLA_v_PLDT_Enterprise_Resolution_w_Dissenting_Opinion.pdf (last accessed 26 Apr. 2022).
493. *Ibid.*, at 11.
494. *Ibid.*
495. *KGR v. BB, et al.*, CID 18-E-040, 12 May 2020, at 4, *available at* https://www.privacy.gov.ph/wp-content/uploads/2022/04/CID-18-E-040-KGR-v.-BB-et-al.-Decision-2020.05.12.pdf (last accessed 26 Apr. 2022).
496. An Act Protecting Individual Personal Information in Information and Communications Systems in the Government and the Private Sector, Creating for this purpose a National Privacy Commission, and For Other Purposes [Data Privacy Act of 2012], Republic Act No. 10173 §11(a) (2012).
497. *Ibid.*, Republic Act No. 10173 §11(d).
498. *Ibid.*, Republic Act No. 10173 §11(b).
499. *Ibid.*, Republic Act No. 10173 §11(c) (2012).

(5) The PIC should retain personal information only for as long as necessary for the fulfillment of the purposes for which the data was obtained.[500] The information should be kept in a form which permits identification of data subjects for no longer than is necessary.[501]

273. The PIC must also implement reasonable and appropriate organizational, physical, and technical measures intended for the protection of personal information.[502] The security obligations of the PIC will be discussed in Chapter 4.

§2. Accountability of PIC

274. The PIC may subcontract or outsource the processing of personal information to a PIP.[503] In such cases, the PIC shall be responsible for ensuring that the PIP implements proper safeguards:

> Section 14. *Subcontract of Personal Information.* – A personal information controller may subcontract the processing of personal information: *Provided,* That the personal information controller shall be responsible for ensuring that proper safeguards are in place to ensure the confidentiality of the personal information processed, prevent its use for unauthorized purposes, and generally, comply with the requirements of this Act and other laws for processing of personal information. The personal information processor shall comply with all the requirements of this Act and other applicable laws.[504]

275. The PIC remains accountable for personal information that is in its control and information that have been outsourced to third parties:

> Section 21. *Principle of Accountability.* Each personal information controller is responsible for personal information under its control or custody, including information that have been transferred to a third party for processing, whether domestically or internationally, subject to cross-border arrangement and cooperation.
>
> (a) The personal information controller is accountable for complying with the requirements of this Act and shall use contractual or other reasonable means to provide a comparable level of protection while the information are being processed by a third party.
> (b) The personal information controller shall designate an individual or individuals who are accountable for the organization's compliance with this

---

500. *Ibid.*, Republic Act No. 10173 §11(e) (2012).
501. *Ibid.*, Republic Act No. 10173 §11(f) (2012).
502. *Ibid.*, Republic Act No. 10173 §20(a) (2012).
503. *Ibid.*, Republic Act No. 10173 §14 (2012).
504. *Ibid.*

Act. The identity of the individual(s) so designated shall be made known to any data subject upon request.[505]

276. In NPC BN 21-035, the Commission held that the PIC cannot assign all fault to its PIP since it remains accountable for the actions of its PIP:

> Although a PIC may subcontract the processing of personal data to another entity, the PIC is still responsible for ensuring the confidentiality of the personal data processed, prevention of any unauthorized processing, and compliance with the DPA, Implementing Rules and Regulations (IRR) and other laws for processing of personal data.
>
> . . .
>
> The Commission recognizes the outsourcing or subcontracting of the processing of personal data to third parties, under Section 43 of the IRR of the DPA. In such cases, however, the PIC continues to bear the responsibility of ensuring the security of the personal data and that the PIP has established proper safeguards 'to … comply with the requirements of the Act, these Rules, other applicable laws for processing of personal data, and other issuances of the Commission.'
>
> Even if the personal data involved was outsourced to [the PIP] for processing, [the PIC] is still accountable for the data breach.[506]

277. Pursuant to the principle of accountability, the PIC remains accountable for the violations of the DPA and other privacy regulations even if the processing of the personal information has been subcontracted or outsourced to a PIP.[507] Section 51 of the IRR provides:

> Section 51. *Accountability for Violation of the Act, these Rules and Other Issuances of the Commission.*
>
> a. Any natural or juridical person, or other body involved in the processing of personal data, who fails to comply with the Act, these Rules, and other issuances of the Commission, shall be liable for such violation, and shall be subject to its corresponding sanction, penalty, or fine, without prejudice to any civil or criminal liability, as may be applicable.
> b. In cases where a data subject files a complaint for violation of his or her rights as data subject, and for any injury suffered as a result of the processing of his or her personal data, the Commission may award indemnity on the basis of the applicable provisions of the New Civil Code.
> c. In case of criminal acts and their corresponding personal penalties, the person who committed the unlawful act or omission shall be recommended for prosecution by the Commission based on substantial evidence. If the

505. *Ibid.*, Republic Act No. 10173 §21 (2012).
506. NPC Case No. 21-035, 8 Jul. 2021, at 5-6 (NPC 2021) (unreported).
507. National Privacy Commission, Rules and Regulations Implementing the Data Privacy Act of 2012, Republic Act No. 10173, §51 (2016).

> offender is a corporation, partnership, or any juridical person, the responsible officers, as the case may be, who participated in, or by their gross negligence, allowed the commission of the crime, shall be recommended for prosecution by the Commission based on substantial evidence.[508]

278. Following this, the IRR requires the PIC to 'use contractual or other reasonable means to ensure that proper safeguards are in place'[509] when the processing of personal data is outsourced to a PIP.[510] In NPC 19-910, the Commission faulted the PIC for entering into an agreement that essentially surrendered all accountability to its PIP:

> [T]hey should have been aware that the provisions of the Master Service Agreement contradicted the principles in the DPA. It included a provision that sought to surrender its accountability as a Personal Information Controller to [the PIP], thus:
>
> Article I
>
> Scope of Service
>
> Section 5. Methods of Work. *The service shall be performed by the Contractor in accordance with means and methods of work determined solely by it,* on the understanding that the company shall exercise control over the contractor only in regard to the results of the service.
>
> This provision is contrary to DPA which is very clear that the subcontracting of personal information by Personal Information Controllers cannot include the responsibility to prevent unauthorized processing[.][511]

279. While a PIC may outsource the processing to a PIP, the PIC remains accountable for the processing.[512] The duty to ultimately comply with the DPA remains with the PIC. The PIC's act of outsourcing its accountability to the PIP is contrary to its obligations under the DPA. Nevertheless, the specific persons who will be recommended for prosecution will still be determined following section 34 of the DPA.[513]

508. *Ibid.*
509. *Ibid.*, §43.
510. *See ibid.*, §§43 & 44 (2016).
511. In re: FLI Operating ABC Online Lending Application, NPC Case No. 19-910, 17 Dec. 2020, at 35-36, available at https://www.privacy.gov.ph/wp-content/uploads/2021/02/NPC-19-910-In-re-FLI-Decision-LYA-Final-pseudonymized-17Dec2020-.pdf (last accessed 24 Apr. 2022).
512. An Act Protecting Individual Personal Information in Information and Communications Systems in the Government and the Private Sector, Creating for this purpose a National Privacy Commission, and For Other Purposes [Data Privacy Act of 2012], Republic Act No. 10173 §21 (2012).
513. *Ibid.*, Republic Act No. 10173 §34.

§3. Registration and Compliance Obligations with the Commission

280. In addition to the PIC's obligations related to the general privacy principles of transparency, legitimate purpose, and proportionality, the PIC is required to fulfil additional registration and compliance requirements.

281. The PIC is required to register its personal data processing systems operating in the Philippines if it processes sensitive personal information of at least one thousand individuals, notify the Commission of automated processing systems when used as the sole basis for making decisions that would significantly affect the data subject, and submit an annual report of security incidents and data breaches:

> Section 46. *Enforcement of the Data Privacy Act.* Pursuant to the mandate of the Commission to administer and implement the Act, and to ensure the compliance of personal information controllers with its obligations under the law, the Commission requires the following:
>
> a. Registration of personal data processing systems operating in the country that involves accessing or requiring sensitive personal information of at least one thousand (1,000) individuals, including the personal data processing system of contractors, and their personnel, entering into contracts with government agencies;
> b. Notification of automated processing operations where the processing becomes the sole basis of making decisions that would significantly affect the data subject;
> c. Annual report of the summary of documented security incidents and personal data breaches;
> d. Compliance with other requirements that may be provided in other issuances of the Commission.[514]

282. As a general rule, a PIC or a PIP who employs less than 250 individuals is not required to register its data processing system.[515] A PIC or a PIP, however, must register its data processing system, even if it employs less than 250 individuals, if any one of the following situations applies: (1) the processing is likely to pose a risk to the rights and freedoms of data subjects; (2) the processing is not occasional; or (3) the processing includes sensitive personal information of at least one thousand individuals:[516]

> Section 47. *Registration of Personal Data Processing Systems.*
> The personal information controller or personal information processor that employs fewer than two hundred fifty (250) persons shall not be required to register unless the processing it carries out is likely to pose a risk to the rights

514. National Privacy Commission, Rules and Regulations Implementing the Data Privacy Act of 2012, Republic Act No. 10173, §46 (2016).
515. *Ibid.*, §47.
516. *Ibid.*

and freedoms of data subjects, the processing is not occasional, or the processing includes sensitive personal information of at least one thousand (1,000) individuals.

a. The contents of registration shall include:
   1. The name and address of the personal information controller or personal information processor, and of its representative, if any, including their contact details;
   2. The purpose or purposes of the processing, and whether processing is being done under an outsourcing or subcontracting agreement;
   3. A description of the category or categories of data subjects, and of the data or categories of data relating to them;
   4. The recipients or categories of recipients to whom the data might be disclosed;
   5. Proposed transfers of personal data outside the Philippines;
   6. A general description of privacy and security measures for data protection;
   7. Brief description of the data processing system;
   8. Copy of all policies relating to data governance, data privacy, and information security;
   9. Attestation to all certifications attained that are related to information and communications processing; and
   10. Name and contact details of the compliance or data protection officer, which shall immediately be updated in case of changes.
b. The procedure for registration shall be in accordance with these Rules and other issuances of the Commission.[517]

283. A PIC or a PIP that performs automated processing of personal information is required to notify the Commission when the automated processing becomes the sole basis for making decisions about a data subject and when the decision would significantly affect the data subject:

Section 48. *Notification of Automated Processing Operations.* The personal information controller carrying out any wholly or partly automated processing operations or set of such operations intended to serve a single purpose or several related purposes shall notify the Commission when the automated processing becomes the sole basis for making decisions about a data subject, and when the decision would significantly affect the data subject.

a. The notification shall include the following information:
   1. Purpose of processing;
   2. Categories of personal data to undergo processing;
   3. Category or categories of data subject;
   4. Consent forms or manner of obtaining consent;

517. *Ibid.*

5. The recipients or categories of recipients to whom the data are to be disclosed;
6. The length of time the data are to be stored;
7. Methods and logic utilized for automated processing;
8. Decisions relating to the data subject that would be made on the basis of processed data or that would significantly affect the rights and freedoms of data subject; and
9. Names and contact details of the compliance or data protection officer.

b. No decision with legal effects concerning a data subject shall be made solely on the basis of automated processing without the consent of the data subject.[518]

284. The registration process for data processing systems and notification of automated processing operations is provided in NPC Circular 17-01.[519] As of this writing, the Circular is being amended.

§4. Data Sharing Agreements Between PICs

285. Data sharing is the transfer or disclosure of personal data under the custody of a PIC or a PIP to a third party:

> Section 3. *Definitions.* Whenever used in these Rules, the following terms shall have the respective meanings hereafter set forth:
>
> . . .
>
> f. 'Data sharing' is the disclosure or transfer to a third party of personal data under the custody of a personal information controller or personal information processor. In the case of the latter, such disclosure or transfer must have been upon the instructions of the personal information controller concerned. The term excludes outsourcing, or the disclosure or transfer of personal data by a personal information controller to a personal information processor[.][520]

518. *Ibid.*, §48.
519. National Privacy Commission, Registration of Data Processing and Notifications regarding Automated Decision-Making, Circular No. 01, Series of 2017 [NPC Circ. No. 17-01] (31 Jul. 2017).
520. National Privacy Commission, Rules and Regulations Implementing the Data Privacy Act of 2012, Republic Act No. 10173, §3(f) (2016).

286. The Commission issued NPC Circular 20-03 governing Data Sharing Agreements (DSAs).[521] The Circular provides that 'only PICs can be parties of [DSAs]', thus clarifying the definition of a DSA in section 3(f) of the IRR.[522]

287. Data Sharing is governed by a DSA, which is defined as:

> Section 3. *Definition of Terms.* For the purpose of this Circular, the following terms are defined, as follows:
>
> . . .
>
> F. 'Data Sharing Agreement' or 'DSA' refers to a contract, joint issuance, or any similar document which sets out the obligations, responsibilities, and liabilities of the personal information controllers involved in the transfer of personal data between or among them, including the implementation of adequate safeguards for data privacy and security, and upholding the rights of the data subjects: *provided*, that only personal information controllers should be made parties to a data sharing agreement[.][523]

A DSA may have more than two parties.[524]

288. DSAs may be reviewed by the Commission when it chooses to do so or if the DSA becomes an important consideration in a pending case:

> Section 49. *Review by the Commission.*
> The following are subject to the review of the Commission, upon its own initiative or upon the filing of a complaint by a data subject:
>
> . . .
>
> c. Any data sharing agreement, outsourcing contract, and similar contracts involving the processing of personal data, and its implementation[.][525]

289. All parties to the DSA remain accountable for personal data in its control or custody and should comply with the DPA and other privacy regulations:

> Section 12. *Accountability.* All parties to a data sharing arrangement should comply with the Act, its IRR, this Circular, and all applicable issuances of the Commission. Subject to the terms of the DSA, *each party will be responsible for any personal data under its control or custody, including those where the*

521. National Privacy Commission, Data Sharing Agreements, Circular No. 03, Series of 2020 [NPC Circ. No. 20-03] (23 Dec. 2020).
522. National Privacy Commission, Rules and Regulations Implementing the Data Privacy Act of 2012, Republic Act No. 10173, §3(f) (2016).
523. National Privacy Commission, Data Sharing Agreements, Circular No. 03, Series of 2020 [NPC Circ. No. 20-03] §2(F) (23 Dec. 2020).
524. National Privacy Commission, Re: Treatment of Insurance Agents under the DPA, Advisory Opinion No. 73, Series of 2018, at 3 (22 Nov. 2018).
525. National Privacy Commission, Rules and Regulations Implementing the Data Privacy Act of 2012, Republic Act No. 10173, §49(c) (2016).

processing has been outsourced or subcontracted to a PIP. This extends to personal data each party shares with or transfers to a third party located outside the Philippines, subject to cross-border arrangement and cooperation.

The DPOs of the parties will sign as witnesses to the DSA.[526]

290. Section 20 of the IRR provides guidelines on the 'further processing of personal data collected from a party other than a data subject':

> Section 20. *General Principles for Data Sharing.* Further Processing of Personal Data collected from a party other than the Data Subject shall be allowed under any of the following conditions:
>
> a. Data sharing shall be allowed when it is expressly authorized by law: Provided, that there are adequate safeguards for data privacy and security, and processing adheres to principle of transparency, legitimate purpose and proportionality.
> b. Data Sharing shall be allowed in the private sector if the data subject consents to data sharing, and the following conditions are complied with:
>   1. Consent for data sharing shall be required even when the data is to be shared with an affiliate or mother company, or similar relationships;
>   2. Data sharing for commercial purposes, including direct marketing, shall be covered by a data sharing agreement.
>   (a) The data sharing agreement shall establish adequate safeguards for data privacy and security, and uphold rights of data subjects.
>   (b) The data sharing agreement shall be subject to review by the Commission, on its own initiative or upon complaint of data subject;
>   3. The data subject shall be provided with the following information prior to collection or before data is shared:
>   (a) Identity of the personal information controllers or personal information processors that will be given access to the personal data;
>   (b) Purpose of data sharing;
>   (c) Categories of personal data concerned;
>   (d) Intended recipients or categories of recipients of the personal data;
>   (e) Existence of the rights of data subjects, including the right to access and correction, and the right to object;
>   (f) Other information that would sufficiently notify the data subject of the nature and extent of data sharing and the manner of processing.

526. National Privacy Commission, Data Sharing Agreements, Circular No. 03, Series of 2020 [NPC Circ. No. 20-03] §12 (23 Dec. 2020). Emphasis supplied.

4. Further processing of shared data shall adhere to the data privacy principles laid down in the Act, these Rules, and other issuances of the Commission.

c. Data collected from parties other than the data subject for purpose of research shall be allowed when the personal data is publicly available, or has the consent of the data subject for purpose of research: Provided, that adequate safeguards are in place, and no decision directly affecting the data subject shall be made on the basis of the data collected or processed. The rights of the data subject shall be upheld without compromising research integrity.

d. Data sharing between government agencies for the purpose of a public function or provision of a public service shall be covered a data sharing agreement.
   1. Any or all government agencies party to the agreement shall comply with the Act, these Rules, and all other issuances of the Commission, including putting in place adequate safeguards for data privacy and security.
   2. The data sharing agreement shall be subject to review of the Commission, on its own initiative or upon complaint of data subject.[527]

291. The Circular also highlights the application of the general privacy principle of transparency in relation to the inclusion of the data subject's personal information in a DSA:

> Section 5. *Transparency.* Each affected data subject should be provided with the following information before personal data is shared or at the next practical opportunity, through an appropriate consent form or privacy notice, whichever is applicable or appropriate to the lawful basis relied upon:
>
> A. Categories of recipients of the personal data: provided, that PICs shall provide a data subject with the identity of the recipients, upon request;
> B. Purpose of data sharing and the objective/s it is meant to achieve;
> C. Categories of personal data that will be shared;
> D. Existence of the rights of data subjects; and
> E. Other information that would sufficiently inform the data subject of the nature and extent of data sharing and the manner of processing involved.
>
> In cases where consent is not required, a privacy notice is sufficient. Where the PIC has already collected the personal data, it should provide the data subjects with the information above as soon as it decides that personal data will be shared or as soon as possible afterwards.

527. National Privacy Commission, Rules and Regulations Implementing the Data Privacy Act of 2012, Republic Act No. 10173, §20 (2016).

It is a good practice for PICs to review their privacy notice regularly to ensure that it continues to reflect accurately the data sharing arrangement they are engaged in.[528]

292. Other than the consent of the data subject, a data subject's personal information may be the subject of data sharing if any of the lawful criteria for processing under sections 12 and 13 of the DPA is present:

> Section 6. *Authorized processing.* Data sharing may be based on any of the criteria for lawful processing of personal data in Sections 12 and 13 of the Act: *provided*, that nothing in this Circular shall be construed as prohibiting or limiting the sharing, disclosure, or transfer of personal data that is already authorized or required by law.[529]

293. Data sharing is also permitted on personal data outside the scope of the DPA:

> Section 7. *Special cases.* Data sharing may also be allowed pursuant to Section 4 of the Act, which specifies the special cases wherein the law and the rules are not applicable, but such data sharing should only be to the minimum extent necessary to achieve the specific purpose, function, or activity, and subject to the requirements of applicable laws, regulations, or ethical standards.[530]

294. Parties may introduce revisions and amendments to DSAs already in effect:

> Section 15. *Revisions and amendments.* Changes to DSAs while it is still in effect should follow the *same procedure observed in the creation of a new agreement.*[531]

295. A DSA may be terminated based on the following grounds:

> Section 16. *Termination.* A data sharing may be terminated:
>
> A. upon the expiration of its term, or any valid extension thereof;
> B. upon the agreement by all parties;
> C. upon breach of any provisions of the DSA by any of the parties;
> D. upon dissolution or death of the PIC;
> E. upon a finding by the Commission that data sharing is:
>   1. no longer necessary for the specified purpose/s and its objective/s has already been achieved; or

528. National Privacy Commission, Data Sharing Agreements, Circular No. 03, Series of 2020 [NPC Circ. No. 20-03] §5 (23 Dec. 2020).
529. *Ibid.*, §6.
530. *Ibid.*, §7.
531. *Ibid.*, §15. Emphasis supplied.

> 2. detrimental to national security, public interest or public policy, or the termination of the same is necessary to preserve and protect the rights of a data subject.
>
> Nothing in this Section prevents the Commission from ordering *motu proprio* the termination of any data sharing, whether or not covered by a DSA, when a party is determined to have violated the Act, its IRR, or any applicable issuance by the Commission.[532]

296. Notably, the Commission may order the termination of data sharing when it finds that (1) data sharing is no longer necessary for the specified purpose; (2) data sharing is detrimental to national security, public interest, or public policy; (3) it is necessary to preserve and protect the rights of a data subject; and (4) a party involved in the data sharing violated the DPA and other privacy regulations.

297. When data sharing is terminated, it is incumbent upon the third party involved to return, destroy, or dispose of the personal data transferred to it:

> Section 17. *Return, destruction, or disposal of transferred personal data.* Unless otherwise provided by the DSA, all personal data transferred to other parties by virtue of a data sharing, whether or not covered by a DSA, should be returned, destroyed, or disposed of, upon the termination of the arrangement.[533]

---

532. *Ibid.*, §16.
533. *Ibid.*, §17.

Chapter 2. National Rules Regarding Joint Controllers

298. The Philippines does not have specific national rules regarding 'joint controllers'. Situations involving joint controllers will still be governed by the provisions of the DPA on the different obligations of PICs. As to the liability of each specific controller, this will be determined by taking into consideration its participation in the specific processing activity that resulted in the violation of the DPA or the rights of the data subject. In the event that the joint controllers are juridical persons, specific responsible officers that will be recommended for criminal prosecution are those who participated in the violation or by their gross negligence allowed the commission of the crime pursuant to section 34 of the DPA.[534]

534. National Privacy Commission, Rules and Regulations Implementing the Data Privacy Act of 2012, Republic Act No. 10173, §51(c) (2016).

Chapter 3. National Rules Regarding Processors

299. A PIP is a person or entity to whom the PIC outsources or instructs the processing of personal information:

> Section. 3. *Definition of Terms.* Whenever used in this Act, the following terms shall have the respective meanings hereafter set forth:
>
> ...
>
> (i) *Personal information processor* refers to any natural or juridical person qualified to act as such under this Act to whom a personal information controller may outsource the processing of personal data pertaining to a data subject.[535]

300. The processing of personal information may be subcontracted or outsourced to the PIP. The PIC and the PIP shall enter into a contract on the processing of personal information.[536] Section 44 of the IRR provides details that must be included in the contract:

> Section 44. *Agreements for Outsourcing.* Processing by a personal information processor shall be governed by a contract or other legal act that binds the personal information processor to the personal information controller.
>
> a. The contract or legal act shall set out the subject-matter and duration of the processing, the nature and purpose of the processing, the type of personal data and categories of data subjects, the obligations and rights of the personal information controller, and the geographic location of the processing under the subcontracting agreement.
> b. The contract or other legal act shall stipulate, in particular, that the personal information processor shall:
>   1. Process the personal data only upon the documented instructions of the personal information controller, including transfers of personal data to another country or an international organization, unless such transfer is authorized by law;
>   2. Ensure that an obligation of confidentiality is imposed on persons authorized to process the personal data;
>   3. Implement appropriate security measures and comply with the Act, these Rules, and other issuances of the Commission;
>   4. Not engage another processor without prior instruction from the personal information controller: Provided, that any such arrangement

535. An Act Protecting Individual Personal Information in Information and Communications Systems in the Government and the Private Sector, Creating for this purpose a National Privacy Commission, and For Other Purposes [Data Privacy Act of 2012], Republic Act No. 10173 §3(i) (2012).
536. National Privacy Commission, Rules and Regulations Implementing the Data Privacy Act of 2012, Republic Act No. 10173, §44 (2016).

shall ensure that the same obligations for data protection under the contract or legal act are implemented, taking into account the nature of the processing;

5. Assist the personal information controller, by appropriate technical and organizational measures and to the extent possible, fulfill the obligation to respond to requests by data subjects relative to the exercise of their rights;
6. Assist the personal information controller in ensuring compliance with the Act, these Rules, other relevant laws, and other issuances of the Commission, taking into account the nature of processing and the information available to the personal information processor;
7. At the choice of the personal information controller, delete or return all personal data to the personal information controller after the end of the provision of services relating to the processing: Provided, that this includes deleting existing copies unless storage is authorized by the Act or another law;
8. Make available to the personal information controller all information necessary to demonstrate compliance with the obligations laid down in the Act, and allow for and contribute to audits, including inspections, conducted by the personal information controller or another auditor mandated by the latter;
9. Immediately inform the personal information controller if, in its opinion, an instruction infringes the Act, these Rules, or any other issuance of the Commission.[537]

301. The contract on the outsourcing or subcontracting of the processing of personal information need not be submitted to the Commission for approval prior to execution by the PIC and the PIP.[538] The Commission, however, in the conduct of compliance checks or investigations, may require the PIC or PIP to submit the outsourcing agreement.[539]

302. The Commission, however, opined in an Advisory Opinion that an outsourcing agreement is not necessary in all instances:

> Based on the wording of the law, the DPA does not require every outsourcing arrangement to be governed by an outsourcing agreement. In fact, it provides that such arrangement may also be governed by any other legal act that clearly indicates the legal obligations of the parties. This way, the PIC can ensure that the PIP is legally bound to it and may be held accountable in case of breach of the agreement. In view of the foregoing, although there is an arrangement wherein the processing of personal data is outsourced to a service provider, the

537. *Ibid.*
538. National Privacy Commission, Re: Data Sharing Agreement/Data Protection Officer, Advisory Opinion No. 005, Series of 2018, at 2 (5 Feb. 2018).
539. *Ibid.*

> wording of the DPA must not be construed literally to the effect that an outsourcing agreement must be entered into by the parties. For instance, the applicable terms and conditions indicated when availing of the email services of [the email provider] or the engagement letter with the terms and conditions provided by a local courier shall suffice for as long as proper safeguards in the protection of personal data are in place, as required by the DPA.[540]

303. When processing personal information, it remains incumbent upon the PIP to comply with the DPA and other privacy regulations as well as its contractual obligations:

> Section 45. *Duty of personal information processor.* The personal information processor shall comply with the requirements of the Act, these Rules, other applicable laws, and other issuances of the Commission, in addition to obligations provided in a contract, or other legal act with a personal information controller.[541]

304. In Advisory Opinion 2020-006, the Commission opined that a collection agency that processes personal information of a data subject acts as a PIP and shall also adhere to section 13 of the DPA:

> We note that the collection agency, allegedly collecting on behalf of a bank, is considered a personal information processor (PIP). Hence, the collection agency must also adhere to the requirements of the DPA in the processing of personal data and must ensure the protection of personal data at all times. Hence, if the purpose of the collection agency's communication to the employer's HR department is to discuss the alleged unsettled loan obligation and the filing of cases in court for an alleged offense/s by one of its employees then such communication/disclosure should have a basis under Section 13 of the DPA dealing with processing of sensitive personal information, the definition of which includes information about any proceeding for any offense committed or alleged to have been committed by such person.[542]

The PIP must also uphold the rights of the data subjects.[543]

305. Characterizing an entity as a PIC or a PIP is not mutually exclusive. In certain instances, a PIP for a particular processing activity may also be considered as

540. National Privacy Commission, Re: Outsourcing the Processing of Personal Data, Advisory Opinion No. 18, Series of 2020, at 2 (31 Mar. 2020).
541. National Privacy Commission, Rules and Regulations Implementing the Data Privacy Act of 2012, Republic Act No. 10173, §45 (2016).
542. National Privacy Commission, Re: Collection Agency Communicating with Human Resource Department, Advisory Opinion No. 006, Series of 2020, at 3 (7 Feb. 2020).
543. National Privacy Commission, Re: Access to Medical Records in CR-DR System, Advisory Opinion No. 81, Series of 2020, at 3 (26 Nov. 2018).

a PIC for another processing activity.[544] The PIP will be responsible for fulfilling all the obligations of a PIC for the processing activities it undertakes in its role as a PIC:

> Where a PIP performs its own operations upon personal data, such as exercising control over its storage, use or retrieval, the PIP may already be considered a PIC. This means that the PIP will be subjected to all the obligations of a PIC under the DPA, including adherence to the data privacy principles of transparency, legitimate purpose and proportionality. Where a PIP processes personal data for its own purposes, including the retention of records, the PIP may risk liability for unauthorized processing and other DPA violations if the processing is done without consent from data subjects or authority from law.[545]

544. *Ibid.*, at 2.
545. *Ibid.*

Chapter 4. Security Obligations

306. It is the obligation of a PIC to implement reasonable and appropriate security measures for the protection of personal information in its custody or outsourced to a PIP:

Section 20. *Security of Personal Information.*

(a) The personal information controller must implement reasonable and appropriate organizational, physical and technical measures intended for the protection of personal information against any accidental or unlawful destruction, alteration and disclosure, as well as against any other unlawful processing.

(b) The personal information controller shall implement reasonable and appropriate measures to protect personal information against natural dangers such as accidental loss or destruction, and human dangers such as unlawful access, fraudulent misuse, unlawful destruction, alteration and contamination.

(c) The determination of the appropriate level of security under this section must take into account the nature of the personal information to be protected, the risks represented by the processing, the size of the organization and complexity of its operations, current data privacy best practices and the cost of security implementation. Subject to guidelines as the Commission may issue from time to time, the measures implemented must include:

  (1) Safeguards to protect its computer network against accidental, unlawful or unauthorized usage or interference with or hindering of their functioning or availability;

  (2) A security policy with respect to the processing of personal information;

  (3) A process for identifying and accessing reasonably foreseeable vulnerabilities in its computer networks, and for taking preventive, corrective and mitigating action against security incidents that can lead to a security breach; and

  (4) Regular monitoring for security breaches and a process for taking preventive, corrective and mitigating action against security incidents that can lead to a security breach.

(d) The personal information controller must further ensure that third parties processing personal information on its behalf shall implement the security measures required by this provision.

(e) The employees, agents or representatives of a personal information controller who are involved in the processing of personal information shall operate and hold personal information under strict confidentiality if the personal information are not intended for public disclosure. This obligation shall continue even after leaving the public service, transfer to another position or upon termination of employment or contractual relations.

(f) The personal information controller shall promptly notify the Commission and affected data subjects when sensitive personal information or other information that may, under the circumstances, be used to enable identity fraud are reasonably believed to have been acquired by an unauthorized person, and the personal information controller or the Commission believes that such unauthorized acquisition is likely to give rise to a real risk of serious harm to any affected data subject. The notification shall at least describe the nature of the breach, the sensitive personal information possibly involved, and the measures taken by the entity to address the breach. Notification may be delayed only to the extent necessary to determine the scope of the breach, to prevent further disclosures, or to restore reasonable integrity to the information and communications system.

(1) In evaluating if notification is unwarranted, the Commission may take into account compliance by the personal information controller with this section and existence of good faith in the acquisition of personal information.
(2) The Commission may exempt a personal information controller from notification where, in its reasonable judgment, such notification would not be in the public interest or in the interests of the affected data subjects.
(3) The Commission may authorize postponement of notification where it may hinder the progress of a criminal investigation related to a serious breach.[546]

307. The PIP also has an obligation to implement reasonable and appropriate security measures as provided in Section 25 of the IRR:

Section 25. *Data Privacy and Security.* Personal information controllers and personal information processors shall implement reasonable and appropriate organizational, physical, and technical security measures for the protection of personal data.

The personal information controller and personal information processor shall take steps to ensure that any natural person acting under their authority and who has access to personal data, does not process them except upon their instructions, or as required by law.

The security measures shall aim to maintain the availability, integrity, and confidentiality of personal data and are intended for the protection of personal data against any accidental or unlawful destruction, alteration, and disclosure, as well as against any other unlawful processing. These measures shall be implemented to protect personal data against natural dangers such as accidental loss or destruction, and human dangers such as unlawful access, fraudulent misuse, unlawful destruction, alteration and contamination.[547]

546. An Act Protecting Individual Personal Information in Information and Communications Systems in the Government and the Private Sector, Creating for this purpose a National Privacy Commission, and For Other Purposes [Data Privacy Act of 2012], Republic Act No. 10173 §20 (2012).
547. National Privacy Commission, Rules and Regulations Implementing the Data Privacy Act of 2012, Republic Act No. 10173, §25 (2016).

308. The security measures that a PIC and PIP shall implement are designed to safeguard the personal information in their respective custody against accidental or unlawful destruction, alteration, and disclosure, and against natural dangers.[548] These security measures should be reasonable and appropriate in consideration of the nature of the personal information to be protected, the risks related to the processing, the size and complexity of the organization, best practices, and the cost of implementation.[549] The implemented security measures shall include organizational, physical, and technical security measures, which are provided in sections 26, 27, and 28 of the IRR:

> Section 26. *Organizational Security Measures.* Where appropriate, personal information controllers and personal information processors shall comply with the following guidelines for organizational security:
>
> a. Compliance Officers. Any natural or juridical person or other body involved in the processing of personal data shall designate an individual or individuals who shall function as data protection officer, compliance officer or otherwise be accountable for ensuring compliance with applicable laws and regulations for the protection of data privacy and security.
> b. Data Protection Policies. Any natural or juridical person or other body involved in the processing of personal data shall implement appropriate data protection policies that provide for organization, physical, and technical security measures, and, for such purpose, take into account the nature, scope, context and purposes of the processing, as well as the risks posed to the rights and freedoms of data subjects.
>   1. The policies shall implement data protection principles both at the time of the determination of the means for processing and at the time of the processing itself.
>   2. The policies shall implement appropriate security measures that, by default, ensure only personal data which is necessary for the specified purpose of the processing are processed. They shall determine the amount of personal data collected, including the extent of processing involved, the period of their storage, and their accessibility.
>   3. The polices shall provide for documentation, regular review, evaluation, and updating of the privacy and security policies and practices.
> c. Records of Processing Activities. Any natural or juridical person or other body involved in the processing of personal data shall maintain records that sufficiently describe its data processing system, and identify the duties and responsibilities of those individuals who will have access to personal data. Records should include:
>   1. Information about the purpose of the processing of personal data, including any intended future processing or data sharing;

548. An Act Protecting Individual Personal Information in Information and Communications Systems in the Government and the Private Sector, Creating for this purpose a National Privacy Commission, and For Other Purposes [Data Privacy Act of 2012], Republic Act No. 10173 §20 (2012).
549. *Ibid.*

2. A description of all categories of data subjects, personal data, and recipients of such personal data that will be involved in the processing;
3. General information about the data flow within the organization, from the time of collection, processing, and retention, including the time limits for disposal or erasure of personal data;
4. A general description of the organizational, physical, and technical security measures in place;
5. The name and contact details of the personal information controller and, where applicable, the joint controller, the its representative, and the compliance officer or Data Protection Officer, or any other individual or individuals accountable for ensuring compliance with the applicable laws and regulations for the protection of data privacy and security.

d. Management of Human Resources. Any natural or juridical person or other entity involved in the processing of personal data shall be responsible for selecting and supervising its employees, agents, or representatives, particularly those who will have access to personal data.

   The said employees, agents, or representatives shall operate and hold personal data under strict confidentiality if the personal data are not intended for public disclosure. This obligation shall continue even after leaving the public service, transferring to another position, or upon terminating their employment or contractual relations. There shall be capacity building, orientation or training programs for such employees, agents or representatives, regarding privacy or security policies.

e. Processing of Personal Data. Any natural or juridical person or other body involved in the processing of personal data shall develop, implement and review:
   1. A procedure for the collection of personal data, including procedures for obtaining consent, when applicable;
   2. Procedures that limit the processing of data, to ensure that it is only to the extent necessary for the declared, specified, and legitimate purpose;
   3. Policies for access management, system monitoring, and protocols to follow during security incidents or technical problems;
   4. Policies and procedures for data subjects to exercise their rights under the Act;
   5. Data retention schedule, including timeline or conditions for erasure or disposal of records.
   6. Contracts with Personal Information Processors. The personal information controller, through appropriate contractual agreements, shall ensure that its personal information processors, where applicable, shall also implement the security measures required by the Act and

these Rules. It shall only engage those personal information processors that provide sufficient guarantees to implement appropriate security measures specified in the Act and these Rules, and ensure the protection of the rights of the data subject.[550]

Section 27. *Physical Security Measures.* Where appropriate, personal information controllers and personal information processors shall comply with the following guidelines for physical security:

a. Policies and procedures shall be implemented to monitor and limit access to and activities in the room, workstation or facility, including guidelines that specify the proper use of and access to electronic media;
b. Design of office space and work stations, including the physical arrangement of furniture and equipment, shall provide privacy to anyone processing personal data, taking into consideration the environment and accessibility to the public;
c. The duties, responsibilities and schedule of individuals involved in the processing of personal data shall be clearly defined to ensure that only the individuals actually performing official duties shall be in the room or work station, at any given time;
d. Any natural or juridical person or other body involved in the processing of personal data shall implement Policies and procedures regarding the transfer, removal, disposal, and re-use of electronic media, to ensure appropriate protection of personal data;
e. Policies and procedures that prevent the mechanical destruction of files and equipment shall be established. The room and workstation used in the processing of personal data shall, as far as practicable, be secured against natural disasters, power disturbances, external access, and other similar threats.[551]

Section 28. *Guidelines for Technical Security Measures.* Where appropriate, personal information controllers and personal information processors shall adopt and establish the following technical security measures:

a. A security policy with respect to the processing of personal data;
b. Safeguards to protect their computer network against accidental, unlawful or unauthorized usage, any interference which will affect data integrity or hinder the functioning or availability of the system, and unauthorized access through an electronic network;
c. The ability to ensure and maintain the confidentiality, integrity, availability, and resilience of their processing systems and services;
d. Regular monitoring for security breaches, and a process both for identifying and accessing reasonably foreseeable vulnerabilities in their computer networks, and for taking preventive, corrective, and mitigating action against security incidents that can lead to a personal data breach;

550. National Privacy Commission, Rules and Regulations Implementing the Data Privacy Act of 2012, Republic Act No. 10173, §26 (2016).
551. *Ibid.*, §27.

e. The ability to restore the availability and access to personal data in a timely manner in the event of a physical or technical incident;
f. A process for regularly testing, assessing, and evaluating the effectiveness of security measures;
g. Encryption of personal data during storage and while in transit, authentication process, and other technical security measures that control and limit access.[552]

309. It is also within the Commission's mandate to monitor the compliance of the PIC or PIP with the implementation of appropriate security measures:

> Section 29. *Appropriate Level of Security.* The Commission shall monitor the compliance of natural or juridical person or other body involved in the processing of personal data, specifically their security measures, with the guidelines provided in these Rules and subsequent issuances of the Commission. In determining the level of security appropriate for a particular personal information controller or personal information processor, the Commission shall take into account the nature of the personal data that requires protection, the risks posed by the processing, the size of the organization and complexity of its operations, current data privacy best practices, and the cost of security implementation. The security measures provided herein shall be subject to regular review and evaluation, and may be updated as necessary by the Commission in separate issuances, taking into account the most appropriate standard recognized by the information and communications technology industry and data privacy best practices.[553]

310. The implementation of appropriate and reasonable measures to prevent security incidents and breaches is the obligation of both the PIC and PIP. It is their responsibility to conduct investigations to ensure that such security measures are in place:

> A PIC should have processes and procedures in place to prevent security incidents and personal data breaches. The DPA and its issuances provide that a PIC should have protocols for investigating a breach, notification of the Commission and the affected data subjects, and for implementation of remediation measures to address the situation and to prevent the incident from recurring.
>
> The Commission notes from [the PIC's] request that it has not even conducted its own investigation and wants to merely rely on the Commission to conduct it for them. The Commission stresses the responsibility of a PIC to conduct its own investigation on any security incident or personal data breach in their systems[.][554]

552. *Ibid.*, §28.
553. *Ibid.*, §29.
554. NPC BN 21-078, 1 Jun. 2021, at 7 (NPC 2021) (unreported).

§1. Security of Sensitive Personal Information in Government

311. The DPA and other privacy regulations provide specific rules for ensuring the security of personal data in the government. The obligation to ensure the implementation of these security measures is entrusted to the head of the government agency:

> Section 22. *Responsibility of Heads of Agencies.* All sensitive personal information maintained by the government, its agencies and instrumentalities shall be secured, as far as practicable, with the use of the most appropriate standard recognized by the information and communications technology industry, and as recommended by the Commission. *The head of each government agency or instrumentality shall be responsible for complying with the security requirements mentioned herein* while the Commission shall monitor the compliance and may recommend the necessary action in order to satisfy the minimum standards.[555]

312. To ensure the security of personal information, the DPA provides rules on on-site and online and off-site access of such information, such as the granting of security clearance and other protective measures by the head of the agency:

> Section 23. *Requirements Relating to Access by Agency Personnel to Sensitive Personal Information.* (a) On-site and Online Access – Except as may be allowed through guidelines to be issued by the Commission, no employee of the government shall have access to sensitive personal information on government property or through online facilities unless the employee has received a security clearance from the head of the source agency.
>
> (b) Off-site Access – Unless otherwise provided in guidelines to be issued by the Commission, sensitive personal information maintained by an agency may not be transported or accessed from a location off government property unless a request for such transportation or access is submitted and approved by the head of the agency in accordance with the following guidelines:
>
> (1) Deadline for Approval or Disapproval – In the case of any request submitted to the head of an agency, such head of the agency shall approve or disapprove the request within two (2) business days after the date of submission of the request. In case there is no action by the head of the agency, then such request is considered disapproved;
>
> (2) Limitation to One thousand (1,000) Records – If a request is approved, the head of the agency shall limit the access to not more than one thousand (1,000) records at a time; and

555. An Act Protecting Individual Personal Information in Information and Communications Systems in the Government and the Private Sector, Creating for this purpose a National Privacy Commission, and For Other Purposes [Data Privacy Act of 2012], Republic Act No. 10173 §22 (2012). Emphasis supplied.

(3) Encryption – Any technology used to store, transport or access sensitive personal information for purposes of off-site access approved under this subsection shall be secured by the use of the most secure encryption standard recognized by the Commission.

The requirements of this subsection shall be implemented not later than six (6) months after the date of the enactment of this Act.[556]

313. The Commission issued NPC Circular No. 2016-01 on the Security of Personal Data in Government Agencies. It enumerates the obligations of the government agency engaged in the processing of personal data in relation to the conduct of a privacy impact assessment (PIA) and regulations on the storage, access, transfer, and disposal of personal data.[557] The Circular provides the minimum standards that government agencies must accomplish in relation to the processing of personal data in its custody.[558]

314. The government agency shall also require its contractors to register their personal information processing system with the Commission if the contract requires the processing of sensitive personal information of at least one thousand individuals.[559] The contractors, acting as PIP, shall also comply with the DPA and other privacy regulations.[560]

§2. Data Breach Notification

315. Section 20(f) of the DPA requires a PIC to promptly notify the Commission and affected data subjects of the breach of personal information:

Section 20. *Security of Personal Information.*

. . .

(f) The personal information controller shall promptly notify the Commission and affected data subjects when sensitive personal information or other information that may, under the circumstances, be used to enable identity fraud are reasonably believed to have been acquired by an unauthorized person, and the personal information controller or the Commission believes that such unauthorized acquisition is likely to give rise to a real risk of serious harm to any affected data subject. The notification shall at least describe the nature of the breach, the sensitive personal information

556. *Ibid.*, Republic Act No. 10173 §23.
557. *See* National Privacy Commission, Security of Personal Data in Government Agencies, Circular No. 01, Series of 2016 [NPC Circ. No. 16-01], rule 1, §5; rules II–V (10 Oct. 2016).
558. *Ibid.*, §2.
559. An Act Protecting Individual Personal Information in Information and Communications Systems in the Government and the Private Sector, Creating for this purpose a National Privacy Commission, and For Other Purposes [Data Privacy Act of 2012], Republic Act No. 10173 §24 (2012).
560. National Privacy Commission, Rules and Regulations Implementing the Data Privacy Act of 2012, Republic Act No. 10173, §33 (2016).

possibly involved, and the measures taken by the entity to address the breach. Notification may be delayed only to the extent necessary to determine the scope of the breach, to prevent further disclosures, or to restore reasonable integrity to the information and communications system.

(1) In evaluating if notification is unwarranted, the Commission may take into account compliance by the personal information controller with this section and existence of good faith in the acquisition of personal information.

(2) The Commission may exempt a personal information controller from notification where, in its reasonable judgment, such notification would not be in the public interest or in the interests of the affected data subjects.

(3) The Commission may authorize postponement of notification where it may hinder the progress of a criminal investigation related to a serious breach.[561]

316. A personal data breach is defined as 'a breach of security leading to the accidental or unlawful destruction, loss, alteration, unauthorized disclosure of, or access to, personal data transmitted, stored, or otherwise processed'.[562] NPC Circular No. 2016-03 on Personal Data Breach Management (NPC Circular 16-03) discusses the different natures of a breach:

Section 3. *Definition of Terms.*

. . .

A personal data breach may be in the nature of:

1. An availability breach resulting from loss, accidental or unlawful destruction of personal data;
2. Integrity breach resulting from alteration of personal data; and/or
3. A confidentiality breach resulting from the unauthorized disclosure of or access to personal data.[563]

317. It is the obligation of the PIC to notify the Commission and its affected data subjects of a breach even if the processing of personal information has been outsourced to a PIP:

Section 15. *Who should Notify.* The personal information controller shall notify the Commission and the affected data subjects upon knowledge of, or when

561. An Act Protecting Individual Personal Information in Information and Communications Systems in the Government and the Private Sector, Creating for this purpose a National Privacy Commission, and For Other Purposes [Data Privacy Act of 2012], Republic Act No. 10173 §20(f) (2012).

562. National Privacy Commission, Rules and Regulations Implementing the Data Privacy Act of 2012, Republic Act No. 10173, §3(k) (2016).

563. National Privacy Commission, Personal Data Breach Management, Circular No. 03, Series of 2016 [NPC Circ. No. 16-03], §3(F) (15 Dec. 2016).

> there is reasonable belief that a personal data breach has occurred. The obligation to notify remains with the personal information controller even if the processing of information is outsourced or subcontracted to a personal information processor.
>
> The personal information controller shall identify the designated data protection officer or other individual responsible for ensuring its compliance with the notification requirements provided in this Circular.[564]

318. The notification to the Commission and the PIC's affected data subjects is required when the PIC or PIP has knowledge or reason to believe that the breach has occurred together with the concurrence of any of the following conditions:

> Section 11. *When notification is required.*
>
> . . .
>
> 1. The personal data involves sensitive personal information or any other information that may be used to enable identity fraud.
>
>   For this purpose, 'other information' shall include, but not be limited to: data about the financial or economic situation of the data subject; usernames, passwords and other login data; biometric data; copies of identification documents, licenses or unique identifiers like Philhealth, SSS, GSIS, TIN number; or other similar information, which may be made the basis of decisions concerning the data subject, including the grant of rights or benefits.
> 2. There is reason to believe that the information may have been acquired by an unauthorized person; and
> 3. The personal information controller or the Commission believes that the unauthorized acquisition is likely to give rise to a real risk of serious harm to any affected data subject.[565]

319. If the PIC is uncertain on whether it should notify the Commission or its affected data subjects, it should consider the following:

> Section 13. *Determination of the Need to Notify.* Where there is uncertainty as to the need for notification, the personal information controller shall take into account, as a primary consideration, the likelihood of harm or negative consequences on the affected data subjects, and how notification, particularly of the data subjects, could reduce the risks arising from the personal data breach reasonably believed to have occurred.
>
> The personal information controller shall also consider if the personal data reasonably believed to have been compromised involves:
>
> 1. Information that would likely affect national security, public safety, public order, or public health;

564. *Ibid.*, §15.
565. *Ibid.*, §11.

2. At least one hundred (100) individuals;
3. Information required by applicable laws or rules to be confidential; or
4. Personal data of vulnerable groups.[566]

320. Notification of the Commission and Notification of Data Subjects are two different and separate requirements.[567] Section 17 of NPC Circular 16-03 discusses the parameters surrounding the Notification of the Commission. It provides that:

> Section 17. *Notification of the Commission.* The personal information controller shall notify the Commission of a personal data breach subject to the following procedures:
>
> A. *When Notification Should be Done.* The Commission shall be notified within seventy-two (72) hours upon knowledge of or the reasonable belief by the personal information controller or personal information processor that a personal data breach has occurred.
>
> B. *Delay in Notification.* Notification may only be delayed to the extent necessary to determine the scope of the breach, to prevent further disclosures, or to restore reasonable integrity to the information and communications system.
>
> The personal information controller need not be absolutely certain of the scope of the breach prior to notification. Its inability to immediately secure or restore integrity to the information and communications system shall not be a ground for any delay in notification, if such delay would be prejudicial to the rights of the data subjects.
>
> Delay in notification shall not be excused if it is used to perpetuate fraud or to conceal the personal data breach.
>
> C. *When delay is prohibited.* There shall be no delay in the notification if the breach involves at least one hundred (100) data subjects, or the disclosure of sensitive personal information will harm or adversely affect the data subject. In both instances, the Commission shall be notified within the 72-hour period based on available information. The full report of the personal data breach must be submitted within five (5) days, unless the personal information controller is granted additional time by the Commission to comply.
>
> D. *Content of Notification.* The notification shall include, but not be limited to:
>
> 1. Nature of the Breach
>   a. description of how the breach occurred and the vulnerability of the data processing system that allowed the breach;
>   b. a chronology of the events leading up to the loss of control over the personal data;
>   c. approximate number of data subjects or records involved;

566. *Ibid.*, §13.
567. NPC BN 20-157, 21 Sep. 2020, at 4 (NPC 2020) (unreported).

d. description or nature of the personal data breach;
e. description of the likely consequences of the personal data breach; and
f. name and contact details of the data protection officer or any other accountable persons.

2. Personal Data Possibly Involved
   a. description of sensitive personal information involved; and
   b. description of other information involved that may be used to enable identity fraud.
3. Measures Taken to Address the Breach
   a. description of the measures taken or proposed to be taken to address the breach;
   b. actions being taken to secure or recover the personal data that were compromised;
   c. actions performed or proposed to mitigate possible harm or negative consequences, and limit the damage or distress to those affected by the incident;
   d. action being taken to inform the data subjects affected by the incident, or reasons for any delay in the notification;
   e. the measures being taken to prevent a recurrence of the incident.

The Commission reserves the right to require additional information, if necessary.

E. *Form.* Notification shall be in the form of a report, whether written or electronic, containing the required contents of notification: *Provided,* that the report shall also include the name and contact details of the data protection officer and a designated representative of the personal information controller: *Provided further,* that, where applicable, the manner of notification of the data subjects shall also be included in the report.

Where notification is transmitted by electronic mail, the personal information controller shall ensure the secure transmission thereof.

Upon receipt of the notification, the Commission shall send a confirmation to the personal information controller. A report is not deemed filed without such confirmation. Where the notification is through a written report, the received copy retained by the personal information controller shall constitute proof of such confirmation.[568]

321. Based on the foregoing, the PIC is required to notify the Commission of a breach by submitting an initial report within seventy-two hours from knowledge of or reasonable belief that a breach has occurred. Within five days from the end of the seventy-two-hour period, the PIC shall submit additional information through a full report of the breach unless it is granted additional time to do so by the Commission.

568. National Privacy Commission, Personal Data Breach Management, Circular No. 03, Series of 2016 [NPC Circ. No. 16-03], §17 (15 Dec. 2016).

322. Section 18 of NPC Circular 16-03 discusses the requirement in relation to the Notification of Data Subjects:

> Section 18. *Notification of Data Subjects.* The personal information controller shall notify the data subjects affected by a personal data breach, subject to the following procedures:
>
> A. *When should notification be done.* The data subjects shall be notified within seventy-two (72) hours upon knowledge of or reasonable belief by the personal information controller or personal information processor that a personal data breach has occurred. The notification may be made on the basis of available information within the 72-hour period if the personal data breach is likely to give rise to a real risk to the rights and freedoms of data subjects. It shall be undertaken in a manner that would allow data subjects to take the necessary precautions or other measures to protect themselves against the possible effects of the breach. It may be supplemented with additional information at a later stage on the basis of further investigation.
>
> B. *Exemption or Postponement of Notification.* If it is not reasonably possible to notify the data subjects within the prescribed period, the personal information controller shall request the Commission for an exemption from the notification requirement, or the postponement of the notification. A personal information controller may be exempted from the notification requirement where the Commission determines that such notification would not be in the public interest or in the interest of the affected data subjects. The Commission may authorize the postponement of notification where it may hinder the progress of a criminal investigation related to a serious breach, taking into account circumstances provided in Section 13 of this Circular, and other risks posed by the personal data breach.
>
> C. *Content of Notification.* The notification shall include, but not be limited to:
>
> 1. nature of the breach;
> 2. personal data possibly involved;
> 3. measures taken to address the breach;
> 4. measures taken to reduce the harm or negative consequences of the breach;
> 5. representative of the personal information controller, including his or her contact details, from whom the data subject can obtain additional information regarding the breach; and
> 6. any assistance to be provided to the affected data subjects.
>
> Where it is not possible to provide the foregoing information all at the same time, they may be provided in phases without undue delay.
>
> D. *Form.* Notification of affected data subjects shall be done individually, using secure means of communication, whether written or electronic. The personal information controller shall take the necessary steps to ensure the proper identity of the data subject being notified, and to safeguard against further unnecessary disclosure of personal data. The personal information controller shall establish all reasonable mechanisms to ensure that all

> affected data subjects are made aware of the breach: *Provided,* that where individual notification is not possible or would require a disproportionate effort, the personal information controller may seek the approval of the Commission to use alternative means of notification, such as through public communication or any similar measure through which the data subjects are informed in an equally effective manner: *Provided further,* that the personal information controller shall establish means through which the data subjects can exercise their rights and obtain more detailed information relating to the breach.[569]

323. As a general rule, the PIC must inform each affected data subject by means of individual notification. The PIC, however, may request the Commission to allow it to notify its affected data subjects through alternative means of notification by means of public communication, such as website postings or newspaper publications.[570] When relying on alternative means of notification, the PIC must show that (1) individual notification is not possible or will require disproportional effort; and (2) the data subjects are informed in a manner equally effective as individual notification.[571]

324. The PIC shall inform its affected data subjects of the breach within seventy-two hours from knowledge of or reasonable belief that a breach has occurred.[572] The PIC may request for postponement of the notice if it is not reasonably possible to inform the affected data subjects of the breach or if the notification may hinder the progress of a criminal investigation related to a serious breach.[573] In a recent breach notification matter, the Commission allowed the postponement of the notification to affected data subjects considering that the PIC is in the process of filing a cybercrime investigation against an individual purporting to be an ethical hacker.[574]

325. The PIC may also request the Commission to grant exceptions from notification of affected data subjects. In addition to section 18(B) on exemptions on notification of affected data subjects, if the Commission believes that the notification 'would not be in the public interest or in the interest of the affected data subjects',[575] the Commission may also grant exemptions from the notification requirements in the following cases:

> Section 19. *Exemption from Notification Requirements.* The following additional factors shall be considered in determining whether the Commission may exempt a personal information controller from notification:

569. *Ibid.*, §18.
570. *Ibid.*, §18(D).
571. *Ibid.*
572. *Ibid.*, §18(A).
573. *Ibid.*, §18(B).
574. NPC BN 21-174, 28 Oct. 2021, at 5 (NPC 2021) (unreported).
575. National Privacy Commission, Personal Data Breach Management, Circular No. 03, Series of 2016 [NPC Circ. No. 16-03], §18(B) (15 Dec. 2016).

A. Security measures that have been implemented and applied to the personal data at the time the personal data breach was reasonably believed to have occurred, including measures that would prevent use of the personal data by any person not authorized to access it;
B. Subsequent measures that have been taken by the personal information controller or personal information processor to ensure that the risk of harm or negative consequence to the data subjects will not materialize;
C. Age or legal capacity of affected data subjects: *Provided*, that in the case of minors or other individuals without legal capacity, notification may be done through their legal representatives.

In evaluating if notification is unwarranted, the Commission may take into account the compliance by the personal information controller with the law and existence of good faith in the acquisition of personal data.[576]

326. It is important to notify the affected data subjects to give them the opportunity to take the necessary precautions or other measures to protect themselves against possible effects of the breach.[577] In NPC BN 20-157, the Commission highlighted the purpose for the notification of affected data subjects:

> It is noteworthy that the avowed purpose of the required notification to data subjects of a breach incident is for them to take the necessary precautions or other measures to protect themselves against possible effects of the breach. Moreover, personal information controllers (PICs) are required to establish all reasonable mechanisms to ensure that all affected data subjects are made aware of the breach. It therefore follows that PICs should guarantee that the notification they sent to data subjects has been received. Otherwise, it defeats the very purpose of notification of data subjects.[578]

327. Since the notification of the Commission and the affected data subjects are important obligations of the PIC in cases of breach, any failure or delay in complying with the notification requirements shall be evaluated by the Commission for possible concealment of a breach punishable under Section 30 of the DPA:

> Section 20. *Failure to Notify.* In case the personal information controller fails to notify the Commission or data subjects, or there is unreasonable delay to the notification, the Commission shall determine if such failure or delay is justified. Failure to notify shall be presumed if the Commission does not receive notification from the personal information controller within five (5) days from knowledge of or upon a reasonable belief that a personal data breach occurred.[579]

576. *Ibid.*, §19.
577. NPC BN 21-054, 15 Apr. 2021, at 3 (NPC 2021) (unreported).
578. NPC BN 20-157, 17 Dec. 2020, at 3 (NPC 2020) (unreported).
579. National Privacy Commission, Personal Data Breach Management, Circular No. 03, Series of 2016 [NPC Circ. No. 16-03], §20 (15 Dec. 2016).

Chapter 5. Data Protection Officer or Similar Functions

328. A Data Protection Officer (DPO) is an individual or group of individuals accountable for ensuring a PIC or PIP's compliance with the DPA and other privacy regulations.[580] The DPO must possess 'specialized knowledge and demonstrate reliability necessary for the performance of his or her duties and responsibilities':[581]

> As such, the DPO should have expertise in relevant privacy or data protection policies and practices. He or she should have sufficient understanding of the processing operations being carried out by the PIC or PIP, including the latter's information systems, data security and/or data protection needs.
>
> Knowledge by the DPO of the sector or field of the PIC or PIP, and the latter's internal structure, policies, and processes is also useful.[582]

329. The duties of a DPO include the monitoring of the PIC's or PIP's compliance with the DPA and other privacy regulations, ensuring the conduct of necessary PIAs, providing insight on the complaints and exercise of data subject rights, ensuring the implementation of proper breach and security measures by the PIC or PIP, and acting as the conduit between the PIC or PIP with the data subjects and the Commission in matters related to data privacy.[583]

330. A PIC or PIP may also designate a Compliance Officer for Privacy (COP) to assist the DPO in fulfilling his or her functions.[584]

331. The functions of a DPO or COP may be outsourced to a third party.[585]

332. A DPO need not be a resident of the Philippines.[586] The Commission, however, opined in an Advisory Opinion that:

> Given its definition, a DPO need not be a resident of the Philippines. However, he or she must be able to fulfill the functions laid out in NPC Advisory No. 2017-01 (Designation of Data Protection Officers). It is worth noting that such functions would require, as a minimum, being familiar with Philippine laws and regulations on data protection and data security.
>
> . . .

580. National Privacy Commission, Designation of Data Protection Officers, Advisory No. 01, Series of 2017, Mandatory Designation (14 Mar. 2017).
581. *Ibid.*, General Qualifications.
582. *Ibid.*
583. *Ibid.*, Duties and Responsibilities of the DPO and COP.
584. *Ibid.*, Mandatory Designation.
585. *Ibid.*, Outsourcing or Subcontracting of Functions.
586. National Privacy Commission, Re: Assignment of a Non-Resident DPO and Requirements for the Contact Details of a DPO, Advisory Opinion No. 21, Series of 2019, at 1–2 (19 Mar. 2019).

[A] DPO must be familiar with the DPA, IRR, and other pertinent Philippine laws and regulations on personal data processing in the Philippines, in order to lessen the risks of violations of the DPA and other applicable laws and policies.[587]

587. *Ibid.*, at 2–3 (19 Mar. 2019).

Part VI. Codes of Conduct

333. The DPA empowers the Commission to review privacy codes prepared by and voluntarily adhered to by the PIC. Section 7(j) of the DPA provides:

> Section 7. *Functions of the National Privacy Commission.* To administer and implement the provisions of this Act, and to monitor and ensure compliance of the country with international standards set for data protection, there is hereby created an independent body to be known as the National Privacy Commission, which shall have the following functions:
>
> . . .
>
> (j) *Review, approve, reject or require modification of privacy codes voluntarily adhered to by personal information controllers:* Provided, That the privacy codes shall adhere to the underlying data privacy principles embodied in this Act: Provided, further, That such privacy codes may include private dispute resolution mechanisms for complaints against any participating personal information controller. For this purpose, the Commission shall consult with relevant regulatory agencies in the formulation and administration of privacy codes applying the standards set out in this Act, with respect to the persons, entities, business activities and business sectors that said regulatory bodies are authorized to principally regulate pursuant to the law: Provided, finally, That the Commission may review such privacy codes and require changes thereto for purposes of complying with this Act[.][588]

Various sectors are allowed to develop specific standards applicable to them, such as additional qualifications of their respective DPOs and minimum security standards that should be implemented for a particular sector.[589] These standards, however, must still comply with the DPA and its general privacy principles.[590]

588. An Act Protecting Individual Personal Information in Information and Communications Systems in the Government and the Private Sector, Creating for this purpose a National Privacy Commission, and For Other Purposes [Data Privacy Act of 2012], Republic Act No. 10173 §7(j) (2012). Emphasis supplied.
589. *See ibid.*, Republic Act No. 10173 §7(j) (2012).
590. *See ibid.*

334. Some sectors have expressed their interest in formulating their own sectoral codes on privacy. None of them, however, have submitted a draft for the Commission's review and approval.

Part VII. International Transfers

335. The DPA has adopted international standards for data protection.[591] The Commission continues to increase its efforts to ease privacy restrictions in cross-border transactions.

336. The Commission is a member of the GPA.[592] As a member of the GPA, the Commission 'operates under a legislation which is compatible with the principal international instruments dealing with data protection or privacy'.[593]

337. In 2017, the Commission was designated as the Philippines' PEA of the APEC-CPEA.[594] The CPEA is a framework for cooperation on privacy investigations and enforcement of privacy laws and regulations among APEC economies.[595] The CPEA encourages PEAs in APEC economies to share information with fellow PEAs to promote effective cross-border privacy cooperation.[596]

338. The Philippines signified its intention to join the CBPR System in 2019.[597] The CBPR requires Member States to adhere to the nine high-level APEC Privacy

591. S. Journal No. 22, at 361, 15th Cong., 2d Reg. Sess. (11 Sep. 2011); An Act Protecting Individual Personal Information in Information and Communications Systems in the Government and the Private Sector, Creating for this purpose a National Privacy Commission, and For Other Purposes [Data Privacy Act of 2012], Republic Act No. 10173 §7 (2012).
592. Global Privacy Assembly, List of Accredited Members, Global Privacy Assembly Website, https://globalprivacyassembly.org/participation-in-the-assembly/list-of-accredited-members/.
593. Global Privacy Assembly, Become a Member, Global Privacy Assembly Website, https://globalprivacyassembly.org/participation-in-the-assembly/become-a-member/.
594. National Privacy Commission, PH Joins APEC Privacy System, National Privacy Commission Website (20 Sep. 2019), https://www.privacy.gov.ph/2019/09/ph-joins-apec-privacy-system/.
595. Asia-Pacific Economic Cooperation, APEC Cooperation Arrangement for Cross-Border Privacy Enforcement, at 1, *available at* https://www.apec.org/docs/default-source/groups/ecsg/cbpr/cpea-2019.pdf (last accessed 29 Apr. 2022).
596. National Privacy Commission, PH Strengthens Extraterritorial Reach through the APEC Cross Border Privacy Enforcement Arrangement, National Privacy Commission Website (5 Dec. 2017), https://www.privacy.gov.ph/2017/12/ph-strengthens-extraterritorial-reach-apec-cross-border-privacy-enforcement-arrangement/.
597. Philippines Submits Notice of Intent to Join the APEC CBPR, Hunton Andrews Kurth (24 Sep. 2019), https://www.huntonprivacyblog.com/2019/09/24/philippines-submits-notice-of-intent-to-join-the-apec-cbpr/#more-17942.

Framework principles and a set of common standards in order to promote cross-border transactions by easing privacy restrictions.[598] The Philippines' membership will allow certified Philippine-based entities to freely transfer personal data to all CBPR Member States.[599] The CBPR requires Member States to establish third-party accountability agents whose main task is to certify that the data privacy policies and practices of participating businesses are compliant with the APEC Privacy Framework.[600] The Commission is currently soliciting applications for third-party accountability agents among interested organizations.

339. As a Member State of the ASEAN, the Philippines also subscribes to the ASEAN Privacy Framework.[601] It promotes the use of MCCs and the ASEAN DMF on Digital Data Governance.[602] The ASEAN MCCs provide standards for the transfer of personal data from one ASEAN Member State to another.[603] The ASEAN DMF aids ASEAN-based businesses to implement a data management system and relevant processes.[604] The use of ASEAN MCCs and the ASEAN DMF is voluntary, and does not create any additional legal rights and obligations.[605] The Commission encourages ASEAN-based businesses to adopt the MCCs and DMF as baseline standards in their data-related business operations.[606]

340. The Philippines is also a signatory to the International Covenant on Civil and Political Rights (ICCPR) and its Option Protocols.[607] It signed the ICCPR on 19 December 1966 and ratified it on 23 October 1986.[608] As such, it is treaty-bound to respect and observe fundamental freedoms such as the right to privacy.[609] Article 17 provides:

Article 17

a. No one shall be subjected to arbitrary or unlawful interference with his privacy, family, home or correspondence, nor to unlawful attacks on his honour and reputation.

---

598. National Privacy Commission, PH Strengthens Extraterritorial Reach through the APEC Cross Border Privacy Enforcement Arrangement, National Privacy Commission Website (5 Dec. 2017), https://www.privacy.gov.ph/2017/12/ph-strengthens-extraterritorial-reach-apec-cross-border-privacy-enforcement-arrangement/.
599. *Ibid.*
600. *Ibid.*
601. *See* National Privacy Commission, Guidance for the Use of the ASEAN Model Contract Clauses and ASEAN Data Management Framework, Advisory No. 02, Series of 2021 (28 Jun. 2021).
602. *Ibid.*
603. *Ibid.*, §3.
604. *Ibid.*, §5.
605. *Ibid.*, §5(A)(1).
606. *Ibid.*
607. United Nations Human Rights Treaty Bodies, View the Ratification Status by Country or by Treaty, UN Treaty Body Database, *available at* https://tbinternet.ohchr.org/_layouts/15/TreatyBodyExternal/Treaty.aspx?CountryID=137&Lang=EN (last accessed 29 Apr. 2022).
608. *Ibid.*
609. International Covenant on Civil and Political rights art. 17, 16 Dec. 1966, 999 U.N.T.S. 171.

b. Everyone has the right to the protection of the law against such interference or attacks.[610]

341. Since 2017, the Philippines has been recognized as an observer to the Council of Europe's Convention 108 or the Convention for the Protection of Individuals with regard to Automatic Processing of Personal Data.[611] The Convention requires its parties to ensure that their respective domestic legislation also applies the principles enshrined in the Convention.[612] Considering that the DPA, its IRR, and other privacy regulations encompass the same principles, the Philippines has also signified its intention to accede to Convention 108 pursuant to Article 27 on the accession by Non-Member States.[613]

342. The Philippines is also a signatory to the Council of Europe's Convention 185 or the Budapest Convention on Cybercrime.[614] It ratified the Convention on 28 March 2018.[615] The Convention entered into force in the Philippines on 1 July 2018.[616]

343. The DPA and other privacy regulations emphasize the principle of accountability in data transfers. The PIC remains accountable for personal data that have been outsourced or transferred to third parties, PIPs, for processing. Section 21 of the DPA states:

> Section 21. *Principle of Accountability.* – Each personal information controller is responsible for personal information under its control or custody, including information that have been transferred to a third party for processing, whether domestically or internationally, subject to cross-border arrangement and cooperation.[617]

---

610. *Ibid.*
611. Treaty Office, Chart of Signatures and Ratifications of Treaty 185, Council of Europe, *available at* https://www.coe.int/en/web/conventions/full-list?module=signatures-by-treaty&treatynum=185 (last accessed 29 Apr. 2022).
612. Council of Europe, *Convention for the Protection of Individuals with regard to Automatic Processing of Personal Data,* art. 4(1), European Treaty Series – No. 108 (28 Jan. 1981) [hereinafter Convention 108].
613. Council of Europe, *Convention for the Protection of Individuals with regard to Automatic Processing of Personal Data,* art. 27, European Treaty Series – No. 108 (28 Jan. 1981) [hereinafter Convention 108].
614. Cybercrime, The Budapest Convention and its Protocols, Council of Europe, *available at* https://www.coe.int/en/web/cybercrime/the-budapest-convention (last accessed 29 Apr. 2022).
615. Treaty Office, Chart of Signatures and Ratifications of Treaty 185, Council of Europe, *available at* https://www.coe.int/en/web/conventions/full-list?module=signatures-by-treaty&treatynum=185 (last accessed 29 Apr. 2022).
616. *Ibid.*
617. An Act Protecting Individual Personal Information in Information and Communications Systems in the Government and the Private Sector, Creating for this purpose a National Privacy Commission, and For Other Purposes [Data Privacy Act of 2012], Republic Act No. 10173 §21 (2012).

344. The DPA highlights the obligations of the PIC pursuant to the principle of accountability. It remains incumbent upon the PIC to:

(a) The personal information controller is accountable *for complying with the requirements of this Act* and shall *use contractual or other reasonable means to provide a comparable level of protection while the information are being processed by a third party.*
(b) The personal information controller shall *designate an individual or individuals who are accountable for the organization's compliance with this Act.* The identity of the individual(s) so designated shall be made known to any data subject upon request.[618]

345. The IRR elaborates on the principle of accountability, particularly when violations of the DPA and other privacy regulations occur. Liability rests on any person involved in the processing of personal data and who failed to comply with the DPA and other privacy regulations. Section 51 of the IRR provides:

> Section 51. *Accountability for Violation of the Act, these Rules and Other Issuances of the Commission.*
>
> a. Any natural or juridical person, or other body involved in the processing of personal data, who fails to comply with the Act, these Rules, and other issuances of the Commission, shall be liable for such violation, and shall be subject to its corresponding sanction, penalty, or fine, without prejudice to any civil or criminal liability, as may be applicable.
> c. In cases where a data subject files a complaint for violation of his or her rights as data subject, and for any injury suffered as a result of the processing of his or her personal data, the Commission may award indemnity on the basis of the applicable provisions of the New Civil Code.
> d. In case of criminal acts and their corresponding personal penalties, the person who committed the unlawful act or omission shall be recommended for prosecution by the Commission based on substantial evidence. If the offender is a corporation, partnership, or any juridical person, the responsible officers, as the case may be, who participated in, or by their gross negligence, allowed the commission of the crime, shall be recommended for prosecution by the Commission based on substantial evidence.[619]

618. *Ibid.* Emphasis supplied.
619. National Privacy Commission, Rules and Regulations Implementing the Data Privacy Act of 2012, Republic Act No. 10173, §51 (2016).

346. Even if the PIC or PIP is found or established outside the Philippines, the DPA and other privacy regulations are still applicable to it; hence, the erring PIC or PIP may be found liable under the mentioned laws.[620]

620. *See* An Act Protecting Individual Personal Information in Information and Communications Systems in the Government and the Private Sector, Creating for this purpose a National Privacy Commission, and For Other Purposes [Data Privacy Act of 2012], Republic Act No. 10173 §4 (2012).

Part VIII. Enforcement

Chapter 1. Supervisory Authorities

347. The DPA created the Commission, an independent body mandated to administer and implement the DPA and other privacy regulations.[621] The Commission is attached to the Department of Information and Communications Technology (DICT) for policy and programme coordination purposes.[622] The DICT is an executive department subordinate to the President of the Philippines focused on developing and promoting the national information communications and technology development agenda of the Philippines.[623] Despite being an attached agency of the DICT, the Commission remains completely independent in the performance of its functions.[624]

348. The Commission serves as the implementing arm in enforcing the DPA and other privacy regulations to protect the right to privacy.[625] In fulfilling its mandate, it aims to promote the rights and interests of data subjects[626] to their personal data and facilitate electronic commerce and modern trade.[627]

621. National Privacy Commission, Rules and Regulations Implementing the Data Privacy Act of 2012, Republic Act No. 10173, §8 (2016).
622. *Ibid.*, §13.
623. An Act Creating the Department of Information and Communications Technology, Defining its Powers and Functions Appropriating Funds Therefor, and for Other Purposes [Department of Information and Communications Technology Act of 2015], Republic Act No. 10844 §4 & 5 (2015).
624. National Privacy Commission, Rules and Regulations Implementing the Data Privacy Act of 2012, Republic Act No. 10173, §13 (2016).
625. S. Journal No. 55, at 1066, 15th Cong., 2d Reg. Sess. (7 Mar. 2012).
626. An Act Creating the Department of Information and Communications Technology, Defining its Powers and Functions Appropriating Funds Therefor, and for Other Purposes [Department of Information and Communications Technology Act of 2015], Republic Act No. 10844 §5 (2015).
627. S. Journal No. 55, at 1067, 15th Cong., 2d Reg. Sess. (7 Mar. 2012).

Chapter 2. Composition

349. At the helm of the Commission is the Commission *En Banc*, which is composed of the Privacy Commissioner and two Deputy Privacy Commissioners.[628] One Deputy Privacy Commissioner shall be responsible for Data Processing Systems, while the other shall be responsible for Policies and Planning.[629]

350. The Commissioners are appointed by the President of the Philippines and serve for a term of three years and may be reappointed for another term of three years.[630] The Commissioners are required to be recognized experts in the fields of information technology and data privacy.[631]

351. The Privacy Commissioner acts as the Chairman of the Commission.[632] He or she must be at least thirty-five years of age and of good moral character, unquestionable integrity, and known probity.[633] Neither the DPA nor its IRR impose a minimum age requirement on the Deputy Privacy Commissioners.

352. The Commission *En Banc* acts as a collegial body in performing its adjudicatory functions.[634] When resolving any complaint or investigation, monitoring of breach notifications, and determining compliance orders,[635] it decides by a majority vote of two out of three Commissioners.[636] It similarly acts as a collegial body in performing its rule-making function through the issuance of Circulars and Advisories.

353. The Commission established a Secretariat that assists in the performance of its mandate to uphold the right to privacy.[637] The current organizational structure of the Secretariat is composed of the Data Security and Compliance Office, the

628. An Act Protecting Individual Personal Information in Information and Communications Systems in the Government and the Private Sector, Creating for this purpose a National Privacy Commission, and For Other Purposes [Data Privacy Act of 2012], Republic Act No. 10173 §9 (2012).
629. National Privacy Commission, Rules and Regulations Implementing the Data Privacy Act of 2012, Republic Act No. 10173, §13 (2016).
630. An Act Protecting Individual Personal Information in Information and Communications Systems in the Government and the Private Sector, Creating for this purpose a National Privacy Commission, and For Other Purposes [Data Privacy Act of 2012], Republic Act No. 10173 §9 (2012).
631. *Ibid.*
632. National Privacy Commission, Rules and Regulations Implementing the Data Privacy Act of 2012, Republic Act No. 10173, §13 (2016).
633. *Ibid.*
634. *Ibid.*, §9(e).
635. An Act Protecting Individual Personal Information in Information and Communications Systems in the Government and the Private Sector, Creating for this purpose a National Privacy Commission, and For Other Purposes [Data Privacy Act of 2012], Republic Act No. 10173 §7 (2012).
636. S. Journal No. 55, at 1067, 15th Cong., 2d Reg. Sess. (7 Mar. 2012).
637. An Act Protecting Individual Personal Information in Information and Communications Systems in the Government and the Private Sector, Creating for this purpose a National Privacy Commission, and For Other Purposes [Data Privacy Act of 2012], Republic Act No. 10173 §10 (2012).

Legal and Enforcement Office, the Privacy Policy Office, the Finance and Administration Office, and the Public Information and Assistance Division (Figure 1).[638]

Figure 1 Organizational Chart

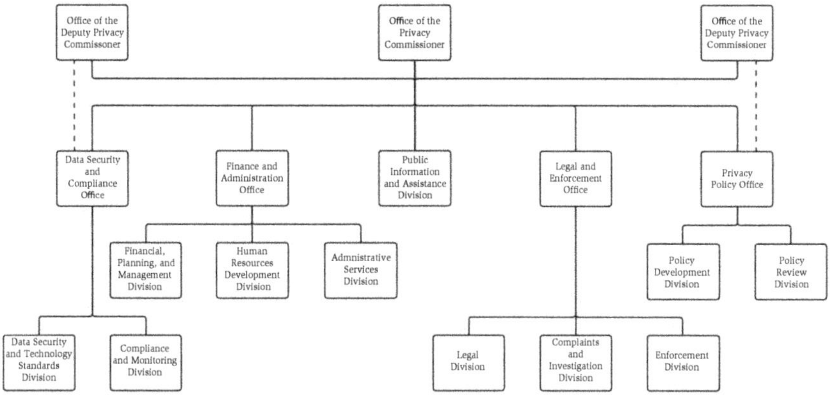

Source: An Act Protecting Individual Personal Information in Information and Communications Systems in the Government and the Private Sector, Creating for this purpose a National Privacy Commission, and For Other Purposes [Data Privacy Act of 2012], Republic Act No. 10173 (2012); National Privacy Commission, Rules and Regulations Implementing the Data Privacy Act of 2012, Republic Act No. 10173 (2016).

354. The Data Security and Compliance Office is composed of the Data Security and Technology Standards Division (DSTSD) and the Compliance and Monitoring Division (CMD). The DSTSD is tasked to develop the most appropriate privacy and data protection industry standards for organizational, physical, and technical security measures based on existing and emerging technologies.[639] The CMD ensures compliance of PICs with the DPA and other privacy regulations.[640] It conducts compliance checks, monitors and investigates data breaches, and manages the registration of data processing systems.[641]

355. The Legal and Enforcement Office (LEO) is composed of the Legal Division (LD), the Complaints and Investigation Division (CID), and the Enforcement Division (EnD). The LD serves as the general counsel of the Commission and

638. National Privacy Commission, Rules and Regulations Implementing the Data Privacy Act of 2012, Republic Act No. 10173, §14 (2016).
639. Operations Manual *by* Data Security and Technology Standards Division, National Privacy Commission (on file with National Privacy Commission).
640. National Privacy Commission, 2020 Annual Report, at 7, *available at* https://www.privacy.gov.ph/wp-content/uploads/2021/11/NPC-2020-ANNUAL-REPORT-REVISED-PAGE-2.pdf (last accessed 29 Apr. 2022).
641. *Ibid.*

provides legal assistance through the evaluation of laws affecting it.[642] The CID's core function is to institute and receive complaints, investigate, gather evidence, and facilitate settlements through alternative modes of dispute resolution on violations of the DPA and other privacy regulations.[643] The EnD manages enforcement and ensures compliance with the Commission's Decisions, Resolutions, and Orders.[644]

356. The Privacy Policy Office (PPO) develops privacy standards for the protection of personal data and facilitates cross-border enforcement of data privacy protection.[645] Through its Policy Development Division (PDD), it formulates and recommends standards in the form of Advisories and Circulars to aid in the implementation of the DPA with the goal of strengthening privacy protection in the Philippines.[646] Through its Policy Review Division (PRD), it prepares Advisory Opinions based on laws and regulations related to privacy.[647] It also assists external stakeholders by conducting seminars on matters involving data privacy.[648]

357. The Commission's internal management is handled by the Finance and Administrative Office (FAO), which is composed of the Financial, Planning, and Management Division (FPMD), Human Resources Development Division (HRDD), and Administrative Services Division (ASD). These divisions undertake the management of the Commission's accounting, human resources, and records-keeping matters.[649]

358. The Public Information and Assistance Division (PIAD) is the Commission's external communications arm. It provides comprehensive information to the public by responding to queries and developing materials for public education and awareness.[650]

---

642. Operations Manual *by* Legal Division, National Privacy Commission (on file with National Privacy Commission).
643. Operations Manual *by* Compliance and Monitoring Division, National Privacy Commission (on file with National Privacy Commission).
644. Operations Manual *by* Enforcement Division, National Privacy Commission (on file with National Privacy Commission).
645. Operations Manual *by* Policy Development Division National Privacy Commission (on file with National Privacy Commission).
646. *Ibid.*
647. National Privacy Commission, 2020 Annual Report, at 14, *available at* https://www.privacy.gov.ph/wp-content/uploads/2021/11/NPC-2020-ANNUAL-REPORT-REVISED-PAGE-2.pdf (last accessed 29 Apr. 2022).
648. Operations Manual *by* Policy Review Division, National Privacy Commission (on file with National Privacy Commission).
649. Operations Manual *by* Financial, Planning, and Management Division, National Privacy Commission (on file with National Privacy Commission).
650. Operations Manual *by* Public Information and Assistance Division, National Privacy Commission (on file with National Privacy Commission).

Chapter 3. Competence, Tasks, and Powers

359. As the independent regulatory body charged with enforcing the primary law on data privacy protection,[651] the Commission is vested with the following functions: rule-making, advisory, public education, compliance and monitoring, complaints and investigation, enforcement, and other functions as may be necessary to fulfil its mandate by law.[652]

§1. Rule-Making

360. Pursuant to its rule-making power, the Commission is tasked to develop, promulgate, and review rules and regulations for the effective implementation of the DPA.[653] These include proposing legislation or amendments to Philippine laws on privacy or data protection[654] and recommending[655] and issuing guidelines[656] on organizational, physical, and technical security measures for personal data protection by entities in the government and private sectors, and specifying electronic format and technical standards for data portability.[657] Corollary to this, the Commission regularly issues Circulars and Advisories to aid in the interpretation and application of the DPA on matters relating to data privacy and data protection.[658] It issued a set of rules to establish procedures for complaints and investigations before the Commission.[659] The Commission promulgated its Rules of Procedure on 15 December 2016,[660] and amended such rules on 28 January 2021.[661] In relation to this and pursuant to its authority to facilitate and enable the settlement of complaints through the use of alternative dispute resolution processes,

---

651. An Act Protecting Individual Personal Information in Information and Communications Systems in the Government and the Private Sector, Creating for this purpose a National Privacy Commission, and For Other Purposes [Data Privacy Act of 2012], Republic Act No. 10173 §7 (2012).
652. National Privacy Commission, Rules and Regulations Implementing the Data Privacy Act of 2012, Republic Act No. 10173, §9 (2016).
653. *Ibid.*, §9(a).
654. An Act Protecting Individual Personal Information in Information and Communications Systems in the Government and the Private Sector, Creating for this purpose a National Privacy Commission, and For Other Purposes [Data Privacy Act of 2012], Republic Act No. 10173 §7(m) (2012).
655. National Privacy Commission, Rules and Regulations Implementing the Data Privacy Act of 2012, Republic Act No. 10173, §9(a)(1) (2016).
656. *Ibid.*
657. *Ibid.*, §9(a)(2).
658. *Ibid.*, §10.
659. *Ibid.*
660. National Privacy Commission, Rules of Procedure, Circular No. 04, Series of 2016 [NPC Circ. No. 16-04] (15 Dec. 2016).
661. National Privacy Commission, Rules of Procedure, Circular No. 01, Series of 2021 [NPC Circ. No. 21-01] (28 Jan. 2021).

it published its Rules on Mediation on 18 December 2018.[662] It also published issuances on the registration of data processing systems,[663] breach notification,[664] and application for cease and desist orders,[665] among others. The Commission is likewise entrusted to regulate the cross-border enforcement of data privacy protection,[666] coordinate with data privacy regulators of foreign countries, and participate in international initiatives geared towards data privacy and protection.[667]

§2. ADVISORY AND PUBLIC EDUCATION

361. As part of its advisory function, the Commission is charged with commenting on proposed national or local statutes, regulations, or procedures related to data privacy protection,[668] reviewing privacy codes voluntarily adhered to by PICs to ensure its compliance with the DPA and other privacy regulations,[669] and assisting entities and data subjects on matters relating to privacy and data protection.[670]

362. The Commission is also tasked with informing and educating the public on the right to privacy, data protection, and fair information rights and responsibilities.[671] In its efforts to educate the public, it regularly publishes guides on all laws related to data privacy and protection and other materials geared towards raising awareness and strengthening the value of data privacy in the Philippines.[672]

---

662. *See* National Privacy Commission, Rules on Mediation before the National Privacy Commission, Circular No. 03, Series of 2018 [NPC Circ. No. 18-03] (18 Dec. 2018); *See also* An Act Protecting Individual Personal Information in Information and Communications Systems in the Government and the Private Sector, Creating for this purpose a National Privacy Commission, and For Other Purposes [Data Privacy Act of 2012], Republic Act No. 10173 §7(b) (2012).
663. National Privacy Commission, Registration of Data Processing and Notifications regarding Automated Decision-Making, Circular No. 01, Series of 2017 [NPC Circ. No. 17-01] (31 Jul. 2017).
664. National Privacy Commission, Personal Data Breach Management, Circular No. 03, Series of 2016 [NPC Circ. No. 16-03] (15 Dec. 2016).
665. National Privacy Commission, Rules on the Issuance of Cease and Desist Orders, Circular No. 02, Series of 2020 [NPC Circ. No. 20-02] (6 Oct. 2020).
666. National Privacy Commission, Rules and Regulations Implementing the Data Privacy Act of 2012, Republic Act No. 10173, §9(d)(4) (2016).
667. *Ibid.*, Republic Act No. 10173, §9(a)(7).
668. An Act Protecting Individual Personal Information in Information and Communications Systems in the Government and the Private Sector, Creating for this purpose a National Privacy Commission, and For Other Purposes [Data Privacy Act of 2012], Republic Act No. 10173 §7(l) (2012).
669. National Privacy Commission, Rules and Regulations Implementing the Data Privacy Act of 2012, Republic Act No. 10173, §9(b)(2) (2016).
670. *Ibid.*, §9(b)(3).
671. *Ibid.*, §9(c) (2016).
672. An Act Protecting Individual Personal Information in Information and Communications Systems in the Government and the Private Sector, Creating for this purpose a National Privacy Commission, and For Other Purposes [Data Privacy Act of 2012], Republic Act No. 10173 §7(g) (2012).

363. The Commission has solidified its public education mandate by introducing several programmes such as Privacy Awareness Week, Kabataang Digital, and Data Protection Officer Accountability, Compliance, and Ethics (DPO ACE) Program.[673]

364. Presidential Proclamation No. 527 declared the last week of May of each year as Privacy Awareness Week in recognition of the 'need to inform and educate the public about data privacy, data protection and fair information rights and responsibilities as part of reinforcing the efforts of the NPC in protecting personal data and ensuring the Philippines' compliance with international standards set for data protection'.[674] During this period, the NPC organizes a summit with the purpose of educating stakeholders on the basics and recent developments in data privacy protection.[675]

365. Kabataang Digital, meaning 'digital youth' in Filipino, is an advocacy campaign that aims to promote the creation of a safe online environment for the youth.[676] It seeks to educate the youth on appropriate digital citizenship, promoting safe choices, and elaborating on the implications of the digital environment for children's privacy rights.[677]

366. DPO ACE is a training programme that aims to establish the capacity-building of privacy professionals in the Philippines.[678] The programme is composed of three skill levels equipping candidates with the necessary knowledge of the DPA and other privacy regulations.[679]

367. In relation to DPO ACE, the Commission established the Training the Trainers Program (T3P) as a means of accrediting qualified trainers who are able to educate the public on key concepts involving the DPA and other privacy regulations.[680]

---

673. National Privacy Commission, 2020 Annual Report, *available at* https://www.privacy.gov.ph/wp-content/uploads/2021/11/NPC-2020-ANNUAL-REPORT-REVISED-PAGE-2.pdf (last accessed 29 Apr. 2022).
674. Office of the President, Declaring the Last Week of May of Every Year as National Data Privacy Awareness Week, Presidential Proclamation No. 527 (3 Jul. 2018).
675. National Privacy Commission, Valuing Privacy in the Time of Digital Transformation, *available at* https://paw2021.privacy.gov.ph/ (last accessed 29 Apr. 2022).
676. National Privacy Commission, About Us Kabataang Digital, *available at* https://www.privacy.gov.ph/kd/ (last accessed 29 Apr. 2022).
677. *Ibid.*
678. National Privacy Commission, NPC Launches DPO ACE Program, Sets Benchmark for Data Privacy Training in PH, *available at* https://www.privacy.gov.ph/2018/12/npc-launches-dpo-ace-program-sets-benchmark-for-data-privacy-training-in-ph/ (last accessed 29 Apr. 2022).
679. *Ibid.*
680. National Privacy Commission, About the T3 Program, *available at* https://www.privacy.gov.ph/t3/ (last accessed 29 Apr. 2022).

§3. Compliance and Monitoring

368. A core function of the Commission is to ensure the compliance of PICs and PIPs, whether they belong to the government or the private sector,[681] with the DPA and other privacy regulations. As part of this function, the Commission also coordinates with foreign data privacy authorities to facilitate cross-border application and implementation of data privacy laws.[682] Through the CMD, it conducts proactive compliance checks to identify and take action on instances of non-compliance,[683] as well as manages the registration of personal data processing systems,[684] data protection officers,[685] and mobile applications in certain sectors[686] of the country.

§4. Complaints, Investigation, and Enforcement

369. The Commission is empowered to adjudicate on cases affecting personal data arising from both complaints filed and investigations instituted by the Commission itself.[687] It exercises primary jurisdiction on violations of the DPA and other privacy regulations.[688] As part of its quasi-judicial powers, the Commission is authorized to: receive complaints, institute investigations, and adjudicate on matters concerning personal data breaches and violations;[689] summon witnesses and require the production of evidence;[690] facilitate settlements through alternative modes of dispute resolution;[691] issue cease and desist orders, impose temporary or permanent bans on the processing of personal information;[692] monitor the compliance of any

681. An Act Protecting Individual Personal Information in Information and Communications Systems in the Government and the Private Sector, Creating for this purpose a National Privacy Commission, and For Other Purposes [Data Privacy Act of 2012], Republic Act No. 10173 §7(a) (2012).
682. National Privacy Commission, Rules and Regulations Implementing the Data Privacy Act of 2012, Republic Act No. 10173, §9(d)(4) (2016).
683. National Privacy Commission, Guidelines on Compliance Checks, Circular No. 02, Series of 2018 [NPC Circ. No. 18-02] §2(B) (20 Sep. 2018).
684. National Privacy Commission, Rules and Regulations Implementing the Data Privacy Act of 2012, Republic Act No. 10173, §9(d)(5) (2016).
685. National Privacy Commission, Registration of Data Processing and Notifications regarding Automated Decision-Making, Circular No. 01, Series of 2017 [NPC Circ. No. 17-01] (31 Jul. 2017).
686. National Privacy Commission, Guidelines on the Processing of Personal Data for Loan-Related Transactions, Circular No. 01, Series of 2020 [NPC Circ. No. 20-01] (14 Sep. 2020).
687. National Privacy Commission, Rules and Regulations Implementing the Data Privacy Act of 2012, Republic Act No. 10173, §9(e) (2016).
688. *Ibid.*, §9(e)(1).
689. An Act Protecting Individual Personal Information in Information and Communications Systems in the Government and the Private Sector, Creating for this purpose a National Privacy Commission, and For Other Purposes [Data Privacy Act of 2012], Republic Act No. 10173 §7(b) (2012).
690. National Privacy Commission, Rules and Regulations Implementing the Data Privacy Act of 2012, Republic Act No. 10173, §9(e)(2) (2016).
691. *Ibid.*, §9(e)(3).
692. An Act Protecting Individual Personal Information in Information and Communications Systems in the Government and the Private Sector, Creating for this purpose a National Privacy Commission, and For Other Purposes [Data Privacy Act of 2012], Republic Act No. 10173 §7(c) (2012).

entity;[693] and compel or petition such entity to abide by its orders or take action on a matter affecting data privacy.[694] The Commission is vested with the powers to award indemnity to data subjects whose privacy rights are violated[695] and recommend to the Department of Justice (DOJ) the criminal prosecution of erring parties and the imposition of the criminal penalties specified in the DPA.[696] The Commission is likewise tasked with effectively implementing and enforcing the DPA and other privacy regulations, including its Decisions, Resolutions, and Orders.[697] Such enforcement powers may be utilized during the course of ongoing investigations to order cooperation of the parties or to compel appropriate action to protect the interests of data subjects.[698]

370. In relation to its power to ensure compliance with the DPA and to adjudicate on complaints and investigations, the Commission is likewise empowered to exercise review over the following:

> Section 49. *Review by the Commission.*
>
> The following are subject to the review of the Commission, upon its own initiative or upon the filing of a complaint by a data subject:
>
> a. Compliance by a personal information controller or personal information processor with the Act, these Rules, and other issuances of the Commission;
> b. Compliance by a personal information controller or personal information processor with the requirement of establishing adequate safeguards for data privacy and security;
> c. Any data sharing agreement, outsourcing contract, and similar contracts involving the processing of personal data, and its implementation;
> d. Any off-site or online access to sensitive personal data in government allowed by a head of agency;
> e. Processing of personal data for research purposes, public functions, or commercial activities;
> f. Any reported violation of the rights and freedoms of data subjects;
> g. Other matters necessary to ensure the effective implementation and administration of the Act, these Rules, and other issuances of the Commission.[699]

---

693. *Ibid.*, Republic Act No. 10173 §7(e).
694. *Ibid.*, Republic Act No. 10173 §7(d).
695. *Ibid.*, Republic Act No. 10173 §7(b).
696. *Ibid.*, Republic Act No. 10173 §7(i).
697. National Privacy Commission, Rules and Regulations Implementing the Data Privacy Act of 2012, Republic Act No. 10173, §9(f) (2016).
698. National Privacy Commission, Rules of Procedure, Circular No. 01, Series of 2021 [NPC Circ. No. 21-01], rule I, §5 (28 Jan. 2021).
699. National Privacy Commission, Rules and Regulations Implementing the Data Privacy Act of 2012, Republic Act No. 10173, §49 (2016).

371. To further bolster the independence of the Commission, the DPA expressly provides that the Commissioners or any person acting on their behalf or under their direction shall not be civilly liable for acts done in good faith and in the lawful performance of duty.[700] Wilful or negligent acts that are contrary to law, morals, public policy, and good customs, however, shall subject the public official and his representative to liability even if he or she acted under orders or instructions of superiors.[701]

700. An Act Protecting Individual Personal Information in Information and Communications Systems in the Government and the Private Sector, Creating for this purpose a National Privacy Commission, and For Other Purposes [Data Privacy Act of 2012], Republic Act No. 10173 §9 (2012).
701. *Ibid.*

Chapter 4. Remedies

372. The remedies available against the violation of the DPA or a personal data breach are detailed in the circulars issued by the Commission pursuant to its rule-making power.

373. The 2021 Rules of Procedure provides the process by which the receipt, investigation, alternative dispute resolution, preliminary conference, adjudication, and all other proceedings before the Commission are performed.[702] The 2021 Rules of Procedure are supplemented by other Circulars and Advisories issued by the Commission on particular matters.[703]

§1. Filing of a Complaint

374. Complaints against privacy violations or data breaches may be filed before the Commission. A complaint may be filed either by the aggrieved data subject or by the Commission through a sua sponte investigation.[704]

375. Prior to filing a complaint before the Commission, it is incumbent upon the aggrieved data subject to sufficiently establish and prove the following: (1) he or she has given written notice to the PIC, PIP, or concerned entity of the privacy violation or personal data breach to allow the latter to address the alleged violation, and (2) the latter failed to take timely and appropriate action on the alleged violation or failed to respond within fifteen calendar days from receipt of the written notice.[705]

376. The failure to comply with the requirement to notify the opposing party is a ground for outright dismissal under the 2021 Rules of Procedure.[706] The purpose of this condition precedent is 'to prevent a deluge of vexatious complaints from

702. National Privacy Commission, Rules of Procedure, Circular No. 01, Series of 2021 [NPC Circ. No. 21-01], rule I, §3 (28 Jan. 2021).
703. *See* National Privacy Commission, Personal Data Breach Management, Circular No. 03, Series of 2016 [NPC Circ. No. 16-03] (15 Dec. 2016); National Privacy Commission, Rules of Procedure on Requests for Advisory Opinions, Circular No. 01, Series of 2018 [NPC Circ. No. 18-01] (10 Sep. 2018); National Privacy Commission, Guidelines on Compliance Checks, Circular No. 02, Series of 2018 [NPC Circ. No. 18-02] (20 Sep. 2018); National Privacy Commission, Rules on the Issuance of Cease and Desist Orders, Circular No. 02, Series of 2020 [NPC Circ. No. 20-02] (6 Oct. 2020); National Privacy Commission, Guidelines on the Use of Videoconferencing Technology for the Remote Appearance and Testimony of Parties before the National Privacy Commission, Advisory No. 02, Series of 2020 (3 Aug. 2020).
704. National Privacy Commission, Rules of Procedure, Circular No. 01, Series of 2021 [NPC Circ. No. 21-01], rule II, §1 & rule X, §1 (28 Jan. 2021).
705. *Ibid.*, rule II, §2.
706. *Ibid.*, rule IV, §1.

those who waited for a long period of time to pass before deciding to lodge a complaint with the [the Commission], unduly clogging its dockets'.[707] Aside from this, the rule is intended to avoid instances of deciding cases based on technicalities.[708]

377. The Commission, however, may waive the exhaustion of such remedies if the aggrieved data subject shows good cause for the waiver or if the allegations involve a serious violation or breach of the DPA.[709] In determining whether a waiver of the exhaustion of remedies is proper, the Commission considers the risk of harm to the affected data subject, including but not limited to: (1) when there is grave and irreparable damage that can only be prevented or mitigated by the Commission; (2) when the alleged violator is unable to provide any plain, speedy, or adequate remedy; or (3) when the action of the alleged violator is patently illegal.[710]

378. In several cases, the Commission has waived the requirement of exhaustion of remedies if the complainant is able to show 'a justifiable reason or substantial proof' to persuade the Commission to waive the requirement.[711]

379. In CID Case No. 17-K-003, it waived the requirement of exhaustion of remedies after determining that the allegations on the face of the complaint show a possible serious violation of the DPA:

> Considering the allegations on the face of the complaint that the complainant's [daily time record] and pay slips may have been illegally accessed and disclosed by the respondents, it is well within the authority of the Commission to take action on this serious allegation of a violation of the DPA.[712]

380. In an Order issued in CID Case No. 18-D-012, the Commission held:

> Contrary to the contention of Respondent ..., to require Complainant to first exhaust his remedies with the Respondents would be unreasonable. First, Respondents already accessed and submitted the [Social Service System] documents of Complainant as evidence in the PRC case. These facts were never disputed. Second, there is nothing in the records or the statements and submissions of the Respondents show either their willingness or capability to

---

707. NPC Case No. 18-038, 21 May 2020, at 6 (NPC 2020) (unreported).
708. *MNLC v. PXXX Corporation*, NPC Case No. 19-528, 23 Feb. 2021, at 10–11, *available at* https://www.privacy.gov.ph/wp-content/uploads/2022/01/Resolution-02.23.2021-NPC-19-528-MNLC-vs-PXXX-Corporation.pdf (last accessed 6 Apr. 2022).
709. National Privacy Commission, Rules of Procedure, Circular No. 01, Series of 2021 [NPC Circ. No. 21-01], rule II, §2 (28 Jan. 2021).
710. *Ibid.*
711. *FAT v. XXX*, NPC Case No. 19-043, 17 Dec. 2020, at 5, *available at* https://www.privacy.gov.ph/wp-content/uploads/2021/04/NPC-19-043-FAT-vs.-XXX-Decision-dated-17-Dec.-2020.pdf (last accessed 29 Apr. 2022).
712. *KRL v. University*, AA, MC, NCB, RG GV, GCT, RR, MR, PB, CID 17-K-003, 19 Nov. 2019, at 7, available at https://www.privacy.gov.ph/wp-content/uploads/2022/04/CID-17-K-003-KRL-v.-University-Decision-2019.11.19-.pdf (last accessed 28 Apr. 2022).

provide an adequate remedy to Complainant. The requirement to exhaust available remedies does not contemplate exercises in futility that only delay justice for data subjects whose rights are violated.[713]

381. The Commission may also dismiss complaints outright without prejudice on the following grounds: (1) the complaint is insufficient in form or did not comply with section 3, Rule II of the 2021 Rules of Procedure;[714] (2) the complainant did not give the respondent an opportunity to address the complaints, unless failure to do so is justified, as previously explained; (3) the complaint does not pertain to a violation of the DPA or does not involve a privacy violation of personal data breach; (4) there is insufficient information to substantiate the allegations in the

---

713. CID Case No. 18-D-012, 21 May 2020, at 5 (NPC 2020) (unreported).

714. Section 3. *Form and contents of the complaint.* – The complaint should be in the proper form, as follows: 1. The complaint must be in writing, signed by the party or his or her counsel, and verified in the format prescribed under the Rules of Court. 2. The complaint must specify the identity of the individual claiming to be the subject of a privacy violation or the person so damaged or injured by a data breach, who shall be referred to as the complainant. 3. The complaint shall include the complainant's contact information, and where the complainant or duly authorized representative may be served with orders, issuances, or communications, including an electronic mail address if available. 4. The complaint must identify the person, entity or organization complained of, who shall be referred to as the respondent: Provided, that in the case of juridical persons, the responsible officers may also be included as respondents if they participated in, or by their gross negligence, allowed the commission of the alleged violation of the Data Privacy Act of 2012. If not known, the complainant shall state the circumstances that may lead to the identity of the respondent. 5. The complainant shall also provide in the complaint, if known: (a) respondent's contact information; and (b) where respondent may be served with orders, issuances, or communications from the NPC. 6. The complaint shall include a narration of the material facts and supporting testimonial or documentary evidence, if any, all of which show: (a) the violation of the Data Privacy Act of 2012, its Implementing Rules and Regulations, or NPC issuances; or (b) the acts or omissions allegedly committed by respondent and in the case of juridical persons, employees or agents who committed the offense amounting to a privacy violation or personal data breach. 7. The complaint must include any and all reliefs sought by the complainant. 8. The complainant shall attach any and all correspondence with respondent on the matter complained of and include a statement of the action taken by respondent to address the complaint, if any, showing compliance with the immediately preceding Section. 9. The supporting documents shall consist of copies of any documentary evidence and the affidavits of witnesses, if any, including those affidavits necessary to identify the documents and to substantiate the complaint. 10. A certification against forum shopping must accompany the complaint. The complainant shall certify under oath in the complaint, or in a sworn certification annexed and simultaneously filed with the pleading: (a) that he or she has not commenced any action or filed any claim involving the same issues in any court, tribunal or quasi-judicial agency and, to the best of his or her knowledge, no such other action or claim is pending with such court, tribunal or quasi-judicial agency; (b) if there is such other pending action or claim, a complete statement of its present status; and (c) if he or she should thereafter learn that the same or similar action or claim has been filed or is pending, he or she shall report that fact within five (5) calendar days therefrom to the NPC. Failure to comply with the proper form and contents of the complaint may cause for outright dismissal under Section 1(1), Rule IV: Provided, an application that does not comply with the foregoing requirements may be acted upon if it merits appropriate consideration on its face, or is of such notoriety that it necessarily contains sufficient leads or particulars to enable the taking of further action.

complaint; or (5) the parties, other than the reasonable officers in case of juridical persons, cannot be identified or traced despite diligent effort to determine the same.[715]

382. In NPC 21-031, the Commission, in holding that the case should have been dismissed outright based on procedural grounds, stated:

> The allegations in [Complainant's] Complaint do not establish a good cause or a potential serious violation or breach of the DPA that would warrant the waiver of the procedural requirements. The facts alleged in his Complaint, even assuming they were all true, still do not support his claim that [Respondent] violated the DPA or that [Respondent] acquired the personal information complained of in her role as a guidance counselor. Furthermore, [Complainant] failed to support any of his allegations with substantial proof. Given that [Complainant's] case does not fall under the instances provided under Section 2, Rule II, the Commission, therefore, finds no reason to waive the procedural requirements.[716]

383. A complaint filed before the Commission must be in the proper form.[717] The Commission has also encouraged the filing of complaints through Complaints-Assisted Forms to assist aggrieved data subjects with the process. The filing of a complaint also requires the payment of appropriate fees to the Commission unless any of the following circumstances apply: (1) the complainant is the government, excluding government-owned and controlled corporations organized under the Corporation Code; (2) the complainant is an indigent; or (3) the Commission waives the requirement upon motion by the complainant subject to the discretion and for a good cause shown.[718]

384. When a complaint is deemed proper in form according to the requirements under the 2021 Rules of Procedure, the investigating officer shall require the other party to file a comment stating his defences and submit supporting evidence within a prescribed period.[719] The investigating officer shall also hold a preliminary conference with the parties to determine matters that may aid in the prompt disposition of the action, including the availability of modes of alternative dispute resolution.[720]

385. Parties to a case may consider engaging in a meaningful settlement process through mediation proceedings.[721] If the parties agree to settle, then they shall

715. National Privacy Commission, Rules of Procedure, Circular No. 01, Series of 2021 [NPC Circ. No. 21-01], rule IV, §1 (28 Jan. 2021).
716. NPC Case No. 21-031, 3 Mar. 2022, at 5–6 (NPC 2022) (unreported).
717. National Privacy Commission, Rules of Procedure, Circular No. 01, Series of 2021 [NPC Circ. No. 21-01], rule II, §3 (28 Jan. 2021).
718. *Ibid.*, rule II, §4.
719. *Ibid.*, rule IV, §3.
720. *Ibid.*, rule V, §1.
721. *Ibid.*, rule VI, §1.

jointly prepare and execute a Mediated Settlement Agreement, which shall, once confirmed by the Commission, have the effect of a decision or judgment.[722] During the time a case is being mediated, the complaint proceedings are suspended.[723] The parties may avail themselves of the mediation proceedings at any stage but before the Commission renders its judgment on a particular case.[724]

386. If the parties fail to reach a settlement or refuse to engage in mediation proceedings, then the investigation of the circumstances surrounding the privacy violation or the personal data breach shall proceed.[725] The parties shall be required to submit memoranda containing their actions, claims, and defences.[726] The investigating officer shall then proceed to submit a Fact-Finding Report (FFR) to the Commission, which shall indicate the results of his investigation, evidence gathered, and recommendations.[727] The party who instigated the matter may withdraw the complaint any time before the submission of the FFR to the Commission.[728] In such cases, the investigating officer may recommend the dismissal of the case or the application of the Commission's power to initiate sua sponte investigations.[729]

387. The Commission, on its own initiative, may conduct its own investigation on a possible data privacy violation or personal data breach.[730] A sua sponte investigation may be initiated based on matters arising from pending cases before the Commission, reports from news, trends, or academic studies, information gathered from corroborated and substantiated anonymous tips, or reports from other offices of the Commission.[731] The Commission, through the CID, investigates the circumstances related to the possible data privacy violation or personal data breach. The investigation process may require the submission of additional information, documents, or evidence, or the production of witnesses on the part of the parties subjected to the investigation.[732] It may also include an on-site examination of systems and procedures.[733] The results of the investigation shall be formalized in an FFR, which shall serve as the complaint in sua sponte investigations.[734] To afford due process to the party subjected to such investigations, he or she shall be given an opportunity to present his or her side by submitting a comment to the FFR.[735] While the

722. *Ibid.*, rule VI, §§12 & 14.
723. *Ibid.*, rule VI, §4.
724. *Ibid.*, rule VI, §1.
725. *Ibid.*, rule VI, §§15 & 16.
726. *Ibid.*, rule VII, §2.
727. *Ibid.*, rule VII, §3.
728. *Ibid.*, rule VII, §4.
729. *Ibid.*
730. *Ibid.*, rule X, §1.
731. *Ibid.*
732. *Ibid*, rule X, §4.
733. *Ibid.*
734. In re: FLI Operating ABC Online Lending Application, NPC Case No. 19-910, 17 Dec. 2020, at 14, *available at* https://www.privacy.gov.ph/wp-content/uploads/2021/02/NPC-19-910-In-re-FLI-Decision-LYA-Final-pseudonymized-17Dec2020-.pdf (last accessed 24 Apr. 2022).
735. National Privacy Commission, Rules of Procedure, Circular No. 01, Series of 2021 [NPC Circ. No. 21-01], rule X, §6 (28 Jan. 2021).

investigation process is ongoing, the CID may apply for the issuance of a temporary ban on the processing of personal information.[736]

388. The FFR with the investigating officer's recommendation and other supporting documents are endorsed to the Commission *En Banc* for adjudication. Pursuant to its quasi-judicial powers, the Commission examines the contents of the FFR and the evidence presented in the supporting documents to determine the next course of action.[737] If the Commission believes that it requires further information from the parties to render a Decision, it may require the parties to submit additional information or conduct a clarificatory hearing.[738] A party may not request the Commission for a clarificatory hearing.[739] Parties, however, may raise as an issue any interlocutory order or decision issued by the investigating officer, and the Commission may resolve such issues separately or jointly with the main case.[740]

389. After a thorough review of the documents and evidence presented, the Commission renders a Decision based on its own consideration of the facts and the law.[741] The Commission may grant or deny the prayer and may also include enforcement orders, such as: (1) an award of indemnity on matters affecting personal data protection or rights of the data subject; (2) a permanent ban on the processing of personal data; (3) a recommendation to the DOJ for the prosecution and imposition of penalties specified in the DPA; or (4) an order compelling any entity, government agency or instrumentality to abide by its orders or take action on a matter affecting data privacy; or (5) any order to enforce compliance with the DPA and other privacy regulations.[742] The Commission may also impose fines for violations of the DPA and its issuances, subject to the issuance of a Circular on Administrative Fines.[743]

390. The Commission's Decision becomes final and executory after fifteen calendar days from receipt of the parties.[744] The parties have the opportunity to file one motion for reconsideration to the Commission, and may appeal the Commission's Decision before the proper courts in accordance with the applicable laws and rules.[745]

736. *Ibid.*, rule X, §2.
737. *Ibid.*, rule VIII, §1.
738. *Ibid.*, rule VIII, §1(a).
739. *Ibid.*
740. *Ibid.*, rule VIII, §2.
741. *Ibid.*, rule VIII, §3.
742. *Ibid.*
743. *Ibid.*
744. *Ibid.*, rule VIII, §4.
745. *Ibid.*

§2. BAN ON THE PROCESSING OF DATA

391. The issuance of a temporary or permanent ban to protect national security or the public interest, or if it is necessary to preserve and protect the rights of data subjects, is governed by specific provisions in the 2021 Rules of Procedure.[746]

392. A temporary ban is provisional in nature. An application for the issuance of a temporary ban has the effect of suspending the complaint proceedings of the main case until the application is resolved by the Commission.[747]

393. An aggrieved data subject or the Commission, in the course of a sua sponte investigation, may apply for the issuance of a temporary ban on the PIC or PIP's processing of personal data.[748] The application shall be filed upon the filing of a complaint or at any time before the Commission renders its Decision on a case.[749]

394. The party applying for a temporary ban on the processing of personal data shall satisfy the requisites for the issuance of a temporary ban provided in the 2021 Rules of Procedure:

> Section 3. *Requisites for temporary ban.* A temporary ban on processing of personal data may be granted only when:
>
> 1. it is necessary in order to preserve the rights of the complainant or to protect national security or public interest, or if it is necessary to preserve and protect the rights of data subjects;
> 2. the motion shows facts entitling the complainant to the relief demanded;
> 3. unless exempted from the payment of filing fees as provided for in these Rules, the complainant shall file with the [the Commission] a bond in an amount to be fixed by the investigating officer executed in favor of the party or person so banned from processing personal data; and
> 4. the parties are heard in a summary hearing.[750]

395. The Commission determines if the imposition of a temporary ban is necessary to preserve the rights of the complainant or to protect national security or the public interest, or if it is necessary to preserve and protect the rights of data subjects.[751] In determining the presence of this requisite, the Commission analyses whether the PIC or PIP's processing of personal information is compliant with the DPA and other privacy regulations, including the general privacy principles of transparency, legitimate purpose, and proportionality, as well as the risks posed by allowing such processing to continue.[752]

746. *Ibid.*, rule X, §2.
747. *Ibid.*, rule IX, §2.
748. *Ibid.*, rule IX, §1.
749. *Ibid.*
750. *Ibid.*, rule IX, §3.
751. *Ibid.*, rule X, §2.
752. *See* NPC SS 21-006, 12 Aug. 2021 (NPC 2021) (unreported).

396. In a recent sua sponte case, the Commission imposed a temporary ban on the PIC, an online lending company, since the deficiencies in the processing of personal data, as gleaned from its Privacy Policy and Service Agreement, violate the rights of the data subjects to be informed of the data collected from them and the purpose for which they are collected.[753] The Commission held, among other reasons, that:

> However, preparing and submitting a 'standalone and rectified Privacy Policy' does not necessarily correct deficiencies in the processing of personal data. The purpose of the Privacy Policy, together with the Service Agreement, is to inform the data subject how [the PIC] processes their personal information. The mere act of submitting a revised Privacy Policy is not sufficient to show that [the PIC] effected changes in the manner it processes personal data. Moreover, while [the PIC] provided the Commission with the revised Privacy Policy, it did not provide the same to the public, much less its data subjects. In fact, despite the claim in its Position Paper that 'from the date of this Position Paper [12 August 2021], users may also review the new Privacy Policy in [the] App and [the website],' the link to the 'Privacy Policy' on the … website still directs users to the original Service Agreement.
>
> . . .
>
> The Commission also notes that [the PIC] did not submit a revised Service Agreement. This leads the Commission to reasonably conclude that [the PIC] still uses the existing Service Agreement available on the website and its mobile application. The existing Service Agreement, however, is inconsistent with the revised Privacy Policy. [The PIC] cannot simply revise the Privacy Policy while maintaining the contradictory practices discussed in the Service Agreement. The principles of the DPA should be reflected in both the revised Privacy Policy and Service Agreement and observed throughout [the PIC's] processing of personal data. As seen in their mobile application, it is the Service Agreement that potential borrowers are asked to consent to and is the one that governs the relationship between the borrower and [the PIC]. A privacy policy, on the other hand, is simply a statement made to data subjects describing how the organization collects, uses, retains, and discloses personal information. In this case, what [the PIC's] revised Privacy Policy is describing is detached from the reality of what is provided in their Service Agreement.[754]

397. The second requisite of 'the motion shows facts entitling the complainant to the relief demanded' is satisfied if there is a clear showing that the complaint or the FFR of the CID in sua sponte investigations contains allegations that merit the issuance of a temporary ban.[755]

---

753. *Ibid.*, at 12–13.
754. *Ibid.*, at 8–9.
755. *Ibid.*, at 12.

398. With regard to the third requisite, the payment of a bond is not necessary if the complainant is the government or the application for a temporary ban is filed by the Commission in the course of its sua sponte investigation.[756]

399. The fourth requisite of imposing a temporary ban refers to a summary hearing. Section 6, Rule XI of the 2021 Rules of Procedure, however, allows the Commission to compel the parties to submit position papers in lieu of a summary hearing.[757]

400. In *Flores-Concepcion v. Castañeda*, the Supreme Court stated that:

> In administrative proceedings, the essence of due process is simply the opportunity to explain one's side. *One may be heard, not solely by verbal presentation but also, and perhaps even much more creditably as it is more practicable than oral arguments, through pleadings.* An actual hearing is not always an indispensable aspect of due process. *As long as a party was given the opportunity to defend his interests in due course, he cannot be said to have been denied due process of law, for this opportunity to be heard is the very essence of due process.*[758]

401. The Commission renders its decision on the issuance of a temporary ban when the requisites are satisfied based on the evidence presented by the parties.[759]

402. Once a temporary ban on the processing of personal data is issued, it shall remain in effect until the final resolution of the main case or until the Commission decides otherwise, such as when the grounds relied upon for the issuance of the temporary ban no longer exist or have been remedied by the party subject of the ban.[760] The Commission may also issue a permanent ban on the processing of personal data in its Decision on the case.[761] Further, even if a temporary ban was not previously issued by the Commission, it can still impose a permanent ban on the processing of personal information (Figure 2).[762]

---

756. *Ibid.*, at 14.
757. National Privacy Commission, Rules of Procedure, Circular No. 01, Series of 2021 [NPC Circ. No. 21-01], rule XI, §6 (28 Jan. 2021).
758. *Flores-Concepcion v. Castaneda,* A.M. No. RTJ-15-2438 (2020). Emphasis supplied.
759. National Privacy Commission, Rules of Procedure, Circular No. 01, Series of 2021 [NPC Circ. No. 21-01], rule IX, §7 (28 Jan. 2021).
760. *See ibid.*, rule IX, §8.
761. *See ibid.*, rule IX, §9.
762. *Ibid.*, rule VIII, §3(b).

Figure 2 Process for Imposition of Temporary Ban

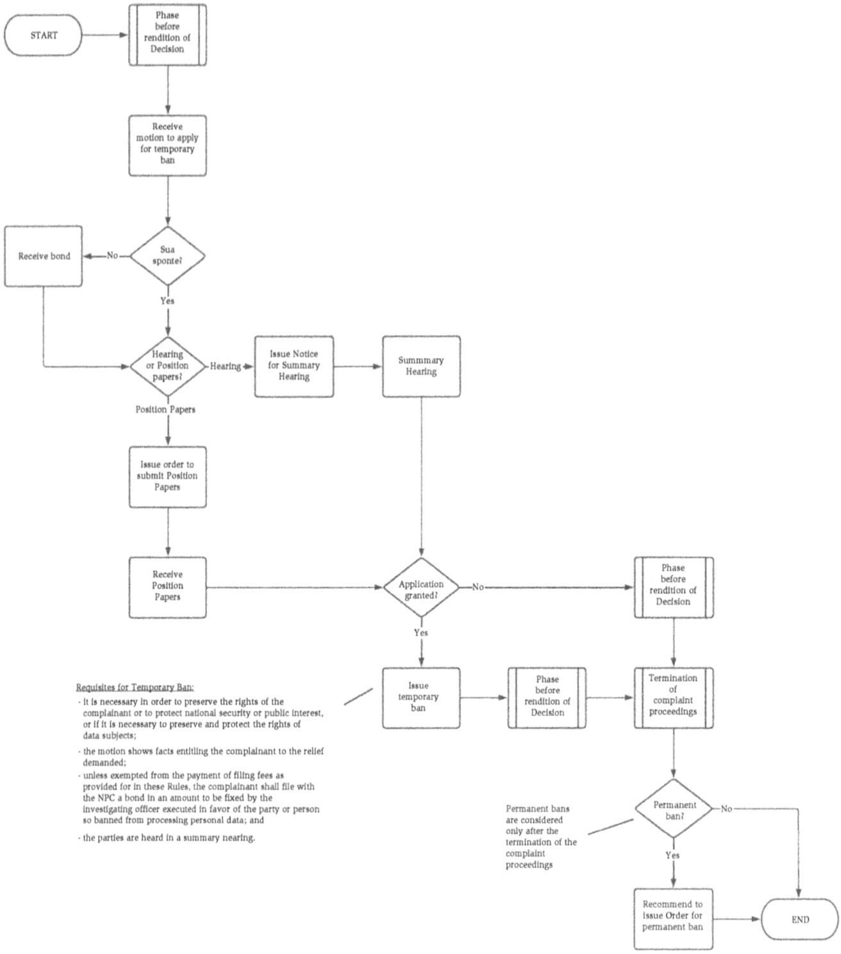

Source: National Privacy Commission, Rules of Procedure, Circular No. 01, Series of 2021 [NPC Circ. No. 21-01] (28 January 2021).

§3. Conduct of Compliance Checks

403. The Commission, through its CMD, may also conduct compliance checks on PICs or PIPs to ensure that these entities are compliant with the DPA and other privacy regulations.[763] In conducting compliance checks, the Commission considers the level of risk to the rights of data subjects posed by the processing, reports received by the Commission, non-registration of a PIC or PIP who is required to register as such with the Commission, unsecured or publicly available personal data on the internet that may be traced to the PIC or PIP, and other considerations that indicate non-compliance with the DPA.[764]

404. A compliance check begins with a privacy sweep of publicly available or accessible information of a PIC or PIP.[765] If the Commission finds a need to clarify certain findings and to determine the level of compliance of such entities, it may require the entity subjected to a compliance check to submit documents and additional information.[766] The Commission may also require and notify the PIC or PIP on the conduct of on-site visits, including the conduct of interviews of relevant personnel who handle personal information, to verify its findings.[767] Upon the finding of deficiencies or non-compliance with the law, the Commission will issue a Notice of Deficiencies to the erring PIC or PIP.[768] Any failure to address the deficiencies within a specific period of time or failure to cooperate with on-site visits shall result in the issuance of a Compliance Order.[769] In the event an erring entity refuses or fails to comply with a Compliance Order, the entity may be subject to the appropriate criminal, civil, or administrative penalties as determined by the Commission.[770] In such cases, the Commission, through the CMD, may also apply for the issuance of a cease and desist order against the PIC or PIP (Figure 3).[771]

763. National Privacy Commission, Guidelines on Compliance Checks, Circular No. 02, Series of 2018 [NPC Circ. No. 18-02] §1 (20 Sep. 2018).
764. *Ibid.*, §5.
765. *Ibid.*, §4.
766. *Ibid.*
767. *Ibid.*
768. *Ibid.*, §8.
769. *Ibid.*, §9.
770. *Ibid.*, §12.
771. National Privacy Commission, Rules on the Issuance of Cease and Desist Orders, Circular No. 02, Series of 2020 [NPC Circ. No. 20-02] §5 (6 Oct. 2020).

Figure 3 Process for Compliance Check

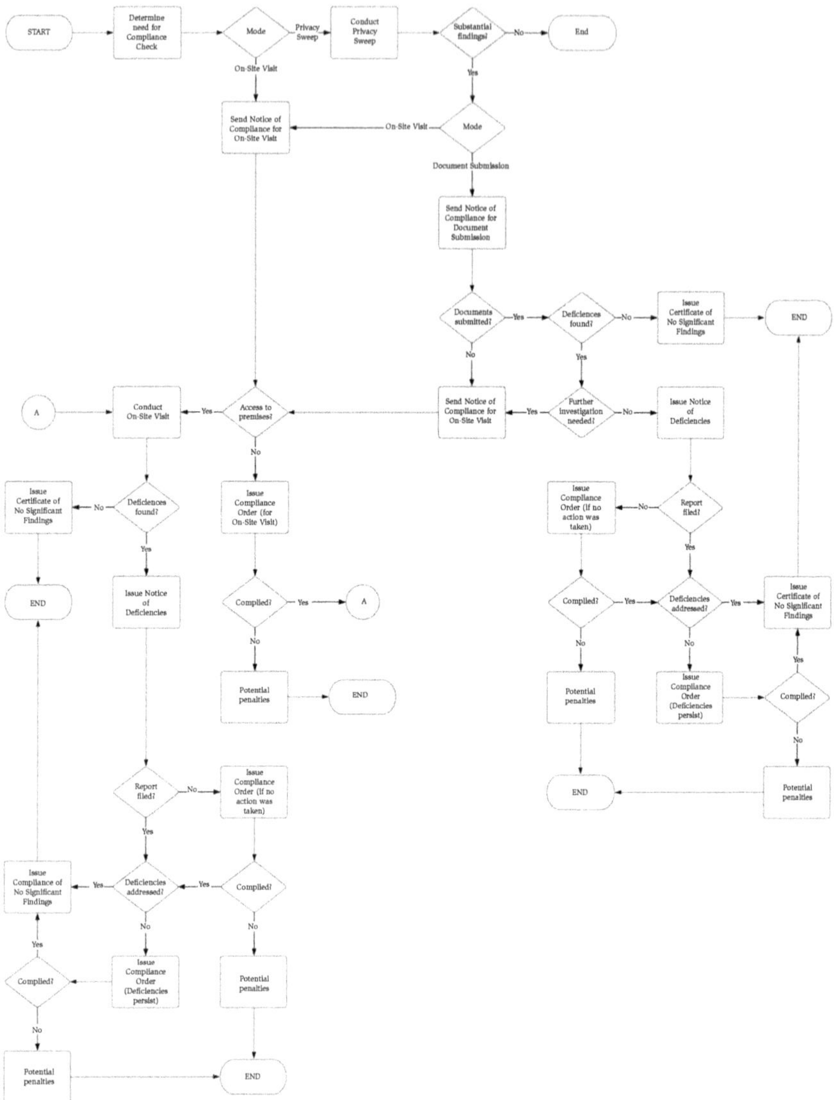

Source: National Privacy Commission, Guidelines on Compliance Checks, Circular No. 02, Series of 2018 [NPC Circ. No. 18-02], (20 September 2018).

§4. Issuance of a Cease and Desist Order

405. The issuance of a cease and desist order is governed by the Circular on the Rules on the Issuance of Cease and Desist Orders. The Commission may issue a cease and desist order (CDO) against the PIC or PIP from processing personal information of data subjects in violation of the DPA and other privacy regulations.[772]

406. A CDO is an independent action and is issued ex parte after the conduct of verification and investigation.[773] It covers the processing of personal information and the conduct of any act or practice in violation of the DPA.[774] On the other hand, a temporary or permanent ban is a provisional remedy that is imposed on the processing of personal information after a summary hearing and notice.[775]

407. An application for the issuance of a CDO may be filed by: (1) the CID in the course of a sua sponte investigation; (2) the CMD through its conduct of a compliance check or handling of breach notifications; or (3) the aggrieved party upon recommendation by the CID after its assessment on the sufficiency of the application.[776]

408. The Commission shall issue a CDO if the following grounds are established by substantial evidence:

> Section 4. *Grounds for the Issuance of Cease and Desist Order.* No CDO shall be issued unless it is established by substantial evidence that all of the following concur:
>
> A. the Adverse Party is doing, threatening or is about to do, is procuring to be done, some act or practice in violation of the DPA, its IRR, or other related issuances;
>
> B. such act or practice is detrimental to national security or public interest, or the CDO is necessary to preserve and protect the rights of a data subject; and
>
> C. the commission or continuance of such act or practice, unless restrained, will cause grave and irreparable injury to a data subject.[777]

409. A hearing is not necessary for the issuance of a CDO.[778] The PIC or the PIP shall be required to comment on the issuance of the CDO.[779] The Commission

772. *Ibid.*, §4(a).
773. *Ibid.*, §8.
774. *Ibid.*, §3(D).
775. National Privacy Commission, Rules of Procedure, Circular No. 01, Series of 2021 [NPC Circ. No. 21-01], rule IX, §1 (28 Jan. 2021).
776. National Privacy Commission, Rules on the Issuance of Cease and Desist Orders, Circular No. 02, Series of 2020 [NPC Circ. No. 20-02] §5 (6 Oct. 2020).
777. *Ibid.*, §4.
778. *Ibid.*, §8.
779. *Ibid.*, §9.

may, however, conduct a clarificatory hearing if it deems that additional information is necessary to make a decision on the issued CDO.[780] The Commission may decide to extend or lift the issued CDO within thirty days from the expiration of the period for comment.[781]

410. If the Commission finds that the act or practice enjoined subsists and there is a need to extend the issued CDO, then the Commission shall extend it until the PIC or the PIP proves that the factual or legal basis for which it was issued no longer exists.[782]

411. While the extended CDO subsists, the PIC or the PIP may file a motion to lift the extended CDO.[783] It is incumbent upon the PIC or the PIP to prove that the factual or legal basis for which the CDO was issued no longer exists.[784]

412. As discussed in a recent case:

> A CDO is issued by the Commission against acts which are potentially harmful and in violation of the Data Privacy Act of 2012 to mitigate the harm that it produced. The lifting of a CDO is dependent on whether such harmful acts had been addressed and remedied to avoid further harm to data subjects. Section 15 of NPC Circular No. 20-02 provides:
> Section 15. Motion to Lift Extended CDO. - At any time during the effectivity of the extended CDO, the Adverse Party may file a motion to lift said order on the ground that *the factual or legal basis for which it was issued no longer exists*, furnishing a copy thereof to the applicant. The motion shall contain or specify the material facts establishing the ground/s relied upon, the relevant documentary, testimonial and object evidence supporting the motion, and the proof of service of the copy of the motion to the applicant.[785]

413. When filing a Motion to Lift Extended CDO, it is incumbent upon the PIC to present evidence concretely showing that the reasons for the issuance of the CDO no longer exist. In cases of breach, the PIC may submit proof that it introduced security measures to address and eliminate the risk of the recurrence of the incident that led to the issuance of the CDO in the first place.[786] It is not sufficient for the PIC to merely claim that it introduced changes, but it must concretely show that such measures are in place and that such measures are adequate and effective based on the conduct of the necessary audits.[787]

---

780. *Ibid.*, §11.
781. *Ibid.*, §12.
782. *Ibid.*, §13.
783. *Ibid.*, §15.
784. *Ibid.*
785. NPC SS 20-001, 24 Jun. 2021, at 3–4 (NPC 2021) (unreported). Emphasis supplied.
786. *See ibid.*
787. *Ibid.*

414. The applicant of the CDO may file a comment or opposition to the motion.[788] The Commission may also require the parties to attend a clarificatory hearing on the motion to lift the extended CDO.[789] The Commission then decides if it shall grant or deny the motion. If the Commission denies the motion, the CDO shall continue to have force and effect.[790]

415. The issuance of a CDO is cumulative, which means that it does not preclude the application of other remedies available to the complainant (Figure 4).[791]

788. National Privacy Commission, Rules on the Issuance of Cease and Desist Orders, Circular No. 02, Series of 2020 [NPC Circ. No. 20-02] §16 (6 Oct. 2020).
789. *Ibid.*, §17.
790. *Ibid.*, §18.
791. *Ibid.*, §21.

Figure 4 Process for Issuance of Cease and Desist Order

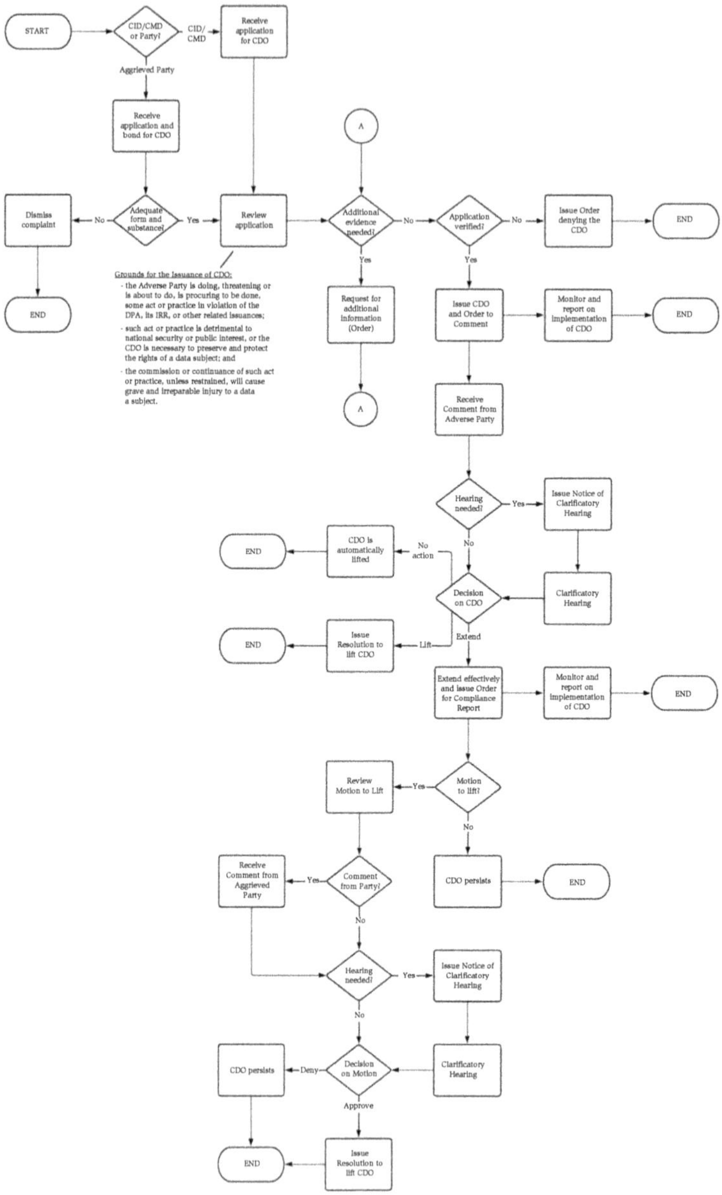

Source: National Privacy Commission, Rules on the Issuance of Cease and Desist Orders, Circular No. 02, Series of 2020 [NPC Circ. No. 20-02] (06 October 2020).

Chapter 5. Liabilities and Penalties

416. A PIC or a PIP may be held liable for the violation of the DPA and other privacy regulations. If the offender is a juridical entity, penalties are imposed upon the responsible officers who participated in, or by their gross negligence, allowed the commission of the crime.[792] Courts may also suspend or revoke the rights under the DPA of a juridical entity.[793] Foreign nationals may also be deported after serving the penalties under the law.[794]

417. The DPA imposes criminal penalties on specific acts that violate the rights of data subjects, which are imposed by courts of law after the conduct of a criminal trial.[795] Upon a finding of a violation, the Commission may recommend to the DOJ the prosecution and imposition of penalties on the violations enumerated under the DPA.[796] These unlawful acts are unauthorized processing of personal or sensitive personal information, processing personal or sensitive personal information for unauthorized purposes, accessing of personal or sensitive personal information, unauthorized access or the intentional breach, improper disposal of personal or sensitive personal information, concealment of security breaches involving sensitive personal information, malicious disclosure, and unauthorized disclosure.[797] The penalties are imposed on the responsible officers of the PIC or the PIP.[798]

§1. Unauthorized Processing of Personal Information and Sensitive Personal Information

418. Unauthorized processing of personal information and sensitive personal information is committed when all the following requisites are present: (1) a person, whether natural or juridical, processed information of the data subject; (2) the information processed is classified as personal information or sensitive personal information; and (3) the processing of personal or sensitive personal information was done without the consent of the data subject, or without being authorized under the DPA or any existing law.[799] The penalty imposed on the unauthorized processing of personal information is imprisonment ranging from one year to three years

792. An Act Protecting Individual Personal Information in Information and Communications Systems in the Government and the Private Sector, Creating for this purpose a National Privacy Commission, and For Other Purposes [Data Privacy Act of 2012], Republic Act No. 10173 §34 (2012).
793. *Ibid.*
794. *Ibid.*
795. *Ibid.*, Republic Act No. 10173, chapter VIII (2012).
796. *Ibid.*, Republic Act No. 10173 §7(i) (2012).
797. *Ibid.*, Republic Act No. 10173 §§25–32 (2012).
798. *Ibid.*, Republic Act No. 10173 §34.
799. In re: FLI Operating ABC Online Lending Application, NPC Case No. 19-910, 17 Dec. 2020, at 17, available at https://www.privacy.gov.ph/wp-content/uploads/2021/02/NPC-19-910-In-re-FLI-Decision-LYA-Final-pseudonymized-17Dec2020-.pdf (last accessed 24 Apr. 2022).

and a fine of not less than PHP 500,000.00 but not more than PHP 2,000,000.00.[800] If the act of unauthorized processing involves sensitive personal information, then the penalty increases to imprisonment ranging from three years to six years and a fine of not less than PHP 500,000.00 but not more than PHP 4,000,000.00.[801]

419. In NPC 19-910, the Commission found the PIC liable for unauthorized processing of personal and sensitive personal information of its data subjects.[802] The PIC, an online lending company, operates ABC's online lending application.[803] ABC online lending application facilitates loans between the PIC and its user-borrowers, the data subjects.[804] FLI, the PIC, collected personal information and sensitive personal information of its data subjects by accessing their mobile phonebook or directory through granting app permissions to 'READ_CONTACTS' and 'READ_EXTERNAL_STORAGE'.[805] The PIC used the information generated from the mobile phonebook or directory to contact third parties who were not nominated as character references.[806] The PIC then contacted such third parties and alleged that the user-borrowers had appointed them as co-makers or character references to the loan.[807] The third parties were often told that they were liable for the loan made by the data subject.[808] The PIC also used the mobile phonebook or directory to harass, threaten, or coerce the data subject and the third parties to settle the loan, thus, damaging the reputation of the data subjects.[809]

420. The Commission held that the PIC processed the mobile phonebook or directory without the consent of ABC online lending application's data subjects, its user-borrowers.[810] The PIC claimed that it obtained the consent of its data subjects when the latter clicked 'Agree' to the Credit Agreement and Privacy Policy.[811] Contrary to the PIC's assertions, the Commission decided that the consent that the PIC purportedly obtained was invalid since the Privacy Policy cannot be the basis for acquiring consent to retain the user-borrowers' entire contacts list.[812] The Privacy Policy limited its declared purpose to collection purposes and it only referred to personal information provided by the user-borrower.[813] The Commission explained that the phrase 'for collection purposes' cannot be considered as a blanket authority to

800. An Act Protecting Individual Personal Information in Information and Communications Systems in the Government and the Private Sector, Creating for this purpose a National Privacy Commission, and For Other Purposes [Data Privacy Act of 2012], Republic Act No. 10173 §25 (2012).
801. *Ibid.*
802. *Ibid.*, at 17–41.
803. *Ibid.*
804. *Ibid.*, at 31.
805. *Ibid.*, at 18–19.
806. *Ibid.*, at 19.
807. *Ibid.*, at 3.
808. *Ibid.*
809. *Ibid.*, at 3.
810. *Ibid.*, at 18–19.
811. *Ibid.*, at 21.
812. *Ibid.*, at 33.
813. *Ibid.*, at 23–26.

allow the PIC to excessively collect and retain information without the data subjects' consent.[814] The user-borrowers could not have reasonably expected the PIC to use their phone contacts other than the reference contacts that the borrower themselves provided to the PIC:[815]

> In this case, Respondent … claimed that the READ_CONTACTS dangerous permission was justified by its need to determine, at the point of the loan application, whether the mobile phone was newly purchased. This is part of their verification process, before approval of the loan. This is determined through the number of entries in the contact list at the moment of application.
>
> While the purpose behind the access of the list of contacts was explained, Respondents have not disputed that it retained the contacts of data subjects and kept the data in a form that allowed them to further process even after the loan applications' approval.
>
> The issue is the retention of these contacts. The excerpts from the cited individual complaints in the Fact-Finding Report pertained to the collection practices made possible because of the retained personal information. Such retention is considered processing of personal information and must be justified under the lawful criteria provided under the DPA. As detailed by the Commission in the Decision, no such lawful criteria is present in this case. Respondent FLI failed to prove that their retention of data is supported by consent or any other lawful criteria provided under the Data Privacy Act.[816]

421. Thus, the PIC is liable for committing unauthorized processing of personal information or sensitive information against its data subjects.

§2. Processing of Personal Information and Sensitive Personal Information for Unauthorized Purposes

422. The act of processing personal or sensitive personal information for unauthorized purposes is committed when the following requisites concur: (1) a person processed information of the data subject; (2) the information processed is classified as personal or sensitive personal information; (3) the person processing the information obtained the consent of the data subject or is granted authority under the DPA or existing laws; (4) the processing of personal or sensitive personal information is for a purpose that is neither covered by the authority given by the data subject and could not have been reasonably foreseen by the data subject nor otherwise authorized by the DPA or existing laws.[817] The law penalizes the commission of the act by imprisonment ranging from one year and six months to five years and a fine of not less than PHP 500,000.00 but not more than PHP 1,000,000.00.[818]

814. *Ibid.*, at 26.
815. *Ibid.*, at 28.
816. NPC Case No. 19-910, 11 Mar. 2021, at 14 (NPC 2021) (unreported).
817. *Ibid.*
818. *Ibid.*

The penalty is increased to imprisonment ranging from two years to seven years and a fine of not less than PHP 500,000.00 but not more than PHP 2,000,000.00 if the act involves sensitive personal information.[819] Public officials held liable for this crime may also suffer perpetual or temporary absolute disqualification from office.[820]

423. On the one hand, the act of unauthorized processing of personal information is committed when the person processing the information unlawfully processed the information without the data subject's consent or without authority under the DPA or any existing law. The person processing the information failed to obtain the consent or authority of the data subject or by law in relation to any act of processing. On the other hand, the act of processing for unauthorized purposes refers to a situation where the person processing the information obtained the data subject's consent or is authorized under the DPA or any existing laws for a declared and specific purpose. The unlawful act of processing is committed when the information is processed for a different purpose that is neither covered by the authority obtained from the data subject or could not have been reasonably foreseen by the data subject or authorized by the DPA or any existing law.

§3. Accessing Personal Information and Sensitive Personal Information Due to Negligence

424. The DPA finds liable any person who provided access to personal or sensitive personal information due to negligence without being authorized by law.[821] The requisites are: (1) there is personal information or sensitive personal information; (2) the personal or sensitive personal information was accessed; (3) the access was not authorized under the DPA or any existing law; and (4) the unauthorized access was due to gross negligence.[822] Access to personal information due to negligence is penalized by imprisonment ranging from one year to three years and a fine of not less than PHP 500,000.00 but not more than PHP 2,000,000.00 shall be imposed on persons who, due to negligence, provided access to personal information without being authorized under this Act or any existing law.[823] If sensitive personal information is accessed due to negligence, then the penalty is imprisonment ranging from three years to six years and a fine of not less than PHP 500,000.00 but not more than PHP 4,000,000.00.[824]

425. While it is true that the law does not qualify the degree of negligence required for criminal liability under this provision, reference may be made to other sections of the DPA.

---

819. *Ibid.*
820. *Ibid.*, Republic Act No. 10173 §34.
821. *Ibid.*, Republic Act No. 10173 §26.
822. *See ibid.*
823. *Ibid.*
824. *Ibid.*

426. Criminal liability is further discussed in section 34 of the same law, which provides:

> Section 34. *Extent of Liability.* – If the offender is a corporation, partnership or any juridical person, the penalty shall be imposed upon the responsible officers, as the case may be, who participated in, or by their *gross negligence*, allowed the commission of the crime. If the offender is a juridical person, the court may suspend or revoke any of its rights under this Act. If the offender is an alien, he or she shall, in addition to the penalties herein prescribed, be deported without further proceedings after serving the penalties prescribed. If the offender is a public official or employee and lie or she is found guilty of acts penalized under Sections 27 and 28 of this Act, he or she shall, in addition to the penalties prescribed herein, suffer perpetual or temporary absolute disqualification from office, as the case may be.[825]

427. Based on section 34, a responsible officer can be subject to the imposable penalties in two instances: (1) participation, or (2) allowing the commission of the crime through gross negligence.[826] This alludes to the definition of felonies under the Revised Penal Code:

> Article 3. *Definition.* - Acts and omissions punishable by law are felonies *(delitos).*
>
> Felonies are committed not only by means of deceit *(dolo)* but also by means of fault *(culpa).*
>
> There is deceit when the act is performed with deliberate intent; and there is fault when the wrongful act results from imprudence, negligence, lack of foresight, or lack of skill.[827]

428. While the intent is not a requirement in the DPA, the first instance in section 34 pertains to positive acts by the offender which contravene the DPA. The second instance, which is the means that is qualified by gross negligence, refers to omissions and a failure to act according to the provisions of the DPA despite a duty under the law to do so.

429. Section 26 speaks of an omission by the responsible officer that allowed access by a third party to the stored personal information. Considering the impossibility of an offender 'participating' in an omission, the offence in section 26 clearly pertains to the second means – that of allowing the commission of the crime by their gross negligence.

---

825. *Ibid.*, Republic Act No. 10173 §34. Emphasis supplied.
826. *Ibid.*
827. An Act Revising the Penal Code and Other Penal Laws [REV. PENAL CODE], Act No. 3815, art. 3 (1930).

430. The Commission has previously categorized the violation in section 26 as a failure to act according to duty, and has qualified 'negligence' in the same provision to refer to gross negligence:

> The higher standard set for government agencies handling sensitive personal information is especially true of COMELEC; COMELEC is no ordinary data controller, it is effectively one of the Philippines' largest data controllers. The COMELEC creates, maintains, and processes data to establish a clean, complete, permanent, and updated list of voters, through the adoption of biometric technology, for us in national and local elections.[828]
>
> . . .
>
> Because of the sensitive nature of this database, the law requires that COMELEC adopt a higher standard of care in the creation, custody, and maintenance of the voters' lists used in elections. The database generated by the creation of the voters' list must be secured; COMELEC must ensure that it not be used for any other purpose other than election exercises.[829]
>
> . . .
>
> It is quite clear from the foregoing that there was very little to no awareness on the part of COMELEC Chairman … regarding his accountability toward handling personal data. There is no documentation that shows there were continuous efforts to increase the level of protection of personal data that was in COMELEC custody, or what other steps were taken to achieve adherence to data protection standards, as required by the Data Privacy Act of 2012.
>
> COMELEC Chairman … 's indifference was manifest with his failure to consider the security implications of his programs; ITD only became relevant in his mind when considering praise given to the Department for its work on the website. *The acts of COMELEC Chairman … partake that of an administrative offense of gross negligence; there is clearly want of even slight care regarding compliance with the provisions of the Data Privacy Act of 2012, when there was a duty to act.* So, when the inevitable injury came, the ITD was completely lost in evaluating and crafting a timely response to the data breach.[830]
>
> . . .
>
> COMELEC could have embedded privacy in the design of its data processing systems, but it missed the opportunity to do so because the head of agency denies any responsibility in complying with the law, even implying that this duty begins only when prompted by subordinate officers. *The willful and intentional disregard of his duties, which he should know or ought to know, is tantamount to gross negligence.* The lack of a clear government policy, particularly in collecting and further processing of personal data, unnecessarily exposed personal and sensitive information of millions of Filipinos to unlawful access.[831]

---

828. *Ibid.*, at 19.
829. *Ibid.*, at 20.
830. *Ibid.*, at 28–29. Emphasis supplied.
831. *Ibid.*, at 30. Emphasis supplied.

. . .

> Considering the negligence on display, the personal liability upon the Head of Agency imposed under Section 22 of the Data Privacy Act of 2012, and the consequent access to personal and sensitive personal information arising from the negligence of COMELEC Chairman …, there is basis to hold him liable for the data breach under Section 26 of the Data Privacy Act of 2012.[832]

431. Section 26 sets out the description of the violation and the elements of its commission, but the penalties it prescribes are criminal in nature and, as such, are only imposed on natural persons. The Commission reiterates that juridical persons, such as the PIC, in this case, cannot be subject to imprisonment or the payment of a criminal fine.

432. Section 34 supplies the lacuna by specifying that the responsible officers of erring corporations are the natural persons to be accused of such violations and explicitly states that gross negligence is the standard to hold them liable.

433. This interpretation is supported by long-standing principles in statutory construction:

> Moreover, under the maxim *noscitur a sociis*, where a particular word or phrase is ambiguous in itself or is equally susceptible of various meanings, its correct construction may be made clear and specific by considering the company of words in which it is founded or with which it is associated. This is because a word or phrase in a statute is always used in association with other words or phrases, and its meaning may, thus, be modified or restricted by the latter. The particular words, clauses and phrases should not be studied as detached and isolated expressions, but the whole and every part of the statute must be considered in fixing the meaning of any of its parts and in order to produce a harmonious whole. *A statute must be so construed as to harmonize and give effect to all its provisions whenever possible.* In short, every meaning to be given to each word or phrase must be ascertained from the context of the body of the statute since a word or phrase in a statute is always used in association with other words or phrases and its meaning may be modified or restricted by the latter.[833]

434. On the assumption that section 26 referred to simple negligence, reading that provision together with section 29 would lead to unreasonableness in the penal provisions of the DPA. Section 29 of the DPA states:

> Section 29. *Unauthorized Access or Intentional Breach.* – The penalty of imprisonment ranging from one (1) year to three (3) years and a fine of not less than Five hundred thousand pesos (Php500,000.00) but not more than Two million pesos (Php2,000,000.00) shall be imposed on persons who *knowingly* and

832. *Ibid.*, at 31).
833. *Chavez v. JBC, et. al.*, G.R. 202242 (2012). Emphasis supplied.

> unlawfully, or violating data confidentiality and security data systems, breaks in any way into any system where personal and sensitive personal information is stored.[834]

435. Notably, section 29 contemplates intentional acts and provides a penalty of imprisonment for one to three years, whether the information involved is personal or sensitive personal information.[835] This is a visibly lighter penalty than the ones meted out in section 26, which provides for one to three years for violations involving personal information, and three to six years for violations involving sensitive personal information.[836]

436. If section 26 contemplated simple negligence, this would lead to a situation where the penalties of responsible officers in cases of misdelivered emails by company employees are graver than the penalties for persons who intentionally violate data confidentiality and security data systems and break into a system where personal and sensitive personal information is stored. This does not lead to a harmonious reading of the law, nor does it allow equitable and effective enforcement of the law against violations of the Data Privacy Act.

437. To consider 'negligence' in section 26 as simple negligence would contradict the intent of the law. While the primary device for statutory construction is *verba legis*, the Commission recognizes that the lack of qualification in the term 'degree' in section 26 is a source of confusion because negligence can only be measured against a standard. The standard is either simple negligence or gross negligence. Hence, it makes reference to the legislative history of the DPA and the Congressional hearings to construe the intent of the lawmakers, following the principle of *ratio legis est.*

438. The Supreme Court discussed the principle as follows:

> Ratio legis est anima. The spirit rather than the letter of the law. A statute must be read according to its spirit or intent, for what is within the spirit is within the statute although it is not within its letter, and that which is within the letter but not within the spirit is not within the statute. Put a bit differently, that which is within the intent of the lawmaker is as much within the statute as if within the letter; and that which is within the letter of the statute is not within the statute unless within the intent of the lawmakers. Withal, courts ought not to interpret and should not accept an interpretation that would defeat the intent of the law and its legislators.[837]

---

834. An Act Protecting Individual Personal Information in Information and Communications Systems in the Government and the Private Sector, Creating for this purpose a National Privacy Commission, and For Other Purposes [Data Privacy Act of 2012], Republic Act No. 10173 §29 (2012). Emphasis supplied.
835. *Ibid.*
836. *Ibid.*, Republic Act No. 10173 §26.
837. *League of Cities of the Philippines v. Commission on Elections*, G.R. 176951, 177499, 178056 (2009).

439. In his Sponsorship speech for the DPA, Senator Edgardo Angara talked about the delicate balance that our data privacy laws need to have:

> Take the case of the IT-BPO industry. It deals with confidential information protected by privacy laws in clients' home countries. Hence, locators also prefer destinations where the security and privacy of their data and intellectual property are upheld.
>
> However, we are cautious not to craft data privacy laws that overreach the original intention of providing a safe and stable environment for businesses. We must look into the experiences of our BPO competitors such as India, and avoid replicating their mistakes in crafting overly stringent privacy regulations.
>
> . . .
>
> Our proposal will keep our information systems safe without unnecessarily restricting our IT-BPO industry and other ICT-driven sectors. This is why we have chosen to follow the Asia-Pacific Economic Cooperation (APEC) Privacy Framework over other private regulations as it provides ample flexibility in implementation.[838]

440. In its documented *Guidance for Domestic Implementation*, the APEC Privacy Framework highlights 'the importance of having a *range of remedies commensurate with the extent of the actual or potential harm* to individuals resulting from such violations'.[839]

441. This need for balance, as discussed by Senator Angara, and the idea of commensurate remedies both argue against interpreting 'negligence' in section 26 as simple negligence.

§4. Unauthorized Access or Intentional Breach

442. A person who knowingly and unlawfully, or by violating data confidentiality and security data systems, breaks in any way into any system where personal or sensitive personal information is stored, commits unauthorized access or intentional breach.[840] The requisites are: (1) there is a data system where personal or sensitive personal information is stored; (2) a person breaks into the system; and (3)

838. S. Journal No. 22, 15th Cong., 2d Reg. Sess. (21 Sep. 2011).
839. APEC Secretariat, APEC Privacy Framework 2005, at 36, *available at* https://www.apec.org/-/media/APEC/Publications/2005/12/APEC-Privacy-Framework/05_ecsg_privacyframewk.pdf (last accessed 29 Apr. 2022). Emphasis supplied.
840. An Act Protecting Individual Personal Information in Information and Communications Systems in the Government and the Private Sector, Creating for this purpose a National Privacy Commission, and For Other Purposes [Data Privacy Act of 2012], Republic Act No. 10173 §29 (2012).

the breakage was done knowingly and unlawfully, or by violating data confidentiality and security. Such a person is liable for imprisonment ranging from one year to three years and a fine of not less than PHP 500,000.00 but not more than PHP 2,000,000.00.[841]

§5. Improper Disposal of Personal Information and Sensitive Personal Information

443. Improper disposal of personal or sensitive personal information is committed when a person who knowingly or negligently disposes, discards or abandons the personal information of an individual in an area accessible to the public or has otherwise placed the personal information of an individual in its container for trash collection.[842]

444. This, however, excludes a situation where the PIC or the PIP has disposed or discarded personal or sensitive personal information in compliance with its obligations under section 19(d)(3) of the IRR:

> Section 19. *General principles in collection, processing and retention.* The processing of personal data shall adhere to the following general principles in the collection, processing, and retention of personal data:
>
> d. Personal Data shall not be retained longer than necessary.
>
> . . .
>
> 3. Personal data shall be disposed or discarded in a secure manner that would prevent further processing, unauthorized access, or disclosure to any other party or the public, or prejudice the interests of the data subjects.[843]

445. If a PIC or PIP has disposed of personal or sensitive personal information that makes further processing, unauthorized access, or disclosure no longer possible, then the personal or sensitive personal information is rendered unusable. In such cases, the place of disposal becomes immaterial.

446. Thus, the requisites are: (1) there is personal or sensitive personal information; (2) the personal or sensitive personal information was disposed, discarded, or abandoned; (3) the manner of disposal, discardment, or abandonment was not in a secure manner that would prevent further processing, unauthorized access, or disclosure; (4) the place of disposal is an area accessible to the public, or the personal or sensitive personal information was placed in a container for trash collection.

---

841. *Ibid.*
842. *Ibid.*, Republic Act No. 10173 §27.
843. National Privacy Commission, Rules and Regulations Implementing the Data Privacy Act of 2012, Republic Act No. 10173, §19(d) (3) (2016).

447. The penalty for improper disposal of personal information is imprisonment ranging from six months to two years and a fine of not less than PHP 100,000.00 but not more than PHP 500,000.00 and the penalty for improper disposal of sensitive personal information is imprisonment ranging from one year to three years and a fine of not less than PHP 100,000.00 but not more than PHP 1,000,000.00.[844] Public officials who commit improper disposal of personal or sensitive personal information may also suffer perpetual or temporary absolute disqualification from office.[845]

§6. CONCEALMENT OF SECURITY BREACHES INVOLVING SENSITIVE PERSONAL INFORMATION

448. The unlawful act of concealment of security breaches involving sensitive personal information is committed when a person who, after having knowledge of a security breach and of the obligation to notify the Commission, intentionally or by omission conceals the fact of such breach incident.[846] The requisites are: (1) a personal data breach occurred; (2) the breach is one that requires notification to the Commission; and (3) the person knowingly conceals the fact of such breach from the Commission.[847] The penalty of imprisonment of one year and six months to five years and a fine of not less than PHP 500,000.00 but not more than PHP 1,000,000.00 is imposed for the commission of the act.[848]

§7. MALICIOUS DISCLOSURE

449. The DPA also penalizes malicious and unauthorized disclosures. Malicious disclosure is committed when any PIC or PIP or any of its officials, employees or agents, with malice or in bad faith, discloses unwarranted or false information relative to any personal or sensitive personal information obtained by him or her.[849] Malicious disclosure is committed when the following requisites concur: (1) the perpetrator is a PIC or PIP or any of its officials, employees, or agents; (2) the perpetrator disclosed personal or sensitive personal information; (3) the disclosure was with malice or in bad faith; and (4) the disclosed information relates to unwarranted

844. *Ibid.*, Republic Act No. 10173 §27.
845. *Ibid.*, Republic Act No. 10173 §34.
846. *Ibid.*, Republic Act No. 10173 §30.
847. *See ibid.*, Republic Act No. 10173 §20(f).
848. An Act Protecting Individual Personal Information in Information and Communications Systems in the Government and the Private Sector, Creating for this purpose a National Privacy Commission, and For Other Purposes [Data Privacy Act of 2012], Republic Act No. 10173 §30 (2012).
849. *Ibid.*, Republic Act No. 10173 §31.

or false information.[850] The penalty imposed is imprisonment ranging from one year and six months to five years and a fine of not less than PHP 500,000.00 but not more than PHP 1,000,000.00.[851]

450. A finding of Malicious Disclosure requires that first, the disclosed personal information is unwarranted or false, and second, the disclosure is malicious or in bad faith.[852] If either of these two requisites is absent, then the offence falls under section 32 or Unauthorized Disclosure.[853]

§8. Unauthorized Disclosure

451. Unauthorized disclosure is committed when a PIC or PIP or any of its officials, employees or agents, discloses to a third party personal or sensitive personal information without the consent of the data subject.[854]

452. The requisites are: (1) the perpetrator is a PIC or a PIP; (2) the perpetrator disclosed information; (3) the information relates to personal or sensitive personal information; (4) the perpetrator disclosed the personal or sensitive personal information to a third party; (5) the disclosure was without any of the lawful basis for processing, consent or otherwise, under sections 12 and 13 of the DPA; and (6) the disclosure is neither malicious nor done in bad faith, and the information disclosed is not unwarranted or false information.[855]

453. In several cases, the Commission had the opportunity to elucidate the requisites of Unauthorized Disclosure.

454. While it is true that criminal and penal statutes must be strictly construed, a strict reading of section 32 of the DPA or Unauthorized Disclosure shows that a PIC or a PIP will be penalized if it discloses personal information without the consent of the data subject even if such disclosure is justified under some other criteria for lawful processing enumerated in sections 12 and 13 of the DPA.[856]

850. *RLA v. PLDT Enterprise*, NPC Case No. 18-010, 10 Dec. 2021, at 30, available at https://www.privacy.gov.ph/wp-content/uploads/2022/03/02-NPC_18_010_RLA_v_PLDT_Enterprise_Resolution_w_Dissenting_Opinion.pdf (last accessed 25 Apr. 2022).
851. An Act Protecting Individual Personal Information in Information and Communications Systems in the Government and the Private Sector, Creating for this purpose a National Privacy Commission, and For Other Purposes [Data Privacy Act of 2012], Republic Act No. 10173 §31 (2012).
852. *RLA v. PLDT Enterprise*, NPC Case No. 18-010, 10 Dec. 2021, at 30, available at https://www.privacy.gov.ph/wp-content/uploads/2022/03/02-NPC_18_010_RLA_v_PLDT_Enterprise_Resolution_w_Dissenting_Opinion.pdf (last accessed 25 Apr. 2022).
853. *Ibid.*, at 31.
854. An Act Protecting Individual Personal Information in Information and Communications Systems in the Government and the Private Sector, Creating for this purpose a National Privacy Commission, and For Other Purposes [Data Privacy Act of 2012], Republic Act No. 10173 §32 (2012).
855. NPC Case No. 21-010, 03 Feb. 2022, at 13 (NPC 2022) (unreported).
856. *See ibid.*, at 12.

455. The rules of statutory construction are clear:

> Where a literal meaning would lead to absurdity, contradiction, or injustice, or otherwise defeat the clear purpose of the lawmakers, the spirit and reason of the statute may be examined to determine the true intention of the provision.[857]

456. If section 32 is understood in its literal sense, then it will result in an absurd situation. A PIC or PIP will be held liable for unauthorized disclosure even if it validly processed personal information based on some other lawful criteria undersections 12 and 13 but failed to obtain the data subjects' consent.

457. Further, section 32 of the DPA on Unauthorized Disclosure should be read together with the entire DPA. As the Supreme Court explained:

> A law must not be read in truncated parts; its provisions must be read in relation to the whole law. It is the cardinal rule in statutory construction that a statute's clauses and phrases must not be taken as detached and isolated expressions, but the whole and every part thereof must be considered in fixing the meaning of any of its parts in order to produce a harmonious whole. Every part of the statute must be interpreted with reference to the context, *i.e.*, that every part of the statute must be considered together with other parts of the statute and kept subservient to the general intent of the whole enactment.[858]

458. Section 32 of the DPA should not be read in isolation. It should be read together with the other provisions of the DPA, particularly sections 12 and 13 on the criteria for lawful processing of personal and sensitive personal information, respectively. A plain reading of sections 12 and 13 will show that consent is just one of the lawful criteria for processing. As such, the presence of any of the criteria listed in either section is sufficient to justify the processing of personal or sensitive personal information as the case may be. To require the consent of the data subject when some other lawful criteria such as law or regulation requires or justifies the processing of the personal information, including its disclosure, will result in absurdity. Such literal interpretation based on an isolated reading of section 32 of the DPA will render sections 12 and 13 of the DPA inoperative:

> The rule is that a construction that would render a provision inoperative should be avoided; *instead, apparently inconsistent provisions should be reconciled whenever possible as parts of a coordinated and harmonious whole.*[859]

---

857. *Metropolitan Bank and Trust Co. v. Liberty Corrugated Boxes Manufacturing Corp.*, G.R. No.184317 (2017).

858. *Fort Bonifacio Development Corp. v. Commissioner of Internal Revenue*, G.R. Nos. 158885 & 170680 (Resolution) (2009).

859. *JMM Promotions & Management, Inc. v. National Labor Relations Commission*, G.R. No. 109835 (1993). Emphasis supplied.

459. A proper reading of section 32 should be that Unauthorized Disclosure is committed when the perpetrator processes personal information without any of the lawful basis for processing under sections 12 and 13. This interpretation is more in line with the principle that 'when two or more interpretations are possible, that interpretation which is favourable or beneficial to the accused must be adopted'.[860] As such, section 32 of the DPA is violated if none of the lawful basis of processing, consent or otherwise, supports the disclosure of personal information. This interpretation is more beneficial to the accused since it actually narrows the extent to which disclosure of personal information may be considered as unauthorized disclosure.[861]

460. The penalty imposed for unauthorized disclosure of personal information is imprisonment ranging from one year to three years and a fine of not less than PHP 500,000.00 but not more than PHP 1,000,000.00.[862] If sensitive personal information is disclosed, then the penalty is imprisonment ranging from three years to five years and a fine of not less than PHP 500,000.00 but not more than PHP 2,000,000.00.[863]

461. If any of the foregoing crimes have been committed in a combination or series of acts, the person liable shall be subject to imprisonment ranging from three years to six years and a fine of not less than PHP 1,000,000.00 but not more than PHP 5,000,000.00.[864] The maximum penalty shall be applied if the personal information of at least 100 persons is affected in the commission of the crimes penalized under the DPA.[865]

§9. Extent of Liability of Responsible Officers

462. The Commission imposes the penalty upon the responsible officers of a corporation, partnership, or any juridical person, if such officers participated in, or by their gross negligence, allowed the commission of a crime:

> Section 34. *Extent of Liability.* – If the offender is a corporation, partnership or any juridical person, the penalty shall be imposed upon the responsible officers, as the case may be, who participated in, or by their gross negligence, allowed the commission of the crime. If the offender is a juridical person, the court may suspend or revoke any of its rights under this Act. If the offender is an alien, he or she shall, in addition to the penalties herein prescribed, be deported without further proceedings after serving the penalties prescribed. If

860. *People v. Liban*, G.R. Nos. 136247 & 138330 (2000).
861. *See* NPC Case No. 21-010, 03 Feb. 2022, at 12 (NPC 2022) (unreported).
862. An Act Protecting Individual Personal Information in Information and Communications Systems in the Government and the Private Sector, Creating for this purpose a National Privacy Commission, and For Other Purposes [Data Privacy Act of 2012], Republic Act No. 10173 §32 (2012).
863. *Ibid.*
864. *Ibid.*, Republic Act No. 10173 §33.
865. *Ibid.*, Republic Act No. 10173 §35.

the offender is a public official or employee and lie or she is found guilty of acts penalized under Sections 27 and 28 of this Act, he or she shall, in addition to the penalties prescribed herein, suffer perpetual or temporary absolute disqualification from office, as the case may be.[866]

463. As discussed by the Commission in a case, the liability of the responsible officers 'does not rely on active participation alone' but requires a showing of gross negligence.[867]

464. The Supreme Court has consistently defined gross negligence as:

> [T]he negligence characterized by the want of even slight care, or by acting or omitting to act in a situation where there is a duty to act, not inadvertently but willfully and intentionally, with a conscious indifference to the consequences, insofar as other persons may be affected. It is the omission of that care that even inattentive and thoughtless men never fail to give to their own property.[868]

465. The Commission found the Board of Directors (BOD) of the PIC grossly negligent because it entered into an agreement that effectively allowed the harassment of the data subjects:

> In this case, the Board of Directors of FLI did not deny the fact that a Master Service Agreement was entered into between Respondent FLI and CSA, with the President as the signatory. The Board of Directors should have been aware of the terms in this Agreement, considering that it concerns a vital aspect of their operations as a lending company.
>
> . . .
>
> It is the persons behind FLI who allowed the harassment of its borrowers through the Master Service Agreement that surrendered all accountability to its subcontractor. These persons provided the approvals for the ABC application's functionalities and dangerous permissions. They were the ones who lacked supervision over the representations it made to all of FLI's borrowers.[869]

466. Based on the facts of the case, it also explicitly authorized the President to enter into the questionable agreement:

---

866. *Ibid.*, Republic Act No. 10173 §34.
867. In re: FLI Operating ABC Online Lending Application, NPC Case No. 19-910, 17 Dec. 2020, at 35, available at https://www.privacy.gov.ph/wp-content/uploads/2021/02/NPC-19-910-In-re-FLI-Decision-LYA-Final-pseudonymized-17Dec2020-.pdf (last accessed 24 Apr. 2022).
868. *Office of the Ombudsman v. De Leon*, G.R. No. 154083 (2013).
869. In re: FLI Operating ABC Online Lending Application, NPC Case No. 19-910, 17 Dec. 2020, at 35–40, available at https://www.privacy.gov.ph/wp-content/uploads/2021/02/NPC-19-910-In-re-FLI-Decision-LYA-Final-pseudonymized-17Dec2020 .pdf (last accessed 24 Apr. 2022).

> The Commission reiterates that it is an undisputed fact that all Respondents were incumbent members of FLI's BOD at the time the violations were committed. The Commission notes that the nature of the DPA violation in this case is tied to the conduct of FLI's business as reflected in the MSA they executed with CSA. Since the authority of the President to enter into the MSA on behalf of the Corporation is not provided in the By-Laws of FLIs, it necessarily means that the FLI's BOD gave him the authority to do so. Consequently, the directors, including Respondents, should have been aware that the provisions of the MSA contradicted the principles in the DPA.
>
> Moreover, as discussed in the Decision, the failure of the BOD to address the violations, which led to the voluminous cases filed with the Commission, shows gross negligence on their part. FLI's counsel stated during the clarificatory hearing on 01 October 2020, that FLI was not aware of specific actions that it took against CSA on the unlawful processing of personal information.[870]

467. Given their gross negligence, the members of the BOD are liable for unlawful processing of personal information.

§10. Other Penalties

468. A public officer responsible for the commission of any crime under the DPA while in the exercise of his or her duties shall be disqualified from occupying public office for a term twice the period of the criminal penalty imposed upon him or her.[871]

469. Other violations that are not expressly enumerated in the DPA shall result in the payment of an administrative fine upon notice and hearing.[872] The amounts of the fines imposed shall be published in a schedule by the Commission.[873] The Commission is in the process of releasing circular imposing administrative fines on violations of the DPA and other privacy regulations.

470. The Commission recently conducted a public hearing on the draft Circular on 22 March 2022, pursuant to the requirements of law. The Circular does not introduce new obligations or penalize new violations. It penalizes acts in violation of the DPA and other privacy regulations.

471. The distinction between the penalties in the DPA and the administrative fines in the draft Circular must be emphasized. The penalties of imprisonment and fines in the DPA are criminal in nature and are imposed by the judicial courts upon

870. NPC Case No. 19-910, 29 Jul. 2021, at 10–11 (NPC 2021) (unreported).
871. An Act Protecting Individual Personal Information in Information and Communications Systems in the Government and the Private Sector, Creating for this purpose a National Privacy Commission, and For Other Purposes [Data Privacy Act of 2012], Republic Act No. 10173 §36 (2012).
872. *Ibid.*, Republic Act No. 10173 §65.
873. *Ibid.*

recommendation of the Commission for criminal prosecution to the DOJ.[874] The criminal penalties in sections 25 to 29 of the DPA are imposed on the responsible officers of the PIC or the PIP, pursuant to section 34 of the DPA.[875]

472. The administrative fines in the draft Circular are administrative in nature and shall be imposed on the PIC or the PIP itself. The administrative fines are imposed on Grave Violations, Major Violations, and Other Violations.[876] The applicable fines imposed for Grave Violations and Major Violations are based on a percentage of the PIC or the PIP's annual gross income of the immediately preceding year of the violation.[877] For other violations, the applicable fine is imposed on a range. The administrative fine shall only be imposed after notice and hearing in accordance with due process.[878]

473. The Commission may also order restitution for any aggrieved party, which shall be governed by the Civil Code.[879]

874. *See ibid.*, Republic Act No. 10173 §7(i).
875. *Ibid.*, Republic Act No. 10173 §34.
876. National Privacy Commission, Guidelines on Administrative Fines, §2 (unpublished Draft Circular).
877. *Ibid.*, §§2–3.
878. *Ibid.*, §4.
879. An Act Protecting Individual Personal Information in Information and Communications Systems in the Government and the Private Sector, Creating for this purpose a National Privacy Commission, and For Other Purposes [Data Privacy Act of 2012], Republic Act No. 10173 §37 (2012).

Part IX. Specific Processing Situations

Chapter 1. Processing for Journalistic Purposes and Academic, Artistic, or Literary Expression

474. The DPA does not apply to the processing of personal or sensitive personal information for journalistic, artistic, or literary purposes:

> Section 4. *Scope.* This Act applies to the processing of all types of personal information and to any natural and juridical person involved in personal information processing including those personal information controllers and processors who, although not found or established in the Philippines, use equipment that are located in the Philippines, or those who maintain an office, branch or agency in the Philippines subject to the immediately succeeding paragraph: Provided, That the requirements of Section 5 are complied with.
> This Act does not apply to the following:
>
> . . .
>
> (d) Personal information processed for *journalistic*, *artistic*, *literary* or research purposes[.][880]

475. The exemption, however, is 'not a carte blanche authorization that journalists can conveniently present to compel potential sources of information to turn over or disclose data under their custody'.[881] The non-applicability of the DPA only applies to personal information to be processed and not to the PIC or PIP undertaking the processing and, even then, only to the minimum extent necessary to achieve the specific purpose, function, or activity concerned:

> Section 5. *Special Cases.* The Act and these Rules shall not apply to the following specified information, only to the minimum extent of collection, access, use, disclosure or other processing necessary to the purpose, function, or activity concerned:
>
> . . .

880. *Ibid.*, Republic Act No. 10173 §4(d) (2012). Emphasis supplied.
881. National Privacy Commission, Various Concerns Regarding the Data Privacy Act, Advisory Opinion No. 051, Series of 2018, at 6 (5 Oct. 2018).

> b. Personal information processed for journalistic, artistic or literary purpose, in order to uphold freedom of speech, of expression, or of the press, subject to requirements of other applicable law or regulations;
>
> . . .
>
> Provided, that the non-applicability of the Act or these Rules do not extend to personal information controllers or personal information processors, who remain subject to the requirements of implementing security measures for personal data protection: Provided further, that the processing of the information provided in the preceding paragraphs shall be exempted from the requirements of the Act only to the minimum extent necessary to achieve the specific purpose, function, or activity.[882]

476. As such, journalists acting as PICs or PIPs still need to comply with the other obligations under the DPA, including implementing the necessary security measures and upholding the general privacy principles and the rights of data subjects.[883] The IRR itself recognizes the obligations of journalists acting as PICs or PIPs:

> Section 7. *Protection Afforded to Journalists and their Sources.*
>
> . . .
>
> b. Publishers, editors, or duly accredited reporters who are likewise personal information controllers or personal information processors within the meaning of the law are *still bound to follow the Data Privacy Act and related issuances with regard to the processing of personal data, upholding rights of their data subjects and maintaining compliance with other provisions* that are not incompatible with the protection provided by Republic Act No. 53.[884]

477. In an Advisory Opinion, the Commission opined that when processing personal information, journalists should remain mindful of the rights of data subjects:

> With this, publishers, editors, or duly accredited reporters reporting on criminal cases should process personal and sensitive personal information fairly and lawfully, *in a manner that would respect the privacy rights of an individual.* The same should avoid prejudicial publicity that may deprive the accused of due process rights to a fair trial.[885]

882. National Privacy Commission, Rules and Regulations Implementing the Data Privacy Act of 2012, Republic Act No. 10173, rule II, §5 (2016).
883. *See* National Privacy Commission, Disclosure of Criminal History, Advisory Opinion No. 024, Series of 2019 (7 May 2019).
884. National Privacy Commission, Rules and Regulations Implementing the Data Privacy Act of 2012, Republic Act No. 10173, rule I, §7(b) (2016). Emphasis supplied.
885. National Privacy Commission, Disclosure of Criminal History, Advisory Opinion No. 024, Series of 2019 (7 May 2019). Emphasis supplied.

478. While the DPA requires journalists acting as PICs or PIPs to comply with its obligations, it also affords them protection from any compulsion to reveal their sources:

> Section 5. *Protection Afforded to Journalists and Their Sources.* Nothing in this Act shall be construed as to have amended or repealed the provisions of Republic Act No. 53, which affords the publishers, editors or duly accredited reporters of any newspaper, magazine or periodical of general circulation protection from being compelled to reveal the source of any news report or information appearing in said publication which was related in any confidence to such publisher, editor, or reporter.[886]

479. Republic Act No. 53 states that journalists and their publishers and editors cannot be compelled to reveal their sources.[887] The protection, however, is not absolute since they can be compelled when the revelation is demanded by the Legislative or Judiciary branch in the interest of the State.[888]

886. An Act Protecting Individual Personal Information in Information and Communications Systems in the Government and the Private Sector, Creating for this purpose a National Privacy Commission, and For Other Purposes [Data Privacy Act of 2012], Republic Act No. 10173 §5 (2012). Emphasis supplied.

887. Section 1. The publisher, editor or duly accredited reporter of any newspaper, magazine or periodical of general circulation cannot be compelled to reveal the source of any news-report or information appearing in said publication which was related in confidence to such publisher, editor or reporter, unless the court or a House or committee of Congress finds that such revelation is demanded by the interest of the State.

An Act to Exempt the Publisher, Editor or Reporter of Any Publication from Revealing the Source of Published News or Information Obtained in Confidence, *Republic Act No. 53*, §1 (1946).

888. *Ibid.*

Chapter 2. Processing of Personal Information Versus Public Access to Official Documents

480. In 2016, the President issued Executive Order No. 2, Series of 2016, on the Freedom of Information (FOI), which is a government mechanism for transparency and full public disclosure of information in the public service:[889]

> Section 3. *Access to information.* Every Filipino shall have access to information, official records, public records and to documents and papers pertaining to official acts, transactions or decisions, as well as to government research data used as basis for policy development.[890]

481. Through the FOI, Filipinos may request from government offices under the Executive Branch information on government transactions and operations, including official records, public records, documents and papers pertaining to official acts, transactions, or decisions, and government research data used as a basis for policy development:[891]

> Section 2. *Coverage.* This order shall cover all government offices under the Executive Branch, including but not limited to the national government and all its offices, departments, bureaus, offices, and instrumentalities, including government-owned or -controlled corporations, and state universities and colleges. Local government units (LGUs) are encouraged to observe and be guided by this Order.[892]

482. It, however, does not allow unlimited access to information, public records, and official records:

> Section 7. Protection of Privacy. While providing access to information, public records, and official records, *responsible officials shall afford full protection to the right to privacy of the individual* as follows:
>
> 1. Each government office per Section 2 hereof shall ensure that personal information in its custody or under its control is disclosed or released only if it is material or relevant to the subject-matter of the request and its disclosure is permissible under this order or existing law, rules or regulations;

---

889. Republic of the Philippines, Frequently Asked Questions on Freedom of Information, *available at* https://www.foi.gov.ph/help (last accessed 25 Apr. 2022).
890. Office of the President, Operationalizing in the Executive Branch the People's Constitutional Right to Information and the State Policies to Full Public Disclosure and Transparency in the Public Service and Providing Guidelines Therefor, Executive Order No. 2, Series of 2016, §3 (23 Jul. 2016).
891. Republic of the Philippines, Frequently Asked Questions on Freedom of Information, *available at* https://www.foi.gov.ph/help (last accessed 25 Apr. 2022).
892. Office of the President, Operationalizing in the Executive Branch the People's Constitutional Right to Information and the State Policies to Full Public Disclosure and Transparency in the Public Service and Providing Guidelines Therefor, Executive Order No. 2, Series of 2016, §2 (23 Jul. 2016).

2. Each government office must protect personal information in its custody or control by making reasonable security arrangements against leaks or premature disclosure of personal information which unduly exposes the individual whose personal information is requested, to vilification, harassment or any other wrongful acts.
3. Any employee, official or director of a government office per Section 2 hereof who has access, authorized or unauthorized, to personal information in the custody of the office, must not disclose that information except when authorized under this order or pursuant to existing laws, rules or regulation.[893]

483. The FOI should be understood in relation to the scope of the DPA. The IRR provides that the non-applicability of the DPA to the following pieces of information of public concern is 'only to the minimum extent of … processing necessary to the purpose, function, or activity concerned':

> Section 5. Special Cases. The Act and these Rules shall not apply to the following specified information, *only to the minimum extent of collection, access, use, disclosure or other processing necessary to the purpose, function, or activity concerned*:
>
> a. Information processed for purpose of allowing public access to information that fall within matters of public concern, pertaining to:
>   1. Information about any individual who is or was an officer or employee of government that relates to his or her position or functions, including:
>   (a) The fact that the individual is or was an officer or employee of the government;
>   (b) The title, office address, and office telephone number of the individual
>   (c) The classification, salary range, and responsibilities of the position held by the individual; and
>   (d) The name of the individual on a document he or she prepared in the course of his or her employment with the government;
>   2. Information about an individual who is or was performing a service under contract for a government institution, but only in so far as it relates to such service, including the name of the individual and the terms of his or her contract;
>   3. Information relating to a benefit of a financial nature conferred on an individual upon the discretion of the government, such as the granting of a license or permit, including the name of the individual and

893. *Ibid.*, §7. Emphasis supplied.

the exact nature of the benefit: Provided, that they do not include benefits given in the course of an ordinary transaction or as a matter of right[.][894]

484. The Commission issued several Advisories on the processing of personal information of public officers while upholding the freedom to access information, public records, and official records under FOI.

485. Advisory No. 2022-01 provides guidelines on requests for personal data of public officers, including individuals performing contractual services for the government:[895]

> Section 4. *Fair and lawful disclosure.* Government agencies shall process various documents which pertain to, and contain personal data of, public officers pursuant to constitutional, statutory, or contractual requirements.
>
> *The access to, or disclosure of, these documents may be regulated, notwithstanding their nature as a public record or public document.* Each government agency shall provide for certain rules or a set of criteria against which a request for such documents shall be evaluated based on the mandate or public service performed and its relevance to the requesting party.[896]

486. As the PIC, the government agency from whom the information or document is requested has to comply with the following obligations:

> Section 5. *Obligations of government agencies as personal information controllers.* Government agencies are considered as personal information controllers (PICs) who exercise control over the processing of personal data.
>
> (1) As PICs, they are required to comply with the provisions of the DPA, its IRR, and issuances of the National Privacy Commission (NPC), specifically adherence to the principles of transparency, legitimate purpose, and proportionality; implement reasonable and appropriate organizational, physical, and technical security measures for the protection of personal data; and uphold the rights of their employees as data subjects.
> (2) Every government agency is responsible for personal data under its control or custody, including personal data that have been transferred to a third party for processing.
> (3) All personal data maintained by the government, its agencies and instrumentalities shall be secured, as far as practicable, with the use of the most reasonable and appropriate standards, taking into account the provisions of

894. National Privacy Commission, Rules and Regulations Implementing the Data Privacy Act of 2012, Republic Act No. 10173, rule I, §5(b) (2016). Emphasis supplied.
895. National Privacy Commission, Guidelines on Requests for Personal Data of Public Officers, Advisory No. 01, Series of 2022 [NPC Advisory No. 22-01], §1 (4 Feb. 2022).
896. *Ibid.*, §4. Emphasis supplied.

NPC Circular No. 16-01 (Security of Personal Data in Government Agencies) and other applicable NPC issuances as may hereafter be issued.[897]

487. The government agency is not mandated to grant all requests for information and documents.[898] The requested information must be a matter of public concern or interest and relevant to the subject matter of the request.[899] The disclosure must not be prohibited by law or regulation and must be in line with the general privacy principles.[900] Section 6 provides:

> Section 6. *Access to information on matters of public concern.* In line with the mandate and thrust for open government, public disclosure, and transparency of government information, personal data may be disclosed to the extent that the requested information is shown to be a matter of public concern or interest: provided, that the information is relevant to the subject matter of the request and disclosure is not prohibited by any law or regulation. Any disclosure of personal data shall be in accordance with the general privacy principles of transparency, legitimate purpose, and proportionality.[901]

488. If the disclosure of the requested information or document is not required by law or regulation, then the public officer to whom the information or document relates to may consent to the disclosure of his personal data:

> Section 9. *Consent of Public Officers.* If the requested document or information specifically relates to the personal data of a public officer, but existing laws or regulations do not require disclosure, the public officer may nevertheless consent to the disclosure of his or her personal data: provided, that consent shall be strictly construed in favor of the data subject:
>
> 1. The government agency has the responsibility to adequately demonstrate that the consent obtained was indeed freely given, informed, specific, indication of will of the public officer; and
> 2. The government agency shall be accountable for the consent mechanisms it has implemented. It shall keep records of consent forms or its equivalent, showing how and when consent was obtained, and the information provided to the public officer at the time the consent was obtained.
>
> Notwithstanding the foregoing, the public officer may nevertheless disclose or release his or her own personal data directly to the requesting party without any intervention from the government agency.[902]

897. *Ibid.*, §5.
898. *See ibid.*
899. *Ibid.*
900. *Ibid.*
901. *Ibid.*
902. *Ibid.*, §9.

489. The Commission also issued an Advisory specific to the Access to Personal Data Sheets[903] of Government Personnel.[904] Advisory No. 2017-02 provides that:

> *[A]ccess to our disclosure of the PDS of a particular government personnel may be regulated despite its nature as a public record and/or public document.* Each government agency or office, acting as its proper custodian, may provide for certain rules or a set criteria against which a request for such document shall be measured or assessed.[905]

490. In recognizing the need to balance the public's right to information with an individual's right to privacy, the Commission advises that government agencies consider the following:

> Thus, when resolving a pending request for access to a PDS, a government agency or office must consider the following:
>
> 1. The information requested falls under matters of public concern
> 2. The individual requesting for personal data has declared and specified the purpose of his or her request
> 3. The declared and specified purpose is not contrary to law, morals, and public policy and
> 4. The personal data requested to the declared, specified, and legitimate purpose.
>
> At the same time, the requesting party is obliged to use the data obtained only for the purpose declared at the time of making the request. The individual must also commit to complying with the provisions of the DPA.
>
> Suffice to say, each request should be evaluated in relation to its declared purpose. In all cases, the rights of the data subject should be respected, including the right to be informed and notified about the processing of his or her personal data.[906]

---

903. A PDS is an official document that the Civil Service Commission (CSC) requires each government employee or official to accomplish prior to his or her assumption of office. It is a repository of information pertaining to that employee or official, including his or her personal background, qualifications, and eligibility. National Privacy Commission, Access to Personal Data Sheets of Government Personnel, Advisory No. 02, Series of 2017 [NPC Advisory No. 17-02], at 4 (3 Apr. 2017).
904. National Privacy Commission, Guidelines on Requests for Personal Data of Public Officers, Advisory No. 01, Series of 2022 [NPC Advisory No. 22-01], §9 (4 Feb. 2022).
905. National Privacy Commission, Access to Personal Data Sheets of Government Personnel, Advisory No. 02, Series of 2017 [NPC Advisory No. 17-02], at 4 (3 Apr. 2017). Emphasis supplied.
906. *Ibid.*, at 5.

Chapter 3. Processing of the National Identification Number

491. The Philippine Identification System Act established the 'Philippine Identification System' (PhilSys), a central national identification system for Filipino citizens and residents.[907] It applies to:

> [A]ll natural persons in all transactions where the PhilSys Number, Philippine Identification (PhilID), or biometric information is required, presented, or used, whether legally or illegally, within or outside the Republic of the Philippines.[908]

492. Each Filipino citizen or resident, upon birth or registration by the Philippine Statistics Authority (PSA), shall be given a PhilSys Number (PSN) or a randomly generated, unique, and permanent identification number.[909] It shall serve as 'the standard number for the individual across all agencies of the government' and 'accepted as sufficient proof of identity'.[910]

493. The PSN and other information collected from all persons registered in the PhilSys shall be stored in the PhilSys Registry.[911] The information collected includes:

> Section 8. *PhilSys Registry Data.* Information to be collected and stored under the PhilSys shall be limited to the following:
>
> (a) Demographic Data
> (1) Full Name;
> (2) Sex;
> (3) Date of Birth;
> (4) Place of Birth;
> (5) Blood Type;
> (6) Address;
> (7) Filipino or Resident Alien;
> (8) Marital Status (optional);
> (9) Mobile Number (optional); and
> (10) E-mail address (optional).
>
> (b) Biometrics Information
> (1) Front-Facing Photograph
> (2) Full set of fingerprints;
> (3) Iris scan; and

907. An Act Establishing the Philippine Identification System [Philippine Identification System Act], Republic Act No. 11055, §2 (2018).
908. *Ibid.*, §4.
909. *Ibid.*
910. *Ibid.*, §7(a).
911. *Ibid.*, §7(b).

(4) If necessary, other identifiable features of an individual as may be determined in the implementing rules and regulations (IRR).[912]

494. The IRR, which was approved and signed on 5 October 2018, adds 'permanent address' and 'present address (optional)' to the list.[913]

495. The PSA is the government agency entrusted to implement the provisions of the PhilSys Act.[914] As such, it 'must ensure that information in the PhilSys is used only in accordance with the intended purpose[915] as set forth in [the PhilSys Act]'.[916]

496. The PhilSys Act also introduces safeguards that echo the principles in the DPA. Section 17 of the PhilSys Act provides privacy measures for the protection against unlawful disclosure of information/records:

> Section 17. *Protection against Unlawful Disclosure of Information/Records.* No person may disclose, collect, record, convey, disseminate, publish, or use any information of registered persons with the PhilSys, give access thereto or give copies thereof to third parties or entities, including law enforcement agencies, national security agencies, or units of the Armed Forces of the Philippines (AFP), except in the following circumstances:
>
> (a) When the registered person has given his or her consent, specific to the purpose prior to the processing; and
> (b) When the compelling interest of public health or safety so requires, relevant information may be disclosed upon order of a competent court, provided that the risk of significant harm to the public is established and the owner of the information is notified within seventy-two (72) hours of the fact of such disclosure.
>
> Information disclosed shall not be used except for the specific purpose for which it was authorized and shall not be divulged by any person to any third party other than the person so authorized.
>
> PSA must ensure that information in the PhilSys is used only in accordance with its intended purpose as set forth in this Act.
>
> Any information obtained as a result of unlawful disclosure under this Act shall be inadmissible in any judicial, quasi-judicial or administrative proceedings.

912. *Ibid.*, §8.
913. Philippine Statistics Authority, Rules and Regulations Implementing the Philippine Identification System Act, Republic Act No. 11055, rule II, 7 (2018).
914. An Act Establishing the Philippine Identification System [Philippine Identification System Act], Republic Act No. 11055, §15 (2018).
915. *See ibid.*, §3.
916. *Ibid.*, §17.

Registered persons may request the PSA to provide access to his or her registered information and record history subject to the guidelines and regulations to be issued by the PSA.[917]

497. In addition to the foregoing protective measures, the PhilSys Act also mandates the implementation of security measures:

> Section 18. *Safeguards on the Philippine Identification System (PhilSys).* The PSA with the technical assistance of the DICT *shall implement reasonable and appropriate organizational, technical, and physical security measures to ensure that the information gathered for the PhilSys, including information stored in the PhilSys Registry*, is protected from unauthorized access, use, disclosure, and against accidental or intentional loss, destruction, or damage. Moreover, *PSA shall ensure that individuals are adequately informed upon registration for PhilSys on how their data will be used and how they can access their registered information and record history.*[918]

498. The IRR of the PhilSys Act further provides for the designation of a DPO for the PhilSys:

> Section 22. *Privacy, Security, and Safeguards on the Philippine Identification System (PhilSys).*
>
> . . .
>
> The PSA shall designate a separate Data Protection Officer for the PhilSys. The PSA shall ensure that applicants are adequately informed upon registration in the PhilSys on how their data will be used and how they can access their registered information and record history. All applicable rights of the registered person shall be upheld.
>
> To ensure the PhilSys is used appropriately and exclusively for its specified purpose, it shall not process personal information and any data from external systems and databases.[919]

917. *Ibid.*
918. *Ibid.*, §18. Emphasis supplied.
919. Philippine Statistics Authority, Rules and Regulations Implementing the Philippine Identification System Act, Republic Act No. 11055, rule V, 22 (2018).

Chapter 4. Processing in the Context of Employment

499. The Commission has not issued any Advisories or Circulars specific to the processing in the context of employment.

500. The DPA and other privacy regulations apply to the processing of personal and sensitive personal information, including processing in the context of employment.[920] Thus, employers processing the personal information of an individual must comply with the provisions of the DPA:

> They are bound to uphold the rights of data subjects, adhere to general data privacy principles of transparency, legitimate purpose and proportionality, and the requirements of lawful processing. They must ensure that data subjects are aware of the nature, purpose, and extent of the processing of their personal data, including the risks and safeguards involved, the identity of personal information controller, their rights as a data subject, and how these may be exercised. Furthermore, they must also provide easy access to information and communication relating to the processing of personal data.[921]

501. When processing personal and sensitive personal information in the context of employment, employers, as PICs, may rely on the criteria for lawful processing under sections 12 and 13 of the DPA.[922] In relation to this, employers shall ensure that the processing complies with the general privacy principles of transparency, legitimate purpose, and proportionality.[923]

502. In several Advisory Opinions, the Commission opined that the employer, as PIC, may collect relevant personal information from their employees for specific purposes:

> An [E]mployee 201 [F]ile, usually containing records pertaining to the employee's personal information, employment contract, duties, salary, performance and employment history, among others, is established and maintained by an employer for specific purposes relating to the employee's employment, i.e. payroll, training and development, performance evaluation, promotion, etc. As this file is compiled and in part, created by and held under the custody of

920. *See* An Act Protecting Individual Personal Information in Information and Communications Systems in the Government and the Private Sector, Creating for this purpose a National Privacy Commission, and For Other Purposes [Data Privacy Act of 2012], Republic Act No. 10173 §4 (2012).
921. National Privacy Commission, Ownership of 201 Files, Advisory Opinion No. 028, Series of 2018 (16 May 2018).
922. *See* An Act Protecting Individual Personal Information in Information and Communications Systems in the Government and the Private Sector, Creating for this purpose a National Privacy Commission, and For Other Purposes [Data Privacy Act of 2012], Republic Act No. 10173 §§12 and 13 (2012).
923. *See ibid.*, Republic Act No. 10173 §11 (2012).

> the company, such files may be considered company property and acquiring a copy thereof may still be governed by certain company rules and regulations.[924]
>
> Upon cessation of employment, the employer may retain the records and files of the employee in accordance with the retention period as may be provided for by existing laws on the matter and/or as stated in its policies.[925]

503. At the same time, employees do not lose their privacy rights in the workplace:

> The DPA does not prevent employers from collecting, maintaining, and using employment records. However, employers should also strive to strike a balance between the need to keep records of their employees and the employees' right to access their personal data. Section 16(c) provides for the right of data subjects to reasonable access to the following: (1) Contents of his or her personal information that were processed; (2) Sources from which personal information were obtained; (3) Names and addresses of recipients of the personal information; (4) Manner by which such data were processed; (5) Reasons for the disclosure of the personal information to recipients; (6) Information on automated processes where the data will or likely to be made as the sole basis for any decision significantly affecting or will affect the data subject; (7) Date when his or her personal information concerning the data subject were last accessed and modified; and (8) The designation, or name or identity and address of the personal information controller.[926]

504. Pursuant to their rights as data subjects, employees may exercise the right to access their own personal information, '[e]specially those they have personally provided the employer during the recruitment and application process'.[927]

505. Employees, however, must still comply with reasonable company protocols when exercising the right to access:

> Accordingly, Employee A, being a data subject, is entitled to have reasonable access to the personal information in her 201 file. She may exercise her right to access in the manner provided under the DPA but she must still abide by company protocols in accessing her 201 file.[928]

---

924. National Privacy Commission, Ownership of 201 Files, Advisory Opinion No. 028, Series of 2018 (16 May 2018).
925. National Privacy Commission, Employee's Right to Access Employment Records, Advisory Opinion No. 042, Series of 2018 (7 Aug. 2018).
926. *Ibid.*, Advisory Opinion No. 051, Series of 2018 (5 Aug. 2018).
927. National Privacy Commission, Employee's Right to Access Employment Records, Advisory Opinion No. 042, Series of 2018 (7 Aug. 2018).
928. National Privacy Commission, Ownership of 201 Files, Advisory Opinion No. 028, Series of 2018 (16 May 2018).

Chapter 5. Processing for Scientific Research, Public Archiving, and Statistical Purposes

506. The DPA does not apply to the processing of personal or sensitive personal information for research purposes:

> Section 4. *Scope.* This Act applies to the processing of all types of personal information and to any natural and juridical person involved in personal information processing including those personal information controllers and processors who, although not found or established in the Philippines, use equipment that are located in the Philippines, or those who maintain an office, branch or agency in the Philippines subject to the immediately succeeding paragraph: Provided, That the requirements of Section 5 are complied with.

507. This Act does not apply to the following:

> . . .
>
> (d). Personal information processed for journalistic, artistic, literary or research purposes[.][929]

508. The IRR elucidates that the exclusion is limited to the personal information to be processed and not to the PIC or PIP undertaking the processing and, even then, only the minimum extent of processing necessary to achieve the specific purpose, function, or activity:

> Section 5. Special Cases. The Act and these Rules shall not apply to the following specified information, *only to the minimum extent of collection, access, use, disclosure or other processing necessary to the purpose, function, or activity concerned*:
>
> . . .
>
> c. Personal information that will be processed for research purpose, intended for a public benefit, subject to the requirements of applicable laws, regulations, or ethical standards[.][930]

509. Thus, it remains incumbent upon the PIC or PIP to ensure that the appropriate security measures are in place to protect the personal data being processed for such purposes and to adhere to the general privacy principles and other DPA provisions.[931]

---

929. An Act Protecting Individual Personal Information in Information and Communications Systems in the Government and the Private Sector, Creating for this purpose a National Privacy Commission, and For Other Purposes [Data Privacy Act of 2012], Republic Act No. 10173 §4(d) (2012).
930. National Privacy Commission, Rules and Regulations Implementing the Data Privacy Act of 2012, Republic Act No. 10173, rule I, §5(c) (2016). Emphasis supplied.
931. National Privacy Commission, Research and the Data Privacy Act of 2012, Advisory Opinion No. 017, Series of 2019 (5 Mar. 2019).

510. The PIC or PIP shall also uphold the rights of data subjects. The data subject has the right to be informed if his or her personal or sensitive personal information will be used for historical, statistical, or scientific purposes:

> Section 34. *Rights of the Data Subject.* The data subject is entitled to the following rights:
>
> a. Right to be informed.
>
> . . .
>
> 2. The data subject shall be notified and furnished with information indicated hereunder before the entry of his or her personal data into the processing system of the personal information controller, or at the next practical opportunity:
>   (a) Description of the personal data to be entered into the system;
>   (b) Purposes for which they are being or will be processed, including processing for direct marketing, profiling or historical, statistical or scientific purpose[.][932]

511. If, however, the processed personal information will only be used for research and no activities are carried out, nor decisions are taken regarding the data subject, then the PIC or PIP need not comply with the requirements provided under the rights of the data subject. Section 19 of the DPA provides:

> Section 19. Non-Applicability. *The immediately preceding sections*[933] *are not applicable if the processed personal information are used only for the needs of scientific and statistical research and, on the basis of such, no activities are carried out and no decisions are taken regarding the data subject: Provided, That the personal information shall be held under strict confidentiality and shall be used only for the declared purpose.* Likewise, the immediately preceding sections are not applicable to processing of personal information gathered for the purpose of investigations in relation to any criminal, administrative or tax liabilities of a data subject.[934]

512. Section 37 of the IRR likewise provides:

> Section 37. *Limitation on Rights.* The immediately preceding sections shall not be applicable if the processed personal data are used only for the needs of scientific and statistical research and, on the basis of such, no activities are carried out and no decisions are taken regarding the data subject: Provided, that

932. National Privacy Commission, Rules and Regulations Implementing the Data Privacy Act of 2012, Republic Act No. 10173, rule VIII, §34(b) (2016).
933. *See* An Act Protecting Individual Personal Information in Information and Communications Systems in the Government and the Private Sector, Creating for this purpose a National Privacy Commission, and For Other Purposes [Data Privacy Act of 2012], Republic Act No. 10173 §§16, 17, and 18 (2012).
934. *Ibid.*, Republic Act No. 10173 §19 (2012). Emphasis supplied.

the personal data shall be held under strict confidentiality and shall be used only for the declared purpose. The said sections are also not applicable to the processing of personal data gathered for the purpose of investigations in relation to any criminal, administrative or tax liabilities of a data subject. Any limitations on the rights of the data subject shall only be to the minimum extent necessary to achieve the purpose of said research or investigation.[935]

513. Personal or sensitive personal information that is further processed for historical, statistical, or scientific purposes may be stored for longer periods.[936] If the information is anonymized or aggregated, then it may be kept longer than necessary for the declared purpose.[937] Section 19 of the IRR provides:

> Section 19. *General principles in collection, processing and retention.* The processing of personal data shall adhere to the following general principles in the collection, processing, and retention of personal data:
>
> . . .
>
> e. Any authorized further processing shall have adequate safeguards.
> 1. Personal data originally collected for a declared, specified, or legitimate purpose may be processed further for historical, statistical, or scientific purposes, and, in cases laid down in law, may be stored for longer periods, subject to implementation of the appropriate organizational, physical, and technical security measures required by the Act in order to safeguard the rights and freedoms of the data subject.
> 2. Personal data which is aggregated or kept in a form which does not permit identification of data subjects may be kept longer than necessary for the declared, specified, and legitimate purpose.[938]

514. If the personal or sensitive personal information is anonymized or aggregated into statistical data where the data subject can no longer be identified, then such is not considered as personal or sensitive personal information.[939] In an Advisory Opinion, the Commission opined:

> We understand that [the PIC's] cloud portal will be used to aggregate and generate reports on the anonymized data collected by the census application. As such, the data that will be processed will be de-identified. Thus, what was previously considered personal and sensitive personal information (collectively,

935. National Privacy Commission, Rules and Regulations Implementing the Data Privacy Act of 2012, Republic Act No. 10173, rule VIII, §37 (2016).
936. National Privacy Commission, Rules and Regulations Implementing the Data Privacy Act of 2012, Republic Act No. 10173, rule IV, §19(e)(1) (2016).
937. *Ibid.*, §19(e)(2).
938. *Ibid.*, §19(e).
939. National Privacy Commission, Collection and Use of Patient Case Number and Appointment of Compliance Officer for Privacy, Advisory Opinion No. 036, Series of 2019 (3 Jul. 2019).

personal data) will be rendered anonymous. Therefore, as previously mentioned, these statistical, aggregate, and de-identified datasets are no longer personal information as defined in the DPA, hence, outside the scope of the law.[940]

515. The personal or sensitive personal information, however, should be truly anonymized. The PIC or PIP should have no access to the original data set even after the anonymization process:

> While the [Electronic Medical Records (EMR)] provider claims that only anonymized information will be accessed, they should clarify the anonymization process. If before, during, and even after the anonymization process, the EMR provider will have direct access to the original data set that still contains personal data, then the said processing will not be exempt from provisions of DPA and its implementing rules and regulations, considering that at any given time, the EMR provider may connect the relevant data sets.[941]

940. *Ibid.*
941. National Privacy Commission, Processing of Anonymized Personal Data By Electronic Medical Records Provider, Advisory Opinion No. 068, Series of 2018 (20 Nov. 2018).

Part X. Specific Data Protection Regimes

Chapter 1. Obligations of Professional Secrecy

516. The DPA defines privileged information as:

> Section 3. *Definition of Terms.* Whenever used in this Act, the following terms shall have the respective meanings hereafter set forth:
>
> . . .
>
> (k) *Privileged information* refers to *any and all forms of data which under the Rules of Court and other pertinent laws constitute privileged communication.*[942]

517. As discussed in Part II, the Rules of Court governs 'the protection and enforcement of constitutional rights, pleading, practice, and procedure in all courts'.[943]

518. Section 24 of Rule 130 of the Rules of Court elucidates on the concept of privileged information on the basis of professional secrecy. The following kinds of communication are deemed privileged since these concern matters learned in confidence by reason of professional secrecy.[944] As such, these are inadmissible as testimony.[945]

> Section 24. *Disqualification by reason of privileged communications.* – The following persons cannot testify as to matters learned in confidence in the following cases:
>
> . . .
>
> (b) An attorney or person reasonably believed by the client to be licensed to engage in the practice of law cannot, without the consent of the client, be examined as to any communication made by the client to him or her, or his

942. An Act Protecting Individual Personal Information in Information and Communications Systems in the Government and the Private Sector, Creating for this purpose a National Privacy Commission, and For Other Purposes [Data Privacy Act of 2012], Republic Act No. 10173 §3(k) (2012). Emphasis supplied.
943. PHIL. CONST. art. VIII, §5(5).
944. *Ibid.*
945. *Ibid.*

or her advice given thereon in the course of, or with a view to, professional employment, nor can an attorney's secretary, stenographer, or clerk, or other persons assisting the attorney be examined, without the consent of the client and his or her employer, concerning any fact the knowledge of which has been acquired in such capacity, except in the following cases:

(i) *Furtherance of crime or fraud.* If the services or advice of the lawyer were sought or obtained to enable or aid anyone to commit or plan to commit what the client knew or reasonably should have known to be a crime or fraud;

(ii) *Claimants through same deceased client.* As to a communication relevant to an issue between parties who claim through the same deceased client, regardless of whether the claims are by testate or intestate or by *inter vivos* transaction;

(iii) *Breach of duty by lawyer or client.* As to a communication relevant to an issue of breach of duty by the lawyer to his or her client, or by the client to his or her lawyer;

(iv) *Document attested by the lawyer.* As to a communication relevant to an issue concerning an attested document to which the lawyer is an attesting witness; or

(v) *Joint clients.* As to a communication relevant to a matter of common interest between two [(2)] or more clients if the communication was made by any of them to a lawyer retained or consulted in common, when offered in an action between any of the clients, unless they have expressly agreed otherwise.

(c) A physician, psychotherapist or person reasonably believed by the patient to be authorized to practice medicine or psychotherapy cannot in a civil case, without the consent of the patient, be examined as to any confidential communication made for the purpose of diagnosis or treatment of the patient's physical, mental or emotional condition, including alcohol or drug addiction, between the patient and his or her physician or psychotherapist. This privilege also applies to persons, including members of the patient's family, who have participated in the diagnosis or treatment of the patient under the direction of the physician or psychotherapist.

A 'psychotherapist' is:

(a) A person licensed to practice medicine engaged in the diagnosis or treatment of a mental or emotional condition, or

(b) A person licensed as a psychologist by the government while similarly engaged.

(d) A minister, priest or person reasonably believed to be so cannot, without the consent of the affected person, be examined as to any communication or confession made to or any advice given by him or her, in his or her professional character, in the course of discipline enjoined by the church to which the minister or priest belongs.

(e) A public officer cannot be examined during or after his or her tenure as to communications made to him or her in official confidence, when the court finds that the public interest would suffer by the disclosure.

The communication shall remain privileged, even in the hands of a third person who may have obtained the information, provided that the original parties to the communication took reasonable precaution to protect its confidentiality. (24a)[946]

519. As provided in the Rules of Court, the obligations of professional secrecy are as follows:

(a) Attorney-Client Privilege
(b) Physician-Patient Privilege
(c) Priest-Penitent Privilege
(d) Privileged Communication to Public Officers in the Exercise of their Duties.[947]

§1. Attorney-Client Privilege

520. Communications between a client and an attorney or persons reasonably believed by the client to be licensed as such shall remain privileged unless the client consents otherwise.[948] The privilege covers communication made by the client to the attorney or the advice of the attorney given in the course of, or with a view to, professional engagement.[949] Thus, communications for the purpose of securing the attorney's services, even if the attorney declines the engagement, are covered by the privilege.[950]

521. The privilege extends to the attorney's secretary, stenographer, clerk, or other persons assisting the attorney.[951] In such cases, both the consent of the client and the employer is necessary before such persons may testify.[952]

522. The privilege has several exceptions:

Section 24. *Disqualification by reason of privileged communications.* The following persons cannot testify as to matters learned in confidence in the following cases:

. . .

946. *Ibid.*
947. *Ibid.*
948. *Ibid.*, §4(b) (1 May 2020).
949. *Ibid.*
950. *Ibid.*
951. *Ibid.*
952. *Ibid.*

(i) Furtherance of crime or fraud. If the services or advice of the lawyer were sought or obtained to enable or aid anyone to commit or plan to commit what the client knew or reasonably should have known to be a crime or fraud;

(ii) Claimants through same deceased client. As to a communication relevant to an issue between parties who claim through the same deceased client, regardless of whether the claims are by testate or intestate or by inter vivos transaction;

(iii) Breach of duty by lawyer or client. As to a communication relevant to an issue of breach of duty by the lawyer to his or her client, or by the client to his or her lawyer;

(iv) Document attested by the lawyer. As to a communication relevant to an issue concerning an attested document to which the lawyer is an attesting witness; or

(v) Joint clients. As to a communication relevant to a matter of common interest between two (2) or more clients if the communication was made by any of them to a lawyer retained or consulted in common, when offered in an action between any of the clients, unless they have expressly agreed otherwise.[953]

523. An attorney is also bound to uphold the trust and confidence that he or she owes to his or her client. Canon 21 of the Code of Professional Responsibility provides:

> CANON 21 - A LAWYER SHALL PRESERVE THE CONFIDENCE AND SECRETS OF HIS CLIENT EVEN AFTER THE ATTORNEY-CLIENT RELATION IS TERMINATED.
>
> Rule 21.01. A lawyer shall not reveal the confidences or secrets of his client except;
>
> (a) When authorized by the client after acquainting him of the consequences of the disclosure;
> (b) When required by law;
> (c) When necessary to collect his fees or to defend himself, his employees or associates or by judicial action.
>
> Rule 21.02 - A lawyer shall not, to the disadvantage of his client, use information acquired in the course of employment, nor shall he use the same to his own advantage or that of a third person, unless the client with full knowledge of the circumstances consents thereto.
> Rule 21.03 - A lawyer shall not, without the written consent of his client, give information from his files to an outside agency seeking such information for auditing, statistical, bookkeeping, accounting, data processing, or any similar purpose.

953. *Ibid.*, §4.

Rule 21.04 - A lawyer may disclose the affairs of a client of the firm to partners or associates thereof unless prohibited by the client.
Rule 21.05 - A lawyer shall adopt such measures as may be required to prevent those whose services are utilized by him, from disclosing or using confidences or secrets of the clients.
Rule 21.06 - A lawyer shall avoid indiscreet conversation about a client's affairs even with members of his family.
Rule 21.07 - A lawyer shall not reveal that he has been consulted about a particular case except to avoid possible conflict of interest.[954]

§2. Physician-Patient Privilege

524. Communications between the patient and a physician, psychotherapist, or person reasonably believed by the patient to be authorized to practice medicine or psychotherapy shall remain privileged when the following requisites concur: (1) the patient did not consent to the disclosure; (2) the communication was for the purpose of diagnosis or treatment of the patient's physical, medical, or emotional condition, including alcohol or drug addiction; (3) and the case involved is a civil case.[955] Further, the privilege 'also applies to persons, including members of the patient's family, who have participated in the diagnosis or treatment of the patient under the direction of the physician or psychotherapist'.[956]

§3. Priest-Penitent Privilege

525. Communications between a minister, priest, or person reasonably believed to be so and the penitent concerned shall remain privileged unless the latter consents otherwise.[957] The communication pertains to communication or confession made to or any advice given by the minister or priest in his or her professional capacity and in the course of the discipline enjoined by the church he or she belongs to.[958]

§4. Privileged Communication to Public Officers in the Exercise of Their Duties

526. Communications made to a public officer in the exercise of his or her duty or in his or her official capacity shall remain privileged when the court determines

954. Code of Professional Responsibility, Canon 21. (21 Jun. 1988).
955. 2019 Amendment to the 1989 Revised Rules on Evidence, A.M. No. 19-08-15-SC, Rule 130, §4(c) (1 May 2020).
956. *Ibid.*
957. *Ibid.*, §4(d) (1 May 2020).
958. *Ibid.*

that the disclosure will affect the public interest.[959] It is the court, and not the public officer, who determines the privileged nature of the communication, and its privileged nature may be invoked even after the tenure of the public officer.[960]

959. *Ibid*, §4(e).
960. *Ibid*.

Chapter 2. Law Enforcement Agencies

527. The personal information and sensitive personal information processed by law enforcement agencies are outside the scope of the DPA:

> Section 4. *Scope.* This Act applies to the processing of all types of personal information and to any natural and juridical person involved in personal information processing including those personal information controllers and processors who, although not found or established in the Philippines, use equipment that are located in the Philippines, or those who maintain an office, branch or agency in the Philippines subject to the immediately succeeding paragraph: Provided, That the requirements of Section 5 are complied with.
>
> This Act does not apply to the following:
>
> . . .
>
> (b) Information necessary in order to carry out the functions of public authority which includes the processing of personal data for the performance by the independent, central monetary authority and *law enforcement and regulatory agencies of their constitutionally and statutorily mandated functions.* Nothing in this Act shall be construed as to have amended or repealed Republic Act No. 1405, otherwise known as the Secrecy of Bank Deposits Act; Republic Act No. 6426, otherwise known as the Foreign Currency Deposit Act; and Republic Act No. 9510, otherwise known as the Credit Information System Act (CISA)[.][961]

528. Thus, disclosure of personal information or sensitive personal information to a law enforcement authority may be permitted if it is in line with the law enforcement authority's mandate to investigate and prevent crimes:

> In the same manner, police officers' act of gathering data is allowed in accordance with Section 24 of the Republic Act No. 69754, which states that the powers and functions of the PNP include, among others, to: 1. Enforce all laws and ordinances relative to the protection of lives and properties; 2. Maintain peace and order and take all necessary steps to ensure public safety; 3. Investigate and prevent crimes, effect the arrest of criminal offenders, bring offenders to justice and assist in their prosecution; and 4. Exercise the general powers to make arrest, search and seizure in accordance with the Constitution and pertinent laws.[962]

---

961. An Act Protecting Individual Personal Information in Information and Communications Systems in the Government and the Private Sector, Creating for this purpose a National Privacy Commission, and For Other Purposes [Data Privacy Act of 2012], Republic Act No. 10173 §4(e) (2012). Emphasis supplied.
962. National Privacy Commission, Re: Reporting of Alleged Criminals' Personal Data, Advisory Opinion No. 014, Series of 2018 (4 May 2018).

529. The disclosure must also be according to existing standard operating procedures of the law enforcement authority:

> Thus, the disclosure of personal information of patients to law enforcement officers may be allowed under the DPA when it is pursuant to its mandate to investigate and prevent crimes, and *strictly following the existing standard operating procedures in the conduct of an investigation and law enforcement operation as stated in the Revised PNP Operational Procedures, and other pertinent laws, rules, and regulations governing the same (i.e. criminal procedures on search and seizure, etc.)* Only these contexts do the exercise of a mandate becomes a lawful basis for processing.[963]

530. This, however, does not mean that law enforcement authorities may indiscriminately process personal information in the guise of exercising their respective mandates:

> Nevertheless, while the DPA recognizes such mandate, *the law is also categorical in stating that the processing of personal information must adhere to the principles of transparency, legitimate purpose and proportionality.* Personal information must be processed for specified and legitimate purposes determined and declared before, or as soon as reasonably practicable after collection. It should also be processed in a way compatible with such declared, specified, and legitimate purposes only. Law enforcement does not have a blanket authority to access medical records of patients in a hospital. These records may be released with patient's consent, or when being requested pursuant to a court order, subpoena or subpoena duces tecum, search warrants, or other administrative orders authorized by law.[964]

531. Law enforcement agencies acting as PICs or PIPs are still bound by the DPA when it comes to their obligations under the DPA and other privacy regulations.[965] These obligations include ensuring that the appropriate security measures are in place to protect the personal data being processed for such purposes and adhering to the general privacy principles and other DPA provisions.[966] Section 5 of the IRR elaborates that the non-applicability of the DPA is only to the minimum extent necessary to achieve the specific purpose, function, or activity concerned:

> Section 5. *Special Cases.* The Act and these Rules shall not apply to the following specified information, only to the minimum extent of collection, access, use, disclosure or other processing necessary to the purpose, function, or activity concerned:

---

963. National Privacy Commission, Re: Pseudonymization of Personal and Sensitive Personal Information, Advisory Opinion No. 029, Series of 2018 (6 Jun. 2018). Emphasis supplied.
964. *Ibid.*
965. National Privacy Commission, Rules and Regulations Implementing the Data Privacy Act of 2012, Republic Act No. 10173, rule II, §5(d) (2016).
966. National Privacy Commission, Re: Research and the Data Privacy Act of 2012, Advisory Opinion No. 017, Series of 2019 (5 Mar. 2019).

. . .

(f) Information necessary in order to carry out the functions of public authority, *in accordance with a constitutionally or statutorily mandated function pertaining to law enforcement or regulatory function*, including the performance of the functions of the independent, central monetary authority, subject to restrictions provided by law. Nothing in this Act shall be construed as having amended or repealed Republic Act No. 1405, otherwise known as the Secrecy of Bank Deposits Act; Republic Act No. 6426, otherwise known as the Foreign Currency Deposit Act; and Republic Act No. 9510, otherwise known as the Credit Information System Act (CISA)[.]

. . .

Provided, that the non-applicability of the Act or these Rules *do not extend to personal information controllers or personal information processors, who remain subject to the requirements of implementing security measures for personal data protection:* Provided further, that the processing of the information provided in the preceding paragraphs shall be exempted from the requirements of the Act *only to the minimum extent necessary to achieve the specific purpose, function, or activity.*[967]

532. Despite the non-applicability of the DPA to the processing of 'information necessary in order to carry out the functions of ... law enforcement and regulatory agencies of their constitutionally and statutorily mandated functions',[968] the DPA and the IRR also provide specific criteria for lawful processing of personal and sensitive personal information that law enforcement agencies may rely on.

533. Section 12(e) of the DPA provides:

Section 12. *Criteria for Lawful Processing of Personal Information.* The processing of personal information shall be permitted only if not otherwise prohibited by law, and when at least one of the following conditions exists:

. . .

f. The processing is necessary in order to respond to national emergency, to comply with the requirements of public order and safety, or *to fulfill functions of public authority which necessarily includes the processing of personal data for the fulfillment of its mandate*[.][969]

534. Section 13(b) and (f) of the DPA provide:

---

967. National Privacy Commission, Rules and Regulations Implementing the Data Privacy Act of 2012, Republic Act No. 10173, rule II, §5(d) (2016). Emphasis supplied.

968. An Act Protecting Individual Personal Information in Information and Communications Systems in the Government and the Private Sector, Creating for this purpose a National Privacy Commission, and For Other Purposes [Data Privacy Act of 2012], Republic Act No. 10173 §4(d) (2012).

969. *Ibid.*, Republic Act No. 10173 §12(c). Emphasis supplied.

> Section 13. *Sensitive Personal Information and Privileged Information.* The processing of sensitive personal information and privileged information shall be prohibited, except in the following cases:
>
> . . .
>
> A. *The processing of the same is provided for by existing laws and regulations: Provided,* That such regulatory enactments guarantee the protection of the sensitive personal information and the privileged information: *Provided, further,* That the consent of the data subjects are not required by law or regulation permitting the processing of the sensitive personal information or the privileged information[.]
>
> . . .
>
> 1. The processing concerns such personal information as is necessary for the protection of lawful rights and interests of natural or legal persons in court proceedings, or the establishment, exercise or defense of legal claims, or *when provided to government or public authority.*[970]

535. Section 22 of the IRR elucidates on section 13(f):

> Section 22. *Sensitive Personal Information and Privileged Information.* The processing of sensitive personal and privileged information is prohibited, except in any of the following cases:
>
> . . .
>
> A. The processing concerns sensitive personal information or privileged information necessary for the protection of lawful rights and interests of natural or legal persons in court proceedings, or the establishment, exercise, or defense of legal claims, or *when provided to government or public authority pursuant to a constitutional or statutory mandate.*[971]

536. The general privacy principles of transparency, legitimate purpose, and proportionality are at the core of the criteria for lawful processing of personal information, as discussed in Part III.

537. The Commission has not had the opportunity to tackle the proper delineation of the scope of the DPA under section 4 of the DPA and section 5 of the IRR, and the application of the criteria for lawful processing under sections 12(b), 13(b) and 13(f) of the DPA and section 22(f) of the IRR.

538. Regardless, it remains the obligation of law enforcement agencies processing personal and sensitive personal information to comply with the same general privacy principles and their obligations as PICs or PIPs under the DPA and other

---

970. *Ibid.*, Republic Act No. 10173 §3(b).
971. National Privacy Commission, Rules and Regulations Implementing the Data Privacy Act of 2012, Republic Act No. 10173, rule V, §22(f) (2016). Emphasis supplied.

privacy regulations.[972] As previously discussed, the non-applicability of the DPA only extends to personal information and sensitive personal information processed by law enforcement agencies, and even then, only to the minimum extent of processing necessary to achieve the specific purpose, function, or activity.[973] Thus, whether the law enforcement agency is relying on the non-applicability of the DPA or on criteria for lawful processing as a basis for processing personal or sensitive personal information pursuant to its mandate, it remains incumbent upon the law enforcement agency to prove the following: (1) the existence of a statutory constitutional mandate to process personal or sensitive personal information; (2) the processing is necessary to the mandate; and (3) the law enforcement agency complies with the general principles of transparency, legitimate purpose, and proportionality as well as the other obligations of a PIC, including the implementation of reasonable and appropriate organizational, physical, and technical security measures.

972. *See Ibid.*, §5 (2016).
973. *See ibid.*

Chapter 3. National Security Services

539. While section 5 of the IRR does not explicitly mention National Security Services, the discussion in the previous chapter is applicable. Section 5(d) of the IRR provides that '[i]nformation necessary in order to carry out the functions of public authority' is outside the scope of the DPA.[974] It may be considered that government agencies who perform national security services following their respective mandates process information for the purpose of performing their functions as a public authority.

540. Following the discussion on Law Enforcement Authorities, the non-applicability of the DPA only applies to personal information to be processed and not to the PIC or PIP undertaking the processing and, even then, only to the minimum extent necessary to achieve the specific purpose, function, or activity concerned.[975]

974. *Ibid.*, §5(d).
975. *Ibid.*, §5.

Chapter 4. Other Specific Regimes

§1. Use of Security Cameras

541. A CCTV is a camera surveillance system that captures images and footage.[976] If the CCTV image or footage contains an identifiable or reasonably ascertainable individual, then the image or footage is personal information.[977] Thus, the DPA, particularly sections 12 and 13 on the criteria for lawful processing, will apply.[978]

542. In an Advisory Opinion, the Commission elaborated on the application of the criteria for lawful processing in relation to CCTV images and footage:

> Concomitant to the above, the processing of CCTV footage is allowed under the DPA if the same is necessary under any of the abovementioned criteria, subject to the implementation of a reasonable and appropriate organizational, physical and technical security measures and adherence to the general data privacy principles of transparency, legitimate purpose and proportionality. In addition, *Section 13(f) of the DPA may likewise apply where a CCTV footage or image would reveal sensitive personal information. Thus, the processing of CCTV footage may be allowed if the same is necessary for the protection of lawful rights and interests of natural or legal persons in court proceedings, or the establishment, exercise or defense of legal claims, or when provided to government or public authority.*
>
> . . .
>
> *Every employer may have a legitimate interest in processing personal information of its employees through the CCTV, particularly in keeping employees safe, preventing crime and detecting employees' misconduct.* Legitimate interest refers to matters that are desired by or important to a PIC, which must not be contrary to law, morals or public policy. This includes business, financial or other reasonable purpose.
>
> Employees must likewise be properly informed and oriented about the policy on CCTV and surveillance cameras, including the place, time, and circumstances of such recording. There must be a privacy notice on conspicuous areas to apprise the data subjects, employees in this case, that the premises or particular areas are under surveillance. Likewise, we wish to emphasize that although employees are within office premises and using company-issued equipment within office hours, they still are entitled to their right to privacy at work. With the emergence of new technologies that provide employers with

---

976. National Privacy Commission, Re: Various Concerns Regarding the Data Privacy Act, Advisory Opinion No. 051, Series of 2018 (5 Oct. 2018).
977. *Ibid.*
978. *See* An Act Protecting Individual Personal Information in Information and Communications Systems in the Government and the Private Sector, Creating for this purpose a National Privacy Commission, and For Other Purposes [Data Privacy Act of 2012], Republic Act No. 10173 §§12, 13 (2012).

vast opportunities to monitor and track employees, unbridled checking can damage trust, disrupt professional relationships and disturb workplace peace and performance.[979]

543. The Commission also issued an Advisory on the use of CCTV systems for processing personal data.[980] It applies to all PICs and PIPs that process personal data through CCTV systems in public and semi-public areas:

> Section 2. *Scope*. This Advisory shall apply to all PICs and PIPs engaged in the processing of personal data through the use of CCTV systems operating in public and semi-public areas. These include CCTV systems that record videos, as well as those systems with both video and audio capabilities.[981]

544. The processing of personal data through CCTV systems shall adhere to the data privacy principles of legitimate purpose, proportionality, and transparency:

> Section 4. *Guidelines*. The processing of personal data in CCTV systems shall be subject to the following guidelines:
>
> A. Legitimate purpose. Prior to installing a CCTV system, *the purpose/s for personal data processing using such system must be clearly determined.* Such processing may be permitted for the following purposes, except where the same are overridden by the fundamental rights and freedoms of the data subject:
>   1. Compliance with a law or regulation, where the same guarantees the protection of personal data;
>   2. Security of properties and protection of vitally important interests of individuals;
>   3. Ensure public order and safety; and
>   4. Other legitimate interests.
>
> . . .
>
> B. Proportionality. The PIC should evaluate *whether the installation and operation of CCTV systems and the nature and kind thereof is necessary for its legitimate purpose, considering whether such purposes could be reasonably fulfilled by other less intrusive means.* Collection and further processing of personal data from CCTV systems should only be to the extent necessary to fulfill the legitimate purpose.
>
> C. Transparency. PICs and PIPs shall *provide CCTV notices which are readily visible and prominent within their premises,* such as at points of entry, or other conspicuous areas. The CCTV notices shall provide information to the public that there is a CCTV system in operation in clear, plain, and concise language.[982]

979. National Privacy Commission, Re: Processing of CCTV Footage Under the Data Privacy Act of 2012, Advisory Opinion No. 023, Series of 2019 (13 Jun. 2019). Emphasis supplied.
980. *See* National Privacy Commission, Guidelines on the Use of Closed-Circuit Television (CCTV) Systems, Circular No. 04, Series of 2020 [NPC Circ. No. 20-04] (16 Nov. 2020).
981. *Ibid.*, §2.
982. *Ibid.*, §4. Emphasis supplied.

545. The Advisory also discusses the location and placement of CCTV systems, which shall only be used to monitor intended spaces according to the legitimate purpose.[983] It proceeds to present specific use cases, particularly household, security, employment, and lawful surveillance:

> Section 5. *Specific use cases.* The use of CCTV systems shall be limited to and consistent with the purpose/s for which the same was established. The use of CCTVs may be for the following instances:
>
> A. Household. Generally, the use of CCTV systems for purely personal, family or household affairs is outside the purview of this Advisory. Nonetheless, the use of these systems shall still bear in mind the rights of every individual to privacy. Where a CCTV faces outwards from an individual's private property and it captures images of individuals beyond the boundaries of such property, particularly where it monitors a public space, the CCTV system cannot be considered as being for a purely personal, family or household purpose. As such, the operator of such CCTV system is deemed as a PIC and will be subjected to the obligations under the DPA and the provisions of this Advisory.
>
> B. Security. The use of CCTVs as mandated by local government units (LGUs) for security and peace and order purposes is recognized. Reference can be made to the Department of Interior and Local Government (DILG) Memorandum Circular No. 2014-1193 on the requirement for the installation of CCTVs for certain business establishments and in strategic areas frequented by the public to support law enforcement and crime prevention, deterrence, detection, and solution efforts of the government.
>
> C. Employment. The DPA recognizes that PICs have a legitimate interest to protect their assets, reputation, and business. To this end, PICs may monitor, through CCTVs, its premises and employees' use of company assets. Note, however, that employees do not lose their privacy rights in the workplace. Personal data of the employees shall only be collected, used, and stored by the employer, through CCTV monitoring, if the purpose sought to be achieved cannot be fulfilled by any other less privacy intrusive means.
>
> The scope and terms of use of monitoring using CCTV in the workplace must be embodied in a company policy and the employees should be informed of the nature and extent of the monitoring specified in the said policy.
>
> D. Lawful surveillance. Law enforcement agencies and other government agencies conducting lawful surveillance are not subject to the provisions of this Advisory. Nonetheless, the same shall be subject to the Constitution and other applicable laws and regulations.[984]

983. *Ibid.*, §5.
984. *Ibid.*

546. Following its obligations under the DPA and other privacy regulations, a PIC has an obligation to implement reasonable and appropriate safeguards to maintain the quality and integrity of data in the CCTV system:

> Section 5. *Specific use cases.* The use of CCTV systems shall be limited to and consistent with the purpose/s for which the same was established. The use of CCTVs may be for the following instances:
>
> . . .
>
> F. *Quality and integrity of data.* CCTV systems shall record images that are of suitable quality to meet the purposes for which it was installed or intended. PICs shall implement reasonable and appropriate safeguards to ensure and maintain the integrity and accuracy of the footage recorded and stored, including any associated meta data (*i.e.* time, date, and location), and to facilitate access requests for CCTV footage.[985]

547. A PIC also has an obligation to ensure proper storage of CCTV images and footage:

> Section 6. *Storage and retention.* Footage recorded by CCTV cameras shall be stored in a secure manner, whereby its confidentiality, integrity, and availability are maintained and protected. The recorded footage shall be encrypted. Access to the area where the CCTV footages are stored shall be secured and restricted to authorized personnel or persons only. Access logs for the CCTV footage shall be updated on a regular basis, including transfers, reproductions, and access requests. Likewise, PICs should restrict monitoring of live CCTV feeds. It should identify responsible persons who are the only ones allowed to monitor such live feeds. There is no specific or fixed minimum or maximum retention periods for CCTV footage. The same shall be retained only for as long as necessary to fulfill of the purposes for which the CCTV footage was obtained. Retention period shall not be determined based solely on the storage capacity of a system. Once determined, such information on retention period shall be clearly documented and form part of the CCTV policies.[986]

548. A PIP operating a CCTV system for a PIC shall also comply with the DPA and other privacy regulations:

> Section 5. *Specific use cases.* The use of CCTV systems shall be limited to and consistent with the purpose/s for which the same was established. The use of CCTVs may be for the following instances:
>
> . . .
>
> G. *Obligations of PIPs.* Entities that operate CCTV systems on behalf of and under the instructions of PICs are considered as PIPs. As such, they shall

985. *Ibid.*, §4(f).
986. *Ibid.*, §6.

likewise comply with all obligations under the DPA, its IRR, and other relevant issuances of the NPC. This includes, among others:

1. Process strictly in accordance with instructions from the PIC;
2. Implement organizational, technical, and physical security measures; and
3. Cooperate and coordinate with the PIC for access requests from data subjects or third parties.[987]

549. A data subject may exercise his right to access his or her own personal information stored in a CCTV system:

> Section 7. *Data subject request for access.* Any person whose image is recorded on a CCTV system has a right to reasonable access and/or be supplied with a copy of their own personal data from the footage, subject to the provisions of Section 13 of this Advisory.[988]

550. A third party may also request access to CCTV images or footage.[989] A third party to whom the CCTV image or footage will be disclosed will have an obligation to comply with the DPA and other privacy regulations in relation to further disclosures:

> Section 8. Third party access request. When a person, other than a data subject, requests for access to CCTV footage, it shall be treated as a third-party access request. The same policies and procedure as outlined in the previous section[990] on data subject access request shall also be applicable. PICs should decide on the merits of the request for disclosure based on its internal policy, the DPA, and other existing laws and regulations. Once a PIC has disclosed information to another, the latter becomes responsible for the copy they hold. It is their responsibility to comply with the DPA in relation to any further disclosures. The method of disclosing information should be secure to ensure they are only seen by the intended recipient. CCTV footage may be disclosed for, but not limited to, the following purposes:
>
> A. Law enforcement and criminal investigations. With respect to request for CCTV footage to be disclosed in relation to a criminal investigation, PICs shall require the law enforcement officer or the requesting party to provide sufficient proof as to the occurrence of a crime and the investigation thereof as well as proof of authority of the law enforcement officer before release of the CCTV footage. This request for CCTV footage shall be done following existing standard operating procedures in the conduct of an investigation and law enforcement operation as stated in the Revised PNP Operational Procedures, and other pertinent laws, rules, and regulations governing the same should be strictly adhered to.

---

987. *Ibid.*, §4(g).
988. *Ibid.*, §7.
989. *Ibid.*, §8.
990. *See Ibid.*, §7.

B. Court Order. Requests for disclosure and use of CCTV footage and images by virtue of a lawful order of a court of competent authority is allowed, taking into consideration the pertinent rules on issuance of subpoena.
C. Administrative investigations. Use of CCTV footage for purposes of an administrative investigation may be allowed. The requesting party must provide sufficient proof of the investigation being conducted or the pending complaint before an administrative body.
D. Request from the media. PICs are not obliged to release CCTV footages to the media, unless there is a lawful basis for processing, and always with due regard to the rights of data subjects and codes of conduct and ethical standards of journalism. PICs are likewise proscribed from disclosing CCTV images of identifiable individuals to the media for entertainment purposes, unless it is with the consent of the said individuals. Law enforcement agencies may release CCTV footage to the media, on a case to case basis, considering the requirements of public order and safety, identification purposes, and other relevant factors. Where images of parties other than the requesting data subject and/or the person/s sought to be identified as part of the request (e.g. identification of malefactors for investigation or law enforcement purposes) appear on the CCTV footage, it is the responsibility of the requesting media personnel or journalist to mask the images of those other parties before making the footage public.
E. Other third-party requests. Third-party access requests for CCTV footage and images shall be approached with care as wider disclosure may be unfair to the individuals concerned. In certain circumstances, it may be appropriate to release information to a third party, where their needs outweigh those of the data subjects whose information is recorded. The PIC must determine on a case to case basis if it will accede to such request taking into consideration the rights and freedoms of the data subjects whose images are recorded by the CCTV system, and considering the provisions of the immediately succeeding section.[991]

551. The right to access is not absolute. The PIC also considers the proportionality of the disclosure to the purpose of the request:

> Section 10. *Response procedure.* Once a PIC or a PIP is notified that a request for access is or will be made, the pertinent CCTV footage shall be taken out of the coverage of the usual retention period to enable the same to be saved and accessed.
>
> Upon fulfillment of the requirements in the immediately preceding sections, the PIC response in allowing access to the CCTV footage shall be tiered: either by viewing or providing a copy to the data subject or the third party, as the case may be. The latter option shall be allowed when proportional to the purpose of the request.
>
> A. *Viewing.* The requesting party may be allowed a reasonable opportunity to view the requested footage; *provided,* that CCTV footages shall be viewed

991. *Ibid.*, §8.

in a secure area; *provided further,* that only the requesting party and the authorized personnel of the PIC shall be allowed to view such footages; *provided finally,* that other security measures to ensure confidentiality of the footage to be viewed may be implemented, such as signing of non-disclosure agreements or prohibiting the capture of the footage through mobile phones and other devices, where appropriate.

B. *Obtaining a copy of the CCTV footage.* If the requesting party opts to obtain a copy of the CCTV footage, PICs shall likewise provide the same. PICs shall ensure that the copying of footages is made in a secure manner that maintains the integrity of the footage and any associated meta data. Such process shall not interrupt the operation of the CCTV system.

In circumstances where there is technical difficulty in providing a copy of the footage in video format, PICs may provide image stills as an alternative. Where image stills are provided, it would be necessary to supply sufficient stills for the duration of the requested footage.[992]

552. The PIC may also deny access to CCTV images and footage in any of the following situations:

Section 13. *Denial of request.* PICs may refuse to provide a copy of CCTV footages or access thereto in the following instances:

A. Incomplete information regarding the requested CCTV footage, as stated in Section 7;
B. The access request is frivolous or vexatious. The determination of what constitutes frivolous or vexatious may be made on the basis of the particular circumstances of the request;
C. Purpose for viewing or obtaining a copy of the footage is contrary to law, morals, or public policy;
D. The burden or expense of providing access would be unreasonable or involve disproportionate effort on the part of the PIC or PIP;
E. The footage has been deleted by the time the PIC receives the request, pursuant to its documented retention policy; or
F. If sharing the footage could put an ongoing criminal investigation at risk.

Should the PIC deny a request for CCTV access, it shall provide the requesting party with a justification for such denial.[993]

553. In an Advisory Opinion, the Commission advised that entities that use CCTV systems, such as hospitals, should develop their own policy on processing personal information through CCTV systems:

Considering the foregoing, it is recommended that the hospital craft and implement its own policy about the collection and processing of photographs and

992. §10.
993. §13.

CCTV, including specific guidelines or instances when [the] taking of photographs is allowed and security measures as to the use and transmission of clinical photographs.

Furthermore, every personal information controller shall recognize the right of data subjects to be informed and notified of the processing activities involving their personal data. The hospital must post a privacy notice on conspicuous areas to apprise the data subjects that the hospital premises or particular areas that are under surveillance of CCTVs.

This notification should sufficiently explain the policy on CCTV and the rights of data subjects. Specifically, it must be able to elaborate on the data subject's right to access CCTV footage and images, and/or request for copies, upon approval of request and with appropriate masking of the personal data of other individuals, where applicable.[994]

§2. E-Health

554. The Commission recently issued a Circular on Guidelines on the Processing of Personal Data During Public Health Emergencies for Public Health Measures. It applies to PICs and PIPs that process personal data during public health emergencies.[995] The Circular defines a public health emergency as:

> Section 2. *Definition of Terms.* For the purpose of this Circular, the following terms are defined, as follows:
>
> . . .
>
> Y. 'Public Health Emergency' refers to an occurrence or imminent threat of an illness or a health condition that poses a high probability of a large number of deaths in the affected population; a large number of serious injuries or long-term disabilities in the affected population; widespread exposure to an infectious or toxic agent that poses a significant risk of substantial harm to a large number of people in the affected population; and international exposure to an infectious or toxic agent that poses a significant risk to the health of citizens of other countries[.][996]

555. The Circular emphasizes that PICs or PIPs that process personal data during public health emergencies must comply with their obligations under the DPA, including the general privacy principles of transparency, legitimate purpose, and proportionality.[997] Section 3 provides:

---

994. National Privacy Commission, Re: Photographs and CCTV Footages in Hospitals, Advisory Opinion No. 053, Series of 2018 (26 Nov. 2018).

995. National Privacy Commission, Guidelines on the Processing of Personal Data During Public Health Emergencies for Public Health Measures, Circular No. 02, Series of 2021 [NPC Circ. No. 21-02], §1 (8 Nov. 2021).

996. *Ibid.*, §2(Y).

997. *Ibid.*, §3.

> Section 3. *General principles.* The processing of personal data in response to public health emergencies as part of a public health measure, specifically the prevention, detection, isolation, treatment, and reintegration strategies such as but not limited to testing, contact tracing, treatment, and activities relating to vaccine deployment, is recognized, and shall be governed by the following principles:
>
> A. Transparency. PICs shall provide the necessary privacy notices at the appropriate instances in relation to all personal data processing activities for public health emergencies to adequately inform data subjects of the details of the processing of their personal data and their rights under the DPA;
>
> B. Legitimate purpose. The specific purpose/s for personal data processing in response to public health emergencies as part of a public health measure shall be clearly determined prior to any personal data processing activities;
>
> C. Proportionality. The processing of personal data shall be limited to the extent necessary to fulfill the identified legitimate purpose/s. Privacy enhancing technologies or privacy-preserving methodologies shall be employed to the end that personal data shall be processed only if the purpose of the processing could not be reasonably fulfilled by other means;
>
> D. Safeguards. PICs shall implement appropriate measures, taking into account the integration of privacy by design and risk management in the development of systems and other digital tools where privacy is embedded into the design and architecture of the same and integral to the system without diminishing functionality;
>
> E. Data subject rights. PICs shall recognize and uphold the rights of affected data subjects, unless otherwise provided by law; and
>
> F. Compliance and accountability. PICs shall fulfill all applicable requirements prescribed by the DPA, its IRR, and other issuances of the NPC.[998]

556. Section 4 of the Circular reiterates that processing personal data under lawful criteria is necessary:

> Section 4. *Criteria for lawful processing; purpose.* A lawful basis for processing is necessary for all personal data processing activities as part of the response to public health emergencies:
>
> A. Personal data processing shall be based on the applicable laws, rules, and regulations requiring the collection and use of personal data for a public health measure[.][999]

557. This, however, does not in any way introduce a different criteria for lawful processing from those enumerated under sections 12 and 13 of the DPA. A PIC or PIP processing personal data in response to a public health emergency must rely on the existing criteria under the DPA.

---

998. *Ibid.*
999. *Ibid.*, §4.

558. Section 4 also explicitly provides that the information collected from data subjects pursuant to the response to public health emergencies 'shall not be repurposed for direct marketing, profiling, or any other analogous purpose, whether commercial or non-commercial'.[1000]

559. The Circular also provides additional safeguards against further processing of personal data. Section 5 states:

> Section 5. *Further processing; limitation.* Further processing of personal data may be allowed in instances which are compatible or consistent with the response to public health emergencies as part of public health measures, such as but not limited to historical, statistical, or scientific purposes.
>
> A. The further processing is considered incompatible when:
>   1. It would be very different from the original purpose of responding to public health emergencies as part of public health measures or there is no clear and reasonable link between such original purpose and the purposes of the intended further processing;
>   2. It would result in an unjustified consequence on the rights and freedoms of the data subject; or
>   3. It would not be reasonably expected by the data subject considering the context in which the personal data has been collected.
>
>   Further processing shall only be allowed when upon examination, it is determined to be compatible with the original purpose communicated to the data subject and not beyond what the data subject may reasonably expect as to the purpose, scope, manner, and extent of the processing of their personal data.
>
> B. The processing for research purposes may be allowed only when the same is intended for a public benefit and subject to the requirements of applicable laws, regulations, and ethical standards such as those prescribed by various research ethics boards or committees of the government, academic institutions, and other similar organizations prescribing such standards: provided, that processing for health research shall involve only aggregate, pseudonymized, or anonymized data. Likewise, all policy and biomedical research related to COVID-19 surveillance and response shall secure an Ethics Board approval prior to implementation.
>
> C. Any authorized further processing shall have adequate safeguards for data privacy and security, such as anonymization, pseudonymization, restriction on access, and shall uphold the rights and freedoms of the data subjects.[1001]

560. The Circular specifically discusses the general privacy principles in the context of application permissions:

1000. *Ibid.*
1001. *Ibid.*, §5.

Section 9. *Application (app) permissions.* Permissions requested by CTAs or Vaccine Card Systems, where applicable, shall be governed by the following:

A. Request minimum permissions. PICs shall assess the proportionality of app permissions and only request for those that are necessary to fulfill its functions.

B. Ask in context. Apps requiring specific permissions shall request them at the most reasonable and appropriate time, such as by means of pop-up notices or just-in-time notices, or any similar manner when the app or the data subject's use requires or triggers it.

C. Provide adequate user choices. Whenever possible, apps shall minimize the time or access window of permissions and provide clear choices to users in managing permissions:

  1. While using the app. The app will only have access to the specific permission when the app is being actively used in the foreground or in the active window of the device;
  2. Only this time. The app will have access temporarily to a specific permission sought from the user, i.e., one-time permission, where such permission shall automatically be withdrawn after the app is closed by the user; and
  3. Deny. The app will be prohibited to use the requested permission. PICs are required to provide mechanisms whereby users are still able to use the app despite this choice.

D. Only access sensitive permissions when necessary and the user reasonably expects it. Apps must provide continuous visual cues, indicators, or notices that are easily understood by users, such as a small icon in the status bar for mobile phones or in the browser's toolbar for websites, that applications are actively accessing sensitive permissions, i.e., camera, location, microphone.

E. Pay attention to libraries. Apps shall be audited with regard to personal data especially sensitive personal information accessed by third-party Application Programming Interfaces (APIs) and libraries. Such third-party APIs and libraries must also be clearly indicated in the app's privacy notice.[1002]

561. While these are not new requirements, the Circular also reminds PICs or PIPs to: (1) conduct a PIA prior to the use of any personal data processing system;[1003] (2) ensure transparency through an appropriate privacy notice;[1004] (3) implement adequate security measures,[1005] storage and retention,[1006] and disposal[1007] policies; and (4) uphold data subject rights.[1008]

1002. *Ibid.*, §9.
1003. *Ibid.*, §7.
1004. *Ibid.*, §8.
1005. *Ibid.*, §10.
1006. *Ibid.*, §12.
1007. *Ibid.*, §13.
1008. *Ibid.*, §10.

List of References

Cases Decided by the Philippine Supreme Court

A.M. No. RTJ-15-2438	*Flores-Concepcion v. Castaneda*
G.R. 109835	*JMM Promotions & Management, Inc. v. NLRC*
G.R. 110318	*Columbia Pictures, Inc. v. Court of Appeals*
G.R. 127685	*Ople v. Torres*
G.R. 136247 & 138330	*People v. Liban*
G.R. 154083	*Office of the Ombudsman v. De Leon*
G.R. 158885 & 170680	*Fort Bonifacio Development Corporation v. CIR, et al.*
G.R. 166715	*Abakada Guro Party List, et al. v. Hon. Purisima*
G.R. 170516	*Akbayan Citizens Action Party, et al. v. Aquino, et al.*
G.R. 174286	*Traders Royal Bank v. Cuison Lumber Co., Inc.*
G.R. 176579	*Gamboa v. Teves*
G.R. 176951, 177499, 178056	*League of Cities of the Philippines v. Commission on Elections*
G.R. 179736	*Spouses Hing v. Choachuy*
G.R. 179408	*Philippine Long Distance Telephone Company v. Alvarez*
G.R. 181881	*Pollo v. Constantino*
G.R. 184317	*Metropolitan Bank and Trust Company v. Liberty Corrugated Boxes Manufacturing Corporation*
G.R. 193914	*Seven Brothers Shipping Corporation v. DMC-Construction Resources, Inc.*
G.R. 201927	*Cabanting v. BPI Family Savings Bank, Inc.*
G.R. 202242	*Chavez v. Judicial and Bar Council, et al.*
G.R. 202666	*Vivares v. St. Theresa's College*
G.R. 203335	*Disini v. Secretary of Justice, et al.*

G.R. 20387	*Morfe v. Mutuc*
G.R. L-19650	*Caltex (Philippines), Inc. v. Palomar*
G.R. L-23825	*Pelaez v. The Auditor General*

Cases Decided by the Philippine Court of Appeals

CA-G.R. SP No. 168952	*PXXX v. MNLC, Inc.*

Cases Decided by the National Privacy Commission

CID 17-047	*JV v. JR*
CID 17-K-003	*KRL v. University, AA, MC, NCB, RG GV, GCT, RR, MR, PB*
CID 18-D-012	Unreported
CID 18-E-040	*KGR v. BB, et al.*
CID BN 18-072	unreported
NPC BN 18-010	*RLA v. PLDT Enterprise*
NPC BN 20-149	unreported
NPC BN 20-157	unreported
NPC BN 21-054	unreported
NPC BN 21-174	unreported
NPC Case No. 16-001	unreported
NPC Case No 19-498	unreported
NPC Case No. 17-018	*EA and TA v. EJ*
NPC Case No. 17-047	unreported
NPC Case No. 18-038	unreported
NPC Case No. 18-141	unreported
NPC Case No. 19-1201	*D.N.T. v K.K. and X.F.*
NPC Case No. 19-043	*FAT v. XXX*
NPC Case No. 19-134	*VVC v. CJB*
NPC Case No. 19-450	*JRG v. CXXX Lending Corporation*
NPC Case No. 19-498	unreported
NPC Case No. 19-528	*MNLC v. PXXX Corporation*
NPC Case No. 19-531	unreported
NPC Case No. 19-621	*AMP v. HXXX Lending Inc.*
NPC Case No. 19-653	*BGM v. IPP*

NPC Case No. 19-910	*In re: FLI Operating ABC Online Lending Application*
NPC Case No. 21-010	unreported
NPC Case No. 21-031	unreported
NPC Case No. 21-035	unreported
NPC SS 20-001	unreported
NPC SS 21-006	unreported

Foreign Cases

389 U.S. 347	*Katz v. US*

Philippine Legislation

Act No. 3815	An Act Revising the Penal Code and Other Penal Laws.
Republic Act No. 53	An Act to Exempt the Publisher, Editor, or Reporter of Any Publication from Revealing the Published News or Information Obtained in Confidence.
Republic Act No. 386	An Act to Ordain and Institute the Civil Code of the Philippines.
Republic Act No, 1405	An Act Prohibiting Disclosure of or Inquiry into Deposits with any Banking Institution and Providing Penalty Therefor.
Republic Act No. 4200	An Act to Prohibit and Penalize Wire Tapping and Other Related Violations of the Privacy of Communication, and For Other Purposes.
Republic Act No. 6426	An Act Instituting a Foreign Currency Deposit System in the Philippines, and for other Purposes.
Republic Act No 7610	An Act Providing for Stronger Deterrence and Special Protection Against Child Exploitation and Discrimination, and For Other Purposes.
Republic Act No. 9262	An Act Defining Violence Against Women and their Children, Providing for Protective Measures for Victims, Prescribing Penalties Therefore, and For Other Purposes.
Republic Act No. 9344	An Act Establishing a Comprehensive Juvenile Justice and Welfare System, Creating the Juvenile Justice and Welfare Council Under the Department of Justice, Appropriating Funds Therefore, and For Other Purposes.

List of References

Republic Act No. 9995	An Act Defining and Penalizing the Crime of Photo and Video Voyeurism. Prescribing Penalties Therefor, and For Other Purposes.
Republic Act No. 10173	An Act Protecting Individual Personal Information in Information and Communications Systems in the Government and the Private Sector, Creating for this Purpose a National Privacy Commission, and For Other Purposes.
Republic Act No. 10175	An Act Defining Cybercrime, Providing for the Prevention, Investigation, Suppression, and the Imposition of Penalties Therefor and For Other Purposes.
Republic Act No. 11055	An Act Establishing the Philippine Identification System.
Republic Act. No. 11166	An Act Strengthening the Philippine Comprehensive Policy on Human Immunodeficiency Virus (HIV) and Acquired Immune Deficiency Syndrome (AIDS) Prevention, Treatment, Care, and Support, and, Reconstituting the Philippine National Aids Council (PNAC), Repealing for the Purpose Republic Act No. 8504, Otherwise Known as The 'Philippine Aids Prevention and Control Act of 1998', and Appropriating Funds Therefor.

Philippine Executive Issuances

Executive Order No 292, Series of 1987	Instituting the 'Administrative Code of 1987'.
Executive Order No. 2, Series of 2016	Operationalizing in the Executive Branch the People's Constitutional Right to Information and the State Policies to Full Public Disclosure and Transparency in the Public Service and Providing Guidelines Therefor.
Memorandum Circular No. 78, Series of 1964	Promulgating Rules Governing Security of Classified Matter in Government Offices.
Memorandum Circular No. 196, Series of 1968	Amending Memorandum Circular 78 dated August 14, 1964, Entitled 'Promulgating Rules Governing Security of Classified Matter in Government Offices'.
Presidential Proclamation No. 527, Series of 2018	Declaring the Last Week of May of Every Year as National Privacy Awareness Week.

Rules and Regulations Implementing The Data Privacy Act of 2012.

Rules and Regulations Implementing the Philippine Identification System Act.

National Privacy Commission Circulars and Advisories

NPC Circular No. 01, Series of 2016	Security of Personal Data in Government Agencies
NPC Circular No. 03, Series of 2016	Personal Data Breach Management
NPC Circular No. 01, Series of 2017	Registration of Data Processing and Notifications regarding Automated Decision-Making
NPC Circular No. 01, Series of 2018	Rules of Procedure on Requests for Advisory Opinions
NPC Circular No. 02, Series of 2018	Guidelines in Compliance Checks
NPC Circular No. 01, Series of 2020	Guidelines on the Processing of Personal Data for Loan-Related Transactions
NPC Circular No. 02, Series of 2020	Rules on the Issuance of Cease and Desist Orders
NPC Circular No. 03, Series of 2020	Data Sharing Agreements
NPC Circular No. 01, Series of 2021	2021 Rules of Procedure of the National Privacy Commission
NPC Circular No. 02, Series of 2022	Guidelines on the Processing of Personal Data During Public Health Emergencies for Public Health Measures
NPC Advisory No. 01, Series of 2017	Designation of Data Protection Officers
NPC Advisory No. 02, Series of 2017	Access to Personal Data Sheets of Government Personnel
NPC Advisory No. 01, Series of 2018	Rules of Procedure on Requests for Advisory Opinions
NPC Advisory No. 02, Series of 2018	Updated Templates on Security Incident and Personal Data Breach Reportorial Requirements
NPC Advisory No. 04, Series of 2020	Guidelines on the Use of Closed-Circuit Television (CCTV) Systems
NPC Advisory No. 01, Series of 2021	Data Subject Rights

List of References

NPC Advisory No. 02, Series of 2021	Guidelines For the Use of the ASEAN Model Contract Clauses and ASEAN Data Management Framework
NPC Advisory No. 01, Series of 2022	Guidelines on Requests for Personal Data of Public Officers

National Privacy Commission Advisory Opinions

Advisory Opinion No. 10, Series of 2017	Re: Rules Governing Certain Information Relating to Corporations
Advisory Opinion No. 27, Series of 2017	Re: Anonymized Data for Marketing Analytics
Advisory Opinion No. 41, Series of 2017	Re: Profiling of Individuals and Collection of Personal Information Based on Publicly Available Data
Advisory Opinion No. 48, Series of 2017	Re: Submission of Credit Information by Cooperatives to the Credit Information Corporation (CIC)
Advisory Opinion No. 05, Series of 2018	Re: Data Sharing Agreement/Data Protection Officer
Advisory Opinion No. 14, Series of 2018	Re: Reporting of Alleged Criminals' Personal Data
Advisory Opinion No. 16, Series of 2018	Re: Compliance of Resident Physicians to the Requirement of Professional Societies for Diplomate Board Exam and Accreditation
Advisory Opinion No. 22, Series of 2018	Re: Scope and Coverage of the Data Privacy Act
Advisory Opinion No. 28, Series of 2018	Re: Ownership of 201 Files
Advisory Opinion No. 29, Series of 2018	Re: Pseudonymization of Personal and Sensitive Personal Information,
Advisory Opinion No. 42, Series of 2018	Re: Employee's Right to Access Employment Records
Advisory No. 44, Series of 2018	Re: Request for Information from Rizal Medical Center
Advisory No. 49, Series of 2018	Re: Disclosure of Personal Information to the Police and Media
Advisory Opinion No. 51, Series of 2018	Re: Various Concerns Regarding the Data Privacy Act

Advisory Opinion No. 53, Series of 2018	Re: Photographs and CCTV Footages in Hospitals
Advisory Opinion No. 58, Series of 2018	Re: Ayala Rewards Circle
Advisory Opinion No. 60, Series of 2018	Re: Disclosure of Personal Information to the Bangko Sentral ng Pilipinas
Advisory Opinion No. 68, Series of 2018	Re: Processing of Anonymized Personal Data by Electronic Medical Records Provider
Advisory Opinion No. 69, Series of 2018	Re: Phone Usage Data Records
Advisory Opinion No. 73, Series of 2018	Re: Treatment of Insurance Agents under the DPA
Advisory Opinion No. 79, Series of 2018,	Re: Authentication of a Marriage Contract for Purpose of Investigation
Advisory No. 83, Series of 2018	Re: Collection of Health Information by the Department of Health
Advisory Opinion No. 10, Series of 2019	Re: Access to Employee 201 Files and Medical Records
Advisory Opinion No. 14, Series of 2019	Re: Proposed Bangko Sentral ng Pilipinas and Department of Interior and Local Government Joint Memorandum Circular in the Issuance of Business License/Permit for Pawnshops and Money Service Businesses
Advisory Opinion No. 17, Series of 2019	Re: Research and the Data Privacy Act of 2012
Advisory Opinion No. 21, Series of 2019	Re: Assignment of a Non-Resident DPO and Requirements for the Contact Details of a DPO
Advisory Opinion No. 23, Series of 2019	Re: Processing of CCTV Footage Under the Data Privacy Act of 2012
Advisory Opinion No. 24, Series of 2019	Re: Disclosure of Criminal History
Advisory Opinion No. 25, Series of 2019	Re: Disclosure of the Names of the Unit Owners/ Members of a Condominium Association
Advisory Opinion No. 27, Series of 2019	Re: Disclosure of the Names of the Unit Owners/ Members of a Homeowners' Association
Advisory Opinion No. 31, Series of 2019	Re: Access to and Processing of Medical Records for Cancer Registries,
Advisory Opinion No. 32, Series of 2019	Re: Storage and Sharing of Electronic Medical Records (EMR)
Advisory Opinion No. 36, Series of 2019	Re: Collection and Use of Patient Case Number and Appointment of Compliance Officer for Privacy

List of References

Advisory Opinion No. 50, Series of 2019	Re: Request for the Last Known Address of a Former Employee
Advisory Opinion No. 06, Series of 2020	Re: Collection Agency Communicating with Human Resource Department
Advisory Opinion No. 09, Series of 2020	Re: Deletion of Electronic Medical Records
Advisory Opinion No. 18, Series of 2020	Re: Outsourcing the Processing of Personal Data
Advisory Opinion No. 21, Series of 2020	Re: Automated Retrieval of Bank Transaction History
Advisory Opinion No. 46, Series of 2020	Re: Common Practices of Schools in Processing Personal Data of Students
Advisory Opinion No. 81, Series of 2020	Re: Access to Medical Records in CR-DR System
Advisory Opinion No. 08, Series of 2021	Re: Request for Official List of Legitimate Taxi Operators
Advisory No. 10, Series of 2021	Re: Private Detective Services
Advisory Opinion No. 28, Series of 2021	Re: Disclosure of Personal Information of Tenants by a Condominium Corporation to the Bureau of Internal Revenue

Philippine Judicial Issuances

A.M. No. 08-1-16-SC	Rule on Writ of Habeas Data
A.M. No. 19-08-15-SC	2019 Amendment to the 1989 Revised Rules on Evidence
A.M. No. 19-10-20-SC	2019 Amendments to the 1997 Rules of Civil Procedure
	Code of Professional Responsibility

Treaties

999 U.N.T.S. 171	International Covenant on Civil and Political Rights
ETS No. 108	Convention for the Protection of Individuals with regard to Automatic Processing of Personal Data
ETS No. 185	The Budapest Convention and its Protocols

Index

The numbers here refer to paragraph numbers.

Index

Index

www.ingramcontent.com/pod-product-compliance
Ingram Content Group UK Ltd.
Pitfield, Milton Keynes, MK11 3LW, UK
UKHW020137290926
15471UKWH00003B/553

9 789403 507262